'A scholarly, sophisticated and clear-headed analysis of the real impact of the last decade's global "populist backlash" against human rights, and the appropriate response by advocates for still-admirable universal principles. Ford challenges us, in effect, to be more introspective and less insulting – to rethink our inclination to blame the "deplorables" for what too often have been shortcomings in our own sensitivity and priority-setting. It's a timely wake-up call.'

Gareth Evans, *Former Australian Foreign Minister, President Emeritus of the International Crisis Group, author of* The Responsibility to Protect: Ending Mass Atrocity Crimes Once and for All, *Distinguished Honorary Professor at the Australian National University*

'The rise of human rights and the decline of colonialism, along with the prohibition on the use of force, were among the signature achievements of international law in the twentieth century. Yet the twenty-first has seen the rise of populist political forces that challenge human rights in form and substance, including explicit denunciations of that discourse by leaders of countries that were once among its greatest champions. In this book, Jolyon Ford examines populism and its impact on human rights, as well as how scholars and activists can and should respond. Importantly, that response goes beyond a counter-populist agenda and embraces the opportunity for a critical evaluation not only of what populism has done to human rights, but also what it has revealed.'

Simon Chesterman, *Vice Provost (Educational Innovation), National University of Singapore*

'The human rights movement has often not reacted well to criticism. This is particularly true of its response to populism. While populism confronts human rights with a great many challenges, it also provides an opportunity for those of us who continue to support human rights with an opportunity to radically evaluate what we stand for and why. This book offers a thoughtful and accessible scholarly tool for undertaking the kind of constructively critical self-analysis the human rights movement urgently needs to engage in. I recommend it to anyone who cares about human rights and social justice.'

Andrew Fagan, *Essex Law School, Director, Human Rights Centre*

HUMAN RIGHTS AND POPULISM

For decades, framing an issue as a 'human rights' issue carried certain power and effect in politics and international relations, one that has been challenged by the recent rise of populist political forces. Ford explores the recent impact of populist politics on the universalist human rights project, in particular, how scholars have framed and responded to this challenge.

Ford offers a provocation to the human rights movement. Rather than 'what have populists done to human rights?', it asks 'how did we, the human rights movement, do this to ourselves?' How did fundamental protections for all become so easily scapegoated as 'us and them,' as claims of small, often foreign, minorities? Did human rights lose some vital connection to ordinary people's interests, their value taken as obvious and self-explanatory? Looking forward, the book asks how – in a post-truth 'fake news' world – we might reimagine human rights as underpinning human flourishing as well as important constraints on public and private concentrations of power.

Traversing relevant scholarly literature on the future of human rights and zooming out to look at wider patterns of political and diplomatic discourse, this book will speak to policymakers, diplomats, journalists, and human rights advocates – and all interested in the crisis of liberal democracies.

Professor Jolyon Ford re-joined the Australian National University (ANU) Law School in 2015 from research positions with the Royal Institute for International Affairs ('Chatham House') and the Global Governance Programme at the University of Oxford's Blavatnik School of Government. He has over 20 years' experience in over 30 countries, working on legal, human rights, and governance issues in government, an inter-governmental organisation, civil society, think tanks, and the private sector. He is the author of *Regulating Business for Peace* (Cambridge, 2015) and co-author of *Regulatory Insights on Artificial Intelligence* (Elgar, 2022). Born and educated in Zimbabwe, he holds degrees from the University of KwaZulu-Natal (South Africa), Cambridge University, and the ANU.

HUMAN RIGHTS AND POPULISM

Jolyon Ford

Routledge
Taylor & Francis Group
LONDON AND NEW YORK

Designed cover image: Getty

First published 2024
by Routledge
4 Park Square, Milton Park, Abingdon, Oxon OX14 4RN

and by Routledge
605 Third Avenue, New York, NY 10158

Routledge is an imprint of the Taylor & Francis Group, an informa business

British Library Cataloguing-in-Publication Data
A catalogue record for this book is available from the British Library

ISBN: 9781032317533 (hbk)
ISBN: 9781032317540 (pbk)
ISBN: 9781003311140 (ebk)

DOI: 10.4324/9781003311140

Typeset in Galliard
by Deanta Global Publishing Services, Chennai, India

CONTENTS

ACKNOWLEDGEMENTS

In addition to thanking the team at Routledge (Kendrick Loo and Payal Bharti, and before them Yong Lin Lam) I would like to acknowledge the support of fellow members of the intellectual community at the Australian National University (ANU) College of Law. In particular, I acknowledge my co-investigators on two projects. These are the ANU-funded project 'Navigating the Populist Backlash against International Law and Institutions' (2018–2020) and now the five-year Australian Research Council (ARC)-funded project 'Reconceiving Engagement with International Law in an Era of Populism' (ARC Discovery Project, DP220101584, 2022–2027). This book draws in part on my thinking developed around and during these projects, and so carries a debt of gratitude to my co-investigators Professor Jeremy Farrall and Associate Professor Imogen Saunders (ANU), and Professors Peter Danchin (University of Maryland) and Shruti Rana (Indiana University). I am grateful for the opportunity to discuss aspects of my work with various other thinkers including Professor Fiona de Londres, the Hon. Gareth Evans, the Hon. Lisa Singh, Professor Sally Wheeler, as well as Dr Cecilia Jacob and various governmental and other participants at our ANU and ARC project workshops. I would also thank then-ANU student Georga Nonnenmacher for her assistance, and Alexandra Bridges for her understanding and support. I dedicate the work to my parents, David and Susan.

Jolyon Ford
Canberra, February 2023

INTRODUCTION

On one view of globalisation, if anything 'globalised' over the last half-century it was the notion of 'human rights.' On this account, what spread was not just the profound idea that any state's power over its population is inherently limited by the need to respect, protect, and fulfil certain basic and universal human rights. What also spread was the reach and relevance of legal and other institutions, mechanisms, and networks to give substance to that politically powerful idea. At the very least, on this account, the human rights lexicon – as a language of political claim or mobilisation, and of inter-state contestation – succeeded in achieving traction and salience in very diverse contexts globally. So it was, riding first on waves of de-colonisation and then of post-Soviet democratisation, that as the 21st century approached leading scholars confidently declared the advent of the 'age of human rights.'[1]

Yet eras, by definition, are not eternal. What then is the future of human rights, including if we unpack this possible association with globalisation? One way to ask this is whether, in future, framing any issue as a 'human rights' one will necessarily give that issue any particular special advantage, urgency, or claim to significance that it might not otherwise have had. For instance, it is conceivable that, in some contexts, invoking human rights might instead be counter-productive for advancing an issue, exposing it to resistance from a significant proportion of the population. With this in mind, this book analyses scholarship on what might be the status and fate of human rights (both the legal-political motif overall, and its institutional manifestations) given the rise of a particular and challenging phenomenon. That phenomenon is 'populism'

1 Louis Henkin, *The Age of Human Rights* (Columbia University Press, 1990).

DOI: 10.4324/9781003311140-1

as a supposedly distinctive style or form of politics and electioneering over the last decade, both in more established market democracies and in so-called emerging or developing ones.

'Populism' is a slippery label, more fully defined later. For present introductory purposes, it refers to a political strategy or style (or for some, an ideology) whereby a 'charismatic' leader and/or party purports finally to speak truthfully and plainly for the 'real' people. That 'people' is itself a construction, perhaps portrayed as an authentic, rump, hitherto-neglected silent virtuous nativist majority, and often differentiated from both troublesome undeserving outsider minorities and corrupt, out-of-touch elites. The 'populist' may say and do many things, but relevantly for a human rights perspective, the term has come to be associated with antagonistic, anti-pluralist political messaging and action to give effect to the people's wishes and at last address their legitimate needs and fears. Those needs and wishes have been frustrated (as the populist might say) by legal obstructions like 'rights,' policed by a privileged, patronising elite class that has long ago chosen to belittle or ignore 'the people,' sometimes by unduly favouring minorities' rights. For now, this characterisation suffices as we outline this book's purpose. However, later we must discuss whether 'populism' is too often and too readily an automatically pejorative or negative label and whether it may create certain analytical blind spots. If so, this would be somewhat ironic given the populists' notion that elites (scholars included) simply do not and cannot see the real concerns of 'ordinary' people.

In any event, since about 2015, human rights scholars and activists have described and engaged with a perceived distinctive, fundamental, and existential 'populist challenge to human rights' (for example, Alston 2017; Roth 2017 and 2018; Garavito and Gomez et al. 2018; Neuman et al. 2020).[2] Their work has catalogued various alarming developments, connecting them as part of a wider trend, typically (but certainly not only) of Right-wing populist-nationalist and illiberal politics with authoritarian instincts or yearnings. On this account, from the United States and the United Kingdom to Poland and Hungary, to India, Brazil and the Philippines, elected leaders and regimes in their populist vein have drawn upon or played to populist sentiment and themes. They have used strategies to stigmatise minorities and to normalise

2 Phillip Alston, 'The Populist Challenge to Human Rights' (2017) 9(1) *Journal of Human Rights Practice*, 1–15; Kenneth Roth, 'Pushback against the Populist Challenge to Human Rights' in Human Rights Watch, *World Report 2018: Events of 2017* (Annual Report, New York, 2018) and 'The Dangerous Rise of Populism: Global Attacks on Human Rights Values' (2017) 70th Anniversary Issue *Journal of International Affairs* 79-84; Cesar Rodriguez-Garavito and Krizna Gomez (eds.), *Rising to the Populist Challenge: A New Playbook for Human Rights* (De Justitia, Bogota, 2018); and Gerald Neuman (ed.) *Human Rights in a Time of Populism* (Cambridge University Press, 2020).

racist, xenophobic or other sentiments and associated discrimination (etc.) in society; to neuter judiciaries and dismantle legal checks and balances on executive power; to reduce independent political, civic, and media space; to curtail freedoms of speech and assembly; to justify torture and other human rights and due process 'shortcuts'; to circumvent criminal justice procedures; and so on.

Yet such scholars and activists have observed something more than just these efforts to undermine rights protections and legal constraints on power or to foster social attitudes antithetical to human rights values. They observe how the leaders that they characterise this way, in order to respond to or energise populist constituencies, have gone further than just backsliding on human rights protections and have challenged the very legitimacy of human rights at all, and of those who might invoke them. For example:

- Rodrigo Duterte, until 2022 the populist elected president of the Philippines, built a domestically effective political brand by, among other things, openly encouraging the extra-judicial killing of alleged drug dealers and users. On his narrative, the president was directly protecting the people where other social and political institutions had failed to do so. When in a 2018 national speech Duterte addressed his critics by saying 'Your concern is human rights; mine is human *lives*,'[3] he was not simply saying that his methods better protected rights. He was saying, and cleverly, that rights arguments and protections at all were at best a distraction, at worst part of society's problem.
- When British Prime Minister David Cameron made statements about the 2011 London riots and looting, it was not to condemn criminality yet reaffirm the value of rights-based safeguards in the justice system. Instead, it was to state that 'human rights are in my sights' because 'phoney' human rights concerns 'get in the way' of bringing criminals to justice.[4]

In such scenarios, it is not just a case of 'populist political actions negatively impact the human rights environment'; it is also 'politicians explicitly denounce human rights to bolster their populist appeal.' In the latter scenario human rights – otherwise potentially a powerful vector of critique of such leaders – is disarmed, dismissed, delegitimised. Human rights is directly part of the problem that the leader must fix in service of 'the people.' It is

3 Third 'State of the Nation' Address, Manila, 24 July 2018, cited in Richard Heydarien, 'Penal Populism in Emerging Markets: Human Rights in an Age of Strongmen,' in Gerald Neuman (ed.) *Human Rights in a Time of Populism* (Cambridge University Press, 2020), Ch. 7, 148.

4 David Cameron, 'Human Rights in My Sights' *Sunday Express* (London, 21 August 2011), cited in Susan Marks, 'Four Human Rights Myths' LSE Law, Society and Economy Working Papers 10/2012, London School of Economics, 1-2.

damned (sometimes as a foreign imposition) by express association with all the other forces that, according to the populist, unaccountable patronising globalist elites are wielding in their self-interested niche agendas to frustrate the legitimate will of the wholesome majority. In this vein, scholarship has emerged on how populists – through their 'nationalistic, xenophobic, misogynistic, and explicitly anti-human rights agenda'[5] – have led or instigated a 'backlash' against (or 'undeclared war' on)[6] human rights more generally.

Questions to explore

The above gives a flavour of the context in which this book addresses three related questions of contemporary global significance:

- What is 'populism' and how might its manifestation in recent years be seen as a significant challenge to the future of 'human rights' – both as a hitherto apparently powerful universal idea, and as a set of particular, partly globalised systems of promotion, protection, and remedy?
- In what ways, and to what extent, do populist politicians' recent attacks on human rights (and its defenders and proponents) account for the challenges that the human rights 'project' is perceived to be facing, or are there other important explanations for those challenges? Might a focus on populism risk the human rights 'movement' misdiagnosing the nature and source of challenges to human rights, diverting attention from internal self-reflection by the movement?
- What is revealed in the way that scholars and activists have framed and responded to the populist challenge in terms of forward-looking prescriptions for renewing, revitalising, reframing (etc.) human rights? What does this reveal about the ability of the human rights 'movement' to reflect upon, adapt to, or indeed learn from challenges, whether or not they can or should be described as 'populist' or other political attacks and critiques?

Empiricism is very difficult, but mostly overlooked, in attempted grand sweeping narratives of the trajectory of the human rights project. Nevertheless, the first two of these questions are partly diagnostic in nature in terms of analysing, interpreting, and contextualising existing trends. Yet as the third question suggests, this book's purpose is mostly forward-looking: to explore what might be involved in re-imagining the future of human rights in a populist,

5 Phillip Alston, 'The Populist Challenge to Human Rights' (2017) 9(1) *Journal of Human Rights Practice*, 1–15, 1.

6 Susan Marks, 'Backlash: The Undeclared War against Human Rights' (2014) 4 *European Human Rights Law Rev.* 319-32.

nationalist, sovereigntist, post-truth era. Part of this must involve asking what various scholarly narratives about the future of human rights, optimistic and pessimistic, imply in terms of assumptions about how healthy the human rights project was *before* certain changes are said to have occurred. It is just not obvious that human rights were an ever-rising 'mighty river'[7] of inevitable progress everywhere before 'the populists' triggered their supposed decline or crisis.

Equally importantly, it is not obvious that if human rights do face some existential threat, that 'populism' is the principal source of that threat. Part of this question must therefore also surely involve exploring how a focus on 'populism' as a problem, as *the* problem for human rights, while no doubt important, also carries potential risks in analytical and strategic terms. Foremost among these is the risk of an incomplete or distorted diagnosis of the source and nature of challenges to greater freedom, security, equality, inclusivity, and well-being in the 21st century. After all, since the early 2000s, scholars have consistently been asking whether, contrary to the 'age of rights' thesis, we might have already moved into a 'post human rights era' (Celermajer 2005), or variously the 'end' (Douzinas 2000), 'end-times' (Hopgood 2013), or 'twilight' (Posner 2014) of human rights.[8] In this context, does the 'populist challenge' narrative give enough space or mention to other issues with significant implications for the future of human rights? Alongside this is the risk, in merely decrying the populist challenge, of obscuring significant opportunities. That is, the chance to reflect on what important lessons the electoral and other political success of right-wing populism (in particular) might tell us in terms of the ongoing struggle to find impactful, legitimate, and inclusive principled ways to advance human freedom, dignity, and flourishing while also providing important constraints on public and private concentrations of power. This book thus offers a provocation to the human rights movement. Rather than '*what have populists done to human rights*?' it asks '*how did we, the human rights movement, do this to ourselves*?' How did fundamental protections for all become so apparently easily scapegoated by populists as 'us and them,' as merely the obstructionist claims of small, often foreign, minorities? Did the human rights project lose some vital connection to ordinary people's interests, the value of rights taken as obvious and self-explanatory? How might we reimagine human rights as underpinning human flourishing within planetary limitations?

7 Jenny Martinez, 'Human Rights and History' (2012) 126 *Harvard Law Review Forum* 121-140, 137.

8 Danielle Celermajer, 'Are We Entering a Post Human Rights Era?' (2005) 14(1) *Human Rights Defender* 2-5; Costas Douzinas, *The End of Human Rights* (Oxford University Press, 2000); Stephen Hopgood, *The End-Times of Human Rights* (Cornell University Press, 2013); Eric Posner, *The Twilight of Human Rights* (Oxford University Press, 2014).

Outline of the book

The balance of this introduction now sets out how this book unfolds – its content and scope.

Part 1 ('Patterns') assesses the ways in which scholars and activists have perceived, described and responded to the populist challenge to human rights after 2010, and especially from 2015-2016 onward. It chronicles patterns of populist backsliding on human rights protections, along with backlash against human rights as a legal-political idiom. In doing so, Part I engages briefly with how 'populism' is defined in this literature, and how this book treats that very complex phenomenon. A comment on the book's timeframe is required. The reference to 2015-16 is not intended to mark any particular event: it is simply when one can discern the emergence of the distinctive contemporary set of scholarly and activist commentaries on 'the populist challenge to human rights.'[9] The mid-2010s period is also a placeholder for populist-nationalist political trends – described in Part I – associated with things such as the Brexit debate and vote in the United Kingdom, the election of President Donald Trump, the ascendancy of Poland's Law and Justice Party and consolidation of its Hungarian equivalent, and so on. However, this book is not by any means confined to the rise of so-called 'illiberal democracy' in Western (North American and European) societies: it engages with a literature that covers contemporary populist-nationalist trends in 'newer' democracies from Brazil to Turkey, Colombia to the Philippines.

In many such places, Left- or Right-wing populism and its ingredient forces (and their impacts on or approach to human rights) obviously predate the middle of the 2010s decade. Of course, a book such as this could seek to explore whether, for instance, political-economic populism in the last decade springs in some way from the fallout from the 2008–2009 global financial crisis and the perceived impunity of those elites whose deal-making fostered first systemic collapse and then state-sponsored bail-outs. In Europe, one could add in the sovereign debt crisis of the 2010s. It might be thought that such shocks came on top of more general growing disillusionment, in both developed and developing countries, with the much-heralded benefits of market integration and economic globalisation. In the mix, too, might perhaps be the deep generalised crisis in the legitimacy and credibility of the liberalising, globalising world order that the 2003 US-led invasion of Iraq appeared to generate. Yet these would be contestable views with tremendous context specificity in different political geographies: while it cannot avoid some commentary, this book does not attempt to fix any timeframes let alone very difficult cause-effect diagnoses. Nor does it posit human rights as some ahistorical

9 See n. 2 above.

phenomenon untouched by populist forces or unrelated to notions of 'populism' before 2015. Instead, it is just the emergence around 2015–2016 of the counter-populist human rights *literature* that explains the book's focus on that period, along with the imperative to limit the scope of study in what is a short-length book. Indeed, the book's true focus is not 'the populist challenge to human rights' itself. The focus is instead on how the human rights movement and academy have framed and responded to that challenge, situating it in the context of the range of internal and external challenges, some of an enduring nature.

Part 2 ('Problems') revisits some enduring 'pre-populist' critiques of human rights, both as a legal-political vocabulary and as a set of normatively grounded institutions, mechanisms, and practices. It asks a range of questions that arguably are not posed or sufficiently treated in the 'populist challenge' literature. Some of these are inconvenient or uncomfortable for those committed to human rights. To what extent might the challenges now faced by the human rights project be part of its own doing, or even a potentially inevitable function of some inescapable paradoxes and contradictions in how human rights are understood or manifested? To what extent might it be said that the human rights firmament was in decline anyway, and so was not necessarily just undermined by populist attack? Can one really analyse a backlash against human rights in isolation from a wider backlash to globalisation in the form of the neoliberal world 'order'? If the populist backlash against human rights has some traction, what is it about patterns in human rights practice and discourse that might have made this more likely or possible? To what extent is there some merit to some of the populist critiques of human rights (or at least the practice and practitioners of human rights), even if these are deployed cynically in service of political advantage?

Most of what has been written in the last decade about populism and human rights can be crudely characterised as saying '*look what populist leaders have done to human rights!*' Sounding this alarm is very important. Yet this book takes a somewhat different, inward-looking and somewhat provocative perspective: '*what did human rights do to itself?*' That is, what has the human rights movement done or not done that might account, in any way, for any traction and force of populism, or for the limited effectiveness of human rights frames, discourses, or strategies in countering this challenge? As outlined above, the book also seeks to disaggregate some of the scholarly analyses in this area, for example in terms of the limits in being able to ascribe certain effects (on human rights protections and discourse) to certain causes (populism); queries about whether the literature has assembled enough evidence that dismissing human rights was explicitly part of (or effective in) populist strategies generally, beyond just some very particular contexts; queries about what reference point of success or effectiveness is being used in accounts either of the decline or persistence of human rights as an ideology; and so on.

Part 3 ('Progress') draws on this to explore the future of the universalist human rights project, especially in terms of the lessons that populism (and counter-populism) might hold for pursuing that agenda in future. Surveying those scholars who see human rights as enduringly robust, or at least worth revitalising, it questions whether a human rights frame is necessarily powerful and effective. This involves exploring arguments about whether overt rights-talk or rights-promotion in some contexts might be counter-productive, especially where populist backlash might be expected. Part III examines some of the prescriptions that scholars have put forward to counter-populist challenges to the human rights project. In particular, it reflects on what we can read into the vagueness that attends some purported solutions (from being 'more pragmatic' (Kennedy 2012), to engaging in 'more innovative thinking and creative strategizing' (Alston 2017) to being 'more nimble' (De Burca 2021).[10]

A clue to one of this book's key messages lies in that term above, 'counter-populism.' The populist challenge is not simply something to be countered, as important as that is. What matters is not just the need for a principled pushback against the populist backlash: the human rights community must not only counter-populism, it must also learn from it and engage with some of its underlying drivers and its communicative techniques. That is, the populist challenge is also a manifest opportunity for some self-reflection and humility as part of the necessary reframing that might accompany a re-dedication to human rights ideals. In some respects – as noted above, and as Part III discusses – a focus on 'populism' might (lesson-learning aside) in many ways be something of a distraction. This is because while the appeal and strategic utility of 'human rights' as a meta-idea is enduring, so too are the problems and paradoxes associated with it. Populism in some polities revealed some of these issues but it is not necessarily a cause or symptom of them. Part III concludes by reflecting on whether, at least in strategy terms in the context of a populist backlash, what matters is societal activism and contestation to protect and advance the underlying values that rights and rights-talk seek to promote and protect, even if we do not explicitly rely on familiar human rights artefacts and instruments to do so. If activism or diplomacy is not being done explicitly or exclusively in the language of human rights (or human rights as enshrined in law), why does this appear to generate so much anxiety in scholars of this subject?

10 David Kennedy, 'The International Human Rights Regime: Still Part of the Problem?' in Rob Dickenson et al. (eds.) *Examining Critical Perspectives on Human Rights* (Cambridge University Press 2012); Phillip Alston, 'The Populist Challenge to Human Rights' (2017) 9(1) *Journal of Human Rights Practice*, 1–15; Grainne de Burca, *Reframing Human Rights in a Turbulent Era* (Oxford University Press, 2021).

Caveat, clarification, caution

First, a brief caveat is required. Both 'populism' and 'human rights' – let alone issues when the two interact – might conceivably be defined and approached from a variety of disciplines, from political science and international relations, to law, to behavioural economics and social psychology. Just the recent literature on the future of human rights alone is bewilderingly large and diverse. It follows that this book is not an attempt at a fully theorised research monograph and so does not comprehensively survey all potentially relevant literatures. Instead, it should be approached as one accessible, short-length scholarly meditation on a topical issue of our times. One consequence of this is that at times some of the literature may be portrayed in a somewhat stylised way, typically for the sake of argument – and of brevity. Another consequence is that the book avoids – or perhaps aims to transcend – particular disciplinary strictures and structures.[11]

Second, at this point, it is worth noting an important clarification, even if we must also revisit this along the way. Scholars engaging with the future of human rights tend to share one thing in common, whether their work relates to the post-2015 populist challenge or to more longstanding critiques of human rights. Indeed, this is something in common with populist leaders themselves, those who might scapegoat or dismiss human rights. This is because it is not always clear whether 'human rights' in these contexts refers to (a) the substantive norms involved, or (b) the institutions, mechanisms, and processes (at various levels from local to global) intended to give these norms effect, or (c) the individuals, groups or organisations that 'do' human rights. Without greater clarity, how can we know which of these is under attack or challenge, let alone whether a purported attack has any actual impact?

Even within these distinct arenas or aspects there is a risk of over-simplification and generalisation. For instance, we will see that much of both the populist-political and scholarly critique of human rights revolves, in effect, around a narrative of elite governance and the problems associated with 'human rights' supposedly being done or run globally by a highly professionalised, unaccountable, legalistic gentrified elite. Part II explores this in greater depth. But it is too easy or lazy to lump actors together as the 'human rights movement' or 'human rights professionals.'[12] Clearly, criticism of the

11 This is the spirit of John Braithwaite, 'In Praise of Tents: Regulatory Studies and Transformative Social Science' (2014) 10 *Annual Review of Law and Social Science* 1-17.

12 See in this regard Hilary Charlesworth, 'Author! Author! A Response to David Kennedy' (2002) 15 *Harvard Human Rights Journal* 127–131, 128–129. More recently, in the context of the populism debate, see Phillip Alston, 'Reply to Dudai and Nagaraj' (2017) 9 *Journal of Human Rights Practice* 25; also Grainne de Burca, *Reframing Human Rights in a Turbulent Era* (Oxford University Press, 2021), 191.

practices of the global head of Human Rights Watch issuing statements from a New York skyscraper is not necessarily criticism of other localised civil society actors that together make up 'the movement' (if indeed it exists as a coherent thing). A populist or other critique or dismissal of 'human rights' might not necessarily be addressed to, or land any significant blows against, all these very diverse sets of actors. Thus throughout the book there is an effort to be clearer, perhaps than some contributions to the literature, about the source of the perceived attack or challenge, and about which conception and/or feature or artefact of human rights is supposedly affected. The analytical task is complicated by the fact, well known to human rights scholars, that the open nature of human rights renders them susceptible to appropriation by all manner of actors in service of all sorts of sometimes contradictory agendas.

Despite noting this, it is not always easy to disaggregate talking about human rights institutions from those working in and around them, from the substantive normative edifices or ecosystems variously underpinning or invoked in this work, or from human rights as either an overall grand idea or conceptual and rhetorical devices of political discourse. At the very least, it is very convenient short-hand for an author to talk about 'the wider human rights project' (or enterprise, or experiment), as in this book. But we must guard against glossing over the different things we could mean when we say 'human rights are under challenge,' and guard against describing something ('the project' or 'movement') into greater coherence than in fact exists. Moreover, the 'project' term does imply that human rights is a viable and inevitable, but merely incomplete, consensus process towards some utopia. Perhaps one part of the scholarly challenge is greater theorisation and attempted empiricism of whether, when, and how alleged agendas against or effects on some of these components (of the overall notion of human rights) affect the legitimacy, effectiveness, utility (etc.) of other component elements. Part of the book's purpose, then, is to seek a clearer set of questions with which a forward research agenda on human rights might need to engage in the context of populism and other forces.

Third and finally, a cautionary point on author ethics. In engaging with the populist-nationalist authoritarian 'moment,' many leading scholars have described human rights as facing profound, existential challenges that are distinct from what may have gone before (see Part I). On this view, at stake are not just substantive rights protections but the very future of human rights as a mobilising discourse with any political salience and emancipatory or protective potency. If this is so, it might well be asked whether it is somewhat indulgent and non-constructive for scholarship such as this to focus internally on some of the shortcomings or contradictions of human rights and its proponents. After all, there is some potential irony in decrying authoritarian backsliding on human rights while giving further oxygen to its shortcomings.

Academics are sometimes wont to adopt postures of critical scepticism as if these elevate the author, including above their own politics.[13] Still, it is enough to be aware of this dilemma and put it aside. This is especially so in a book that asks, ultimately, whether we ought to be learning from populist (or other) critiques and not merely condemning these. Moreover, to refrain from critical perspectives would be to treat human rights as too fragile to withstand robust examination and debate.[14] *That* would suggest the age of human rights has indeed ended.

13 Danielle Celermajer, comments, 6th Australian Human Rights Teachers Workshop, UNSW Law School, Sydney, 17 February 2016. See too Alston, 'The Populist Challenge to Human Rights,' 13 (on the unintended consequences of 'fashionable' critical scholarship disparaging the 'undoubted shortcomings' of human rights in 'dramatic and sometimes destructive ways').

14 See in this regard David Kennedy, *The Dark Sides of Virtue* (Princeton University Press, 2004), 3-4, 35 (human rights is not a 'frail child' in need of protection from critical assessment).

1

PATTERNS

'Populism' and its claimed impact on human rights in recent times

In September 2016, the United Nations High Commissioner for Human Rights (Prince Zeid Ra'an Al Hussein) gave a passionate speech in The Hague denouncing 'populists and demagogues.'[1] This was in the final months of Donald Trump's first US presidential election campaign, in the aftermath of the UK Brexit vote and, across Europe, growing public debate on immigration in the context Syrian refugee intakes, among other things. Zeid spoke of the 'lies and half-truths, manipulation and peddling of fear' that populist politicians in the United States and Europe were increasingly engaged in and – in human rights terms – of the risk that such politicking represented to peaceful, tolerant, inclusive societies. Such concerns and commentary were so widespread in politics and the media at this time, well beyond peak human rights institutional office-holders, that it would be almost impossible to chronicle them (although their assumed prevalence beyond Europe and the US is something we must return to). Within the global human rights 'movement,' higher-profile entities echoed Zeid's concerns by identifying populist leadership and rhetoric as the main threat to human rights not just in Europe and the US but globally.[2] Amnesty International's annual report on the state of human rights for 2016–2017 saw:

1 Prince Zeid Ra'an Al Hussein (UN High Commissioner for Human Rights), 'Zeid Warns Against Populists and Demagogues in Europe and U.S.' Speech, The Hague, 5 September 2016; https://www.ohchr.org/en/NewsEvents/Pages/DisplayNews.aspx?NewsID=20452&LangID=E

2 Amnesty International *2016–2017: The state of the world's human rights* (Annual Report, London, 2017), Kenneth Roth, 'Pushback Against the Populist Challenge to Human Rights' in Human Rights Watch, *World Report 2018: Events of 2017* (Annual Report, New York, 2018) and 'The dangerous rise of populism: global attacks on human rights values' (2017) 70th Anniversary Issue *Journal of International Affairs* 79-84; see too Ian Siederman, 'The UN High Commissioner for Human Rights in the Age of Global Backlash' (2019) 37(1) *Netherlands Quarterly of Human Rights* 5.

DOI: 10.4324/9781003311140-2

> the idea of human dignity and equality, the very notion of a human family, coming under vigorous and relentless assault from powerful narratives of blame, fear and scapegoating, propagated by those who sought to take or cling on to power at almost any cost.[3]

Likewise, the Human Rights Watch report on 2017 warned of political forces that built their constituency by 'demonizing unpopular minorities, attacking human rights principles and fuelling distrust of democratic institutions.'[4] Around this time, the scholarly literature began to echo activists' concern with the populist 'nationalistic, xenophobic, misogynistic, and explicitly anti-human rights agenda.'[5] Scholars came to fix on populism as the most significant challenge in this field through works with such titles as:[6]

- 2017: 'The Populist Challenge to Human Rights';[7]
- 2018: 'Rising to the Populist Challenge: A New Playbook for Human Rights';[8]
- 2019: 'The Rise of Populism and the War on Human Rights';[9]
- 2020: 'Human Rights in a Time of Populism.'[10]

Over this period, some academics felt 'an acute sense of whiplash'[11] at the extent to which hitherto liberal democratic states in particular – apparently acting on or pandering to populist impulses – were backsliding on their commitments to (and becoming increasingly critical of) international norms and governance mechanisms in the areas of human rights and international criminal justice. Most scholarly and transnational advocacy approaches have proceeded on the basis that the populist challenge to human rights:

3 *Amnesty International report 2016–2017: The state of the world's human rights* (London, 2017), 12.

4 Kenneth Roth, 'Pushback Against the Populist Challenge to Human Rights' in Human Rights Watch, *World Report 2018: Events of 2017* (Annual Report, New York, 2018).

5 Phillip Alston, 'The populist challenge to human rights' (2017) 9(1) *Journal of Human Rights Practice*, 1–15, 1.

6 Fagan, meanwhile, uses the 'populist' and 'demagogic' challenge interchangeably: Andrew Fagan, 'The Gentrification of Human Rights' (2019) 41 *Human Rights Quarterly* 283.

7 See in particular Philip Alston, 'The Populist Challenge to Human Rights' (2017) 9(1) *Journal of Human Rights Practice* 1.

8 Cesar Rodriguez-Garavito and Krizna Gomez (eds.), *Rising to the Populist Challenge: A New Playbook for Human Rights* (De Justitia, Bogota, 2018).

9 Darren O'Byrne, 'The Rise of Populism, the Demise of the Neoliberal and Neoconservative Globalist Projects, and the War on Human Rights' (2019) 9(2) *International Critical Thought* 254–268.

10 Gerald Neuman (ed.) *Human Rights in a Time of Populism* (Cambridge University Press, 2020).

11 Diane Orentlicher, 'The Emerging Shape of Global Justice: Retrogression or Course Correction?' (2020) 35 *Maryland Journal of International Law* 61-72, 61.

(a) is new and distinctive;
(b) is only growing;
(c) is a world-wide phenomenon, or (but which mostly is implied) its impact on 'leading' or exemplar liberal democracies nevertheless inevitably has global implications;
(d) has features in common even if it is sometimes noted that the nature and extent of the challenge varies considerably from country to country; and
(e) is an existential challenge for the future of human rights (and, in a wider literature, to the values or institutions of democracy, constitutionalism and the rule of law more generally).[12]

Thus the leading article declared unambiguously that the populist challenge is 'fundamentally different' from what has come before.[13] We live, we are told, in an age of populist resentment against the liberal international order and its core national-level political form: liberal constitutional democracy, based overtly on human rights.[14] Populism is seen as *the* cause of a new crisis in human rights,[15] a 'new type of threat' portending a 'dark future'[16] that poses 'grave obstacles' to internationalised protection of rights, and indeed has already done 'systemic damage.'[17] Yet if populism and populist demagoguery is so significant, and so problematic – 'the crack cocaine of contemporary politics'[18] – what does the term mean or represent?

12 Andrew Arato and Jean Cohen, *Populism and Civil Society: The Challenge to Constitutional Democracy* (Oxford University Press, 2021). See too Cesar Rodriguez-Garavito, 'Disrupting Human Rights: Existential Challenges and a New Paradigm' in Nehal Bhuta, Florian Hoffmann, Sarah Knuckey, Frédéric Mégret, and Margaret Satterthwaite (eds.), *The Struggle for Human Rights Essays in Honour of Phillip Alston* (Oxford University Press, 2021).
13 Phillip Alston, 'The populist challenge to human rights' (2017) 9(1) *Journal of Human Rights Practice*, 1–15, 2.
14 Bojan Bugaric, 'Could Populism Be Good for Constitutional Democracy?' (2019) 15(1) *Annual Review of Law and Social Science* 41-58, 43. For another relatively recent comprehensive review, see Sergei Guriev and Elias Pappaioannou, 'The Political Economy of Populism' (2022) 60(3) *Journal of Economic Literature* 753-832 (I am grateful to Phillip Alston for drawing this to my attention).
15 James Loeffler and Mila Versteeg, 'The Future of Human Rights Scholarship' (2018) 81 *Law and Contemporary Problems* i.
16 Laurence Helfer, 'Populism and International Human Rights Law Institutions: a Survival Guide' in Neuman (ed.) 2020, 218. See too, to the same effect, Jeremy Waldron, 'Rule-of-Law Rights and Populist Impatience' in Neuman (ed.) 2020, 52; also Leslie Vinjamuri, 'Human rights backlash' in Stephen Hopgood, Jack Snyder and Leslie Vinjamuri (eds.), *Human Rights Futures* (Cambridge University Press, 2018), Ch 5. See also (but not specific to populism) Grainne de Burca, *Reframing Human Rights in a Turbulent Era* (Oxford University Press, 2021), 200.
17 Gerald Neuman, 'Populist threats to the international human rights system' in Neuman (ed.) 2020, 4, 15.
18 Andrew Fagan, 'The Gentrification of Human Rights' (2019) 41 *Human Rights Quarterly* 283, 307.

DEFINING 'POPULISM'

First, a brief aside on the 'human rights' portion of the composite phrase 'the populist challenge to human rights.' This book does not attempt to define 'human rights,' although the introduction notes the importance of distinguishing, as we proceed, between rights as norms, rights-talk or discourse, rights activists or defenders, and rights institutions or mechanisms. If anything, the book's intention is to engage with human rights *as practised* in politics and international relations.[19] It does not purport to engage in questions about the true basis for the authority of rights[20] or debate about whether human rights exist as such or are merely products of efforts to articulate and use them instrumentally,[21] or whether they are valuable mostly not in themselves but because of the universal values that they seek to advance or protect.[22] Nevertheless, in all that follows it is important to note that questions of apparent 'mere philosophy' might be of very considerable 'practical' real-world importance. That is, at least part of the vulnerability of the human rights project to challenge (populist or other) remains the enduring uncertainty, disagreement, or doubt about some of these questions on the source or basis, nature, etc., of universal human rights.

If we can put definitions of 'human rights' aside, then, we do need to consider what might be meant by 'populism.' We need not resolve here the scholarly debate on whether populism is an ideology or merely a strategy or even just methodology (style, technique) of politics, or what organisational forms it might take.[23] Mudde describes it as a 'thin-centred' ideology (or, style or strategy, etc.) that views or portrays society as divided into two distinct and antagonistic groups: 'the people' (wholesome, victimised and virtuous) versus 'the elite' (corrupt, illegitimate, and out-of-touch). Moreover, the nation's direction and politics should reflect the 'general will' of the former and should

19 In this sense, the approach is not dissimilar to that adopted in Charles Beitz, *The Idea of Human Rights* (Oxford University Press, 2009).

20 See, for example, the question posed in Conor Gearty, *Can Human Rights Survive?* (Cambridge University Press, 2006), 11, and Ch. 2 generally.

21 David Kennedy, *The Dark Sides of Virtue* (Princeton University Press, 2004), 7.

22 For example, Joseph Raz, 'Human Rights in the Emerging World Order' (2010) 1 *Transnational Legal Theory* 31; or somewhat differently, for example, Jürgen Habermas, 'The Concept of Human Dignity and the Realistic Utopia of Human Rights' (2010) 41(4) *Metaphilosophy* 464-480 (rights are instruments for the effective implementation of core moral values of an 'egalitarian universalism').

23 One recent comprehensive work on populism in democracies distinguishes four main organizational forms: socio-political movement, political party, government, and regime: Andrew Arato and Jean Cohen, *Populism and Civil Society: The Challenge to Constitutional Democracy* (Oxford University Press, 2021). For present purposes it is not necessary to explore these distinctions, or ones between populist individual leaders and the parties or groups that they might lead.

ignore or dismantle legal and other structures that the latter have erected to insulate or enrich themselves and frustrate that popular will.[24] The populist often takes latent, unarticulated feelings of exclusion, disenfranchisement, and resentment among a group (the 'forgotten and despised') and is able to offer them a sense of value and to weave a fairly 'coherent political doctrine promoting profound change.'[25] The dominant strain of analysis relies on the 'ideational' approach:[26] a form or style of politics that employs an exclusionary (and, by definition, exclusively inclusionary) notion of 'the people' (the 'real' people versus unworthy other groups), on whose behalf the populist must rule. On this definition, populism is anti-pluralist, anti-elitist (constructs of 'real virtuous people versus corrupt domineering elites'), and a phenomenon in which the populist leader speaks for and directly with the 'real' people, whose collective [homogenous] will should be enabled without legal constraints (such as human rights).[27]

The better literature observes that the drivers or causes are diverse and highly context-specific, even if scholars certainly attempt to identify some common grievances and conditions such as anti-globalisation, economic insecurity, unmet expectations of democratisation, corruption, unresponsive government, frustration with the criminal justice system, convergence and indistinguishability of mainstream parties, and so on. The literature mostly accepts that this is an identifiable pattern phenomenon even if its specific causes, patterns and circumstances vary quite considerably across different political systems, and notwithstanding that populists in the sense above might hail from a Leftist or Right-wing orientation. For instance, one might attempt to generalise how South American populist leaders tend to be Leftist, whereas North American or northern European ones tend to be

24 Cas Mudde, 'The Populist Zeitgeist' (2004) 39(3) *Government and Opposition* 541, 543; more generally Cas Mudde and Cristobal Rivera Kaltwasser, *Populism: A Very Short Introduction* (Oxford University Press, 2017). See too Dwayne Woods, 'The many faces of populism' in Dwayne Woods and Barbara Wejnert (eds.), *The many faces of populism: current perspectives* (Emerald, Bingley, 2014); Yasha Mounk, 'Pitchfork politics: the populist threat to liberal democracy (2014) 9(3) *Foreign Affairs* 27–36; Benjamin Moffitt, *The global rise of populism* (Stanford University Press, 2016); and Jan-Werner Müller, *What Is Populism?* (Penguin, London, 2017).

25 Hans-George Betz, 'Populist mobilization across time and space' in Kirk Hawkins et al. (eds.), *The Ideational Approach to Populism* (Routledge, New York, 2018), cited in Ronald Pernia, 'Human Rights in a Time of Populism: Philippines under Duterte' (2019) 19(3) *Asia-Pacific Social Science Review* 56–71, 65.

26 See Jan-Werner Müller, *What Is Populism?* (University of Pennsylvania Press, 2016), and Cas Mudde, 'Populism: An Ideational Approach' in Cristóbal Rovira Kaltwasser et al. (eds.) *The Oxford Handbook of Populism* (Oxford University Press, 2017).

27 Gerald Neuman, 'Populist threats to the international human rights system' in Neuman (ed.) 2020, 4. For a review of definitions, see Sergei Guriev and Elias Pappaioannou, 'The Political Economy of Populism' (2022) 60(3) *Journal of Economic Literature* 753-832, especially 758.

found on the political Right,[28] but only a few counter-examples are needed to reveal the problems with such generalisations (e.g., Colombian Right-wing populism, or Left-wing populists in the US Democratic Party). South-East Asian populism, meanwhile, may not be readily explicable along a Left–Right axis, instead being character-driven (Philippines' Joseph Estrada and Rodrigo Duterte) or organised on nationalist (Prabowo Subianto of Indonesia) or rural-urban (Thailand: Thaksin Shinawatra) lines.[29] Populism is not a binary concept (President X is either 'populist' or not) and, if it is indeed a distinctive phenomenon at all, is observable in matters of degree.[30] What all forms are said to have in common is the deployment of 'simplifying narratives'[31] around certain themes that arguably make populism a distinctive enough phenomenon to analyse and work with: anti-pluralism ('us' versus 'them'), anti-institutionalism (personalised rule of governance), and anti-elitism.[32] The latter has been described as *the* 'common denominator' of populism, marked by fostering, or giving expression to, popular dissatisfaction with some often vaguely identified local or global 'cosmopolitan elite' to whom the people are morally superior.[33]

Stereotypical populists such as Presidents Duterte (Philippines, 2016–2022) or Trump (United States, 2017–2021) are portrayed as creating the image of a tough but benevolent 'patriarch' of a nation under threat from within, a patriot who cares deeply for his or her people. This image is contrasted to the 'detached and callous technocrats' that have governed hitherto.[34] A common theme, then, is a challenge to the 'establishment' or 'elites' by outsiders on behalf of the common people or, in some cases, by insiders who claim a mandate from the common people.[35] Populism 'promises to protect

28 For an example of this, see Nienke Grossman, 'Populism, International Courts, and Women's Human Rights' (2020) 35 *Maryland Journal of International Law* 104-126.

29 Pernia 2019, 60, citing Olli Hellmann, 'Populism in East Asia' in Cristobal Rivera Kaltwasser et al. (eds.) *The Oxford Handbook on Populism* (Oxford University Press, 2017).

30 Sergei Guriev and Elias Pappaioannou, 'The Political Economy of Populism' (2022) 60(3) *Journal of Economic Literature* 753-832, 763.

31 Andrew Fagan, 'The Gentrification of Human Rights' (2019) 41 *Human Rights Quarterly* 283, 285.

32 Cesar Rodriguez-Garavito and Krizna Gomez (eds.), (Editors' introduction) in *Rising to the Populist Challenge: A New Playbook for Human Rights* (De Justitia, Bogota, 2018), 17: populists come equally from the Right (Modi, Erdoğan, Putin, Trump) and the Left (Maduro, Correa, Ortega).

33 Darren O'Byrne, 'The Rise of Populism, the Demise of the Neoliberal and Neoconservative Globalist Projects, and the War on Human Rights' (2019) 9(2) *International Critical Thought* 254-268, 255.

34 Shamila Parmanand, 'Duterte as the Macho Messiah: chauvinist populism and the feminisation of human rights in the Philippines' (2020) 29(2) *Review of Women's Studies* 1-30, 29.

35 Eric Posner, 'Liberal Internationalism and the Populist Backlash' (2020) 49 *Arizona State Law Journal* 795, 796.

the ordinary people abandoned by the liberal elite.'[36] For many of its supporters, populism appears to offer the types of political options and choices which (typically more liberal) elites managed to exclude from the ticket or consign to the margins for so long.[37] Where 'reformism' is about gradual and inclusionary approaches to better governance, 'populism' is explicit about its rejection of (and blame against) elitist governance.[38] This strong emphasis on anti-elitism is accompanied by prioritising popular sovereignty, more direct democracy, and personal (not institutional) rule.[39]

One meta-study of populism literature sees this as a 'spectre haunting the West' in contrast, supposedly, to being confined previously to Latin America.[40] In any event, perhaps the clearest or archetypal version of contemporary (Right-wing) nationalist populism in the literature is the Eastern and Central Europe version. It is not necessary to explore whether or not this is in fact a product of the European sovereign debt crisis, concern about immigration and/or terrorism, or any manner of potential drivers and causes. It is enough to snapshot the pattern that this version of populism posits liberalism as an external phenomenon, a 'non-national and even anti-national project' that 'subordinates the interests of the nation to foreign capital, on the one hand, and to foreign models of multiculturalism, [minority and] LGBT rights, and refugee protection.'[41] Of course, many of these features are not common to populism as experienced outside of Europe. Still, if there is a broad populist-nationalist-sovereigntist meta-trend at all, it can be summarised, perhaps, as attacking supra-national governance mechanisms along with other symbols of the prevailing order: liberal democracy, neoliberal economics, migration and multiculturalism, orthodox histories, political correctness, and socio-cultural tolerance, moderate political parties, and the mainstream media.[42]

Is there inevitably a gendered dimension to this phenomenon? While recent elected populist strongmen have used sexualised rhetoric and exhibited very patronising, chauvinistic, or sexist views of women, populism as a concept

36 Bojan Bugaric, 'Could Populism Be Good for Constitutional Democracy?' (2019) 15(1) *Annual Review of Law and Social Science* 41-58, 43.

37 Andrew Fagan, 'Human Rights in a Time of Populism 2021, by Gerald Neuman (ed.): Book Review' (2021) 43(2) *Human Rights Quarterly* 416-421, 416-417.

38 See Mark Thompson, 'Reformism vs. Populism in the Philippines' (2010) 21(4) *Journal of Democracy* 154-168, 158, cited in Pernia 2019.

39 Bojan Bugaric, 'Could Populism Be Good for Constitutional Democracy?' (2019) 15(1) *Annual Review of Law and Social Science* 41-58, 44.

40 For the most recent comprehensive review, see Sergei Guriev and Elias Pappaioannou, 'The Political Economy of Populism' (2022) 60(3) *Journal of Economic Literature* 753-832. I am grateful to Phillip Alston for drawing this to my attention.

41 Bojan Bugaric, 'Could Populism Be Good for Constitutional Democracy?' (2019) 15(1) *Annual Review of Law and Social Science* 41-58, 49-51.

42 Bojan Bugaric, 'Could Populism Be Good for Constitutional Democracy?' (2019) 15(1) *Annual Review of Law and Social Science* 41-58, 52.

or phenomenon has a somewhat complex relationship with gender issues. At the very least, this is true in terms of the promotion of women's rights and empowerment issues (which a populist may well purport to champion, even if from a very paternalistic and traditionalist approach, for example of 'feminine vs. feminist') along with promoting women's political participation (for example, Eva Peron's Argentina).[43] Nevertheless, the classic 'populist leader' traits tend to smack of the sort of paternalism and patriarchy and patronising that the gender studies tradition has helped to show are so problematic in society generally. Moreover, in practical terms, it has been part of a populist tactic, in more than one setting, to portray movements for greater women's independence or inclusion as merely the schemes of a foreign, 'transnational, non-autochthonous, nefarious elite' rather than 'the people.'[44]

Aside from gender issues, where does or do human rights come into this?[45] Mudde's core definition of 'populism' turns on a politics that promises to reduce, remove, or dismiss constraints on the fulfilment of the popular will and destiny. At least, as observed by scholars in recent years in liberal democracies, human rights standards are just those sorts of constraints. If anything, they are the most high-profile ones, unduly inhibiting the nation from reaching its manifest destiny. Thus one part of the intensely political project of an elected populist such as Duterte is to convey the image of someone who understands the country's problems (and cares for the people's wellbeing) much better than 'obstructionist human rights defenders.'[46] Values and frameworks such as 'due process' or 'human rights' and ideologies of gradual institutional reform are portrayed as obstacles to solving the nation's problems,[47] if not also part of a sophisticated elite conspiracy to govern eternally. Human rights scholars have observed that populists make a connection between elites and marginalised or minority groups that is 'as empirically implausible as it is symbolically and politically powerful.'[48] This connection is as follows: that liberal elites ignore the legitimate concerns, insecurities and deprivations of

43 Nienke Grossman, 'Populism, International Courts, and Women's Human Rights' (2020) 35 *Maryland Journal of International Law* 104-126, 105, 109-110, 114-116, 120. See also Shamila Parmanand, 'Duterte as the Macho Messiah: chauvinist populism and the feminisation of human rights in the Philippines' (2020) 29(2) *Review of Women's Studies* 1-30.

44 Nienke Grossman, 'Populism, International Courts, and Women's Human Rights' (2020) 35 *Maryland Journal of International Law* 104-126, 126.

45 For one compilation defining populism as a human rights problem, albeit mostly in terms of law and legal process, see Jure Vidmar (ed.), *European Populism and Human Rights* (Brill Nijhoff 2020).

46 Shamila Parmanand, 'Duterte as the Macho Messiah: chauvinist populism and the feminisation of human rights in the Philippines' (2020) 29(2) *Review of Women's Studies* 1-30, 29.

47 Shamila Parmanand, 'Duterte as the Macho Messiah: chauvinist populism and the feminisation of human rights in the Philippines' (2020) 29(2) *Review of Women's Studies* 1-30, 19.

48 Cesar Rodriguez-Garavito and Krizna Gomez (eds.), (Editors' introduction) in *Rising to the Populist Challenge: a New Playbook for Human Rights* (De Justitia, Bogota, 2018), 18.

the majority, and unduly promote the claims and interests of an (often immigrant) undeserving, fawned-over minority – and use the language and systems of human rights to do so.

Backsliding and attacks on human rights standards (and on their defenders) are certainly nothing new. However, the 'populist challenge' literature is framed by noting what is said to be a new dimension that raises the stakes: that such attacks are coming from *elected* governments in states hitherto committed to human rights values, creating tension and potential de-coupling between the 'liberal' and 'democratic' components of liberal democracy.[49] Thus Mudde and Kaltwasser argue that while populism may be *democratic* (manifesting popular sovereignty and majority rule), it is threatening to *liberal* democracy with the latter's insistence on independent institutions that exist to protect the rule of law and human rights standards, and to prevent the 'tyranny of the majority.'[50] The 'democratic' element creates a particular tension in how populism relates to constitutionalism, the rule of law, and human rights.[51] If we see human rights demands as invariably tending to be counter-majoritarian,[52] and as having a role in taming 'the effects of collective (majoritarian) irrationality,'[53] we can also see how supporters of populists are sceptical of (or supportive of attacks on) counter-majoritarian institutions that in effect – and in the popular/populist perception, if not in design – operate to protect minorities.[54]

One meta-study tracks the notable rise of populism and references to it since 2010, including in terms of the term's prevalence on internet searches.[55] The geographic spread of the populist challenge narrative appears, at least at first glance, fairly diverse, from Brexit-era UK[56] and Trump-era US,[57] to East

49 Cesar Rodriguez-Garavito and Krizna Gomez (eds.), (Editors' introduction) in *Rising to the Populist Challenge: a New Playbook for Human Rights* (De Justitia, Bogota, 2018), 15, 20.

50 Cas Mudde and Cristobal Rivera Kaltwasser, *Populism: A Very Short Introduction* (Oxford University Press, 2017).

51 Danielle Celermajer and Don Avnon, 'Human Rights Under "Democratic" Pressure: Navigating a Path Between Truth and Politics' (2019) 41(3) *Human Rights Quarterly* 672-700.

52 Kathryn Sikkink, 'A Cautionary Note about the Frame of Crisis and Peril in Human Rights Activism' in Cesar Rogriguez-Garavito and Krizna Gomez (eds.), (Editors' introduction) in *Rising to the Populist Challenge: a New Playbook for Human Rights* (De Justitia, Bogota, 2018), 171-184, 173.

53 Andrew Fagan, 'Human Rights in a Time of Populism 2021, by Gerald Neuman (ed.): Book Review' (2021) 43(2) *Human Rights Quarterly* 416-421, 421.

54 William Galston, 'The Populist Challenge to Liberal Democracy' (2018) 20 *Journal of Democracy* 5, 11.

55 Sergei Guriev and Elias Pappaioannou, 'The Political Economy of Populism' (2022) 60(3) *Journal of Economic Literature* 753-832.

56 Jeremy Waldron, 'Rule-of-Law Rights and Populist Impatience' in Neuman (ed.) 2020.

57 Steven Pomper and Daniel Levine-Spound, 'US Human Rights Policy and the Trump Administration' in Neuman (ed.) 2020, Ch. 2.

and Central Europe,[58] to Erdogan's Turkey and Modi's India, to South-East Asia,[59] to Latin America.[60] Heydarian would distinguish between developed country populism (anti-immigration, economic stagnation, and culture wars) and emerging market populism (democratic deficit or fatigue, and/or unmet expectations of liberalisation, fragile institutions, and in equality in the context of rapid low-quality growth).[61] This distinction is useful since much of the literature assumes that concerns about immigration are common to all post-2010s populist regimes or parties, but is confined largely to those in Europe, Australasia and North America (although Modi's populist Hindu nationalism seeks to portray India's sizeable Muslim minority as 'foreign'). The pattern in much of the literature is of elected-but-authoritarian-leaning governments in places that have only relatively recently become democratic (such as Hungary, Poland, and Romania) 'backsliding' on the rule of law in democratic terms: undermining governance structures and media ecosystems that limit (and hold to account) executive power in government power. Law and legality hold ambiguous places in these patterns of 'autocratic legalism'[62] or 'populist constitutionalism.'[63] But anti-immigration and anti-elite populism is also a feature of more established democracies (for example, in recent years, the *National Front* in France, the *UK Independence Party*, and *Alternative for Germany*, along with Spain's *Podemos*, *Five-Star* in Italy, *Syriza* in Greece, the *People's Party* in Denmark, and so on). As used in the 'populist challenge to human rights' literature, populism certainly has implied or expressed inevitable connotations of authoritarianism.[64] We ought not to presuppose that the phenomenon inevitably has an 'authoritarian logic.' Still, it is the authoritarian instincts or leanings of (elected) populist leaders of recent years that is at issue in how the challenge to human rights is framed in the literature.[65] Whether or not a populist leader is necessarily authoritarian in tendency, in any event, we can proceed on the basis that modern political populisms are inherently anti-institutional and anti-pluralist and so make a bend towards authoritarianism more likely and appealing.[66] Indeed, Latin America shows how Left-wing populism (Chavez in Venezuela) and Right-wing populism

58 Wojciech Sadurski, 'Populism and Human Rights in Poland' in Neuman (ed.) 2020, Ch. 4.

59 Richard Javad Heydarian, 'Penal Populism in Emerging Markets: Human Rights and Democracy in the Age of Strongmen' in Neuman (ed.) 2020, Ch. 7, 156.

60 Helena Alviar Garcia, 'The Legal Architecture of Populism' in Neuman (ed.) 2020, Ch. 5, 83.

61 Richard Javad Heydarian, 'Penal Populism in Emerging Markets: Human Rights and Democracy in the Age of Strongmen' in Neuman (ed.) 2020, 137-139.

62 Kim Scheppele, 'Autocratic Legalism' (2018) 85 *University of Chicago Law Review* 545.

63 David Landau, 'Populist Constitutions' (2018) 85 *University of Chicago Law Review* 521.

64 Pernia 2019, 59.

65 See generally, for example, Andrew Arato and Jean Cohen, *Populism and Civil Society: The Challenge to Constitutional Democracy* (Oxford University Press, 2021).

66 Nienke Grossman, 'Populism, International Courts, and Women's Human Rights' (2020) 35 *Maryland Journal of International Law* 104-126, 106.

(Uribe in Colombia) might have different ideologies but have very similar styles and approaches.[67]

Of course, there is a separate and very important question here, of what drives populism or creates the conditions in which this form of politicking has traction. That question is well beyond this book's scope,[68] even if (in Part III) we explore the point that the human rights movement ought to make more 'effort' to understand the phenomenon of populism (and indeed, in Part II, how it might have contributed to its rise), rather than merely push back against it. Other books might deal better or more fully with diagnosis (or blame), such as the argument that the ascendancy of Right-wing nationalist populism today is a symptom of the perceived failure of below-expectations progressive politics.[69] The most comprehensive review of studies would suggest the confluence of growing anti-globalisation economic dislocation and disillusionment from about 2008–2009 (alongside de-industrialisation, austerity, and increasing automation), concerns about cultural imposition (and, in the West, immigration ones), together with the rise of internet connectivity and social media.[70] As that study noted, these various drivers might trigger or compound one another and interact in complex ways in particular polities. For now, in ways that relate to some of the discussion below and in Part II, it is enough to note that for many scholars, populism is best understood as a 'creation of its opponents.'[71] That is, the rise of populism tends to follow from a crisis in perceived political representation, particularly the failure of liberal democratic governance to deliver on its promises or include a large proportion of the populace. Thus recent 'ideational approach' scholars argue that while the features of populism are largely latent in most societies and are always contingent on, and indeed produced by, historical and regional context, the populism we see today is a function of perceived dysfunction and non-delivery in democracies.[72] Indeed the same high-profile institutions that helped raise the alarm about the populist challenge to human rights have shown some recognition that the phenomenon is not wholly driven by calculating political players manipulating the population. For the head of Human Rights Watch, for example, the populist era is a function of those discontent with the status quo,

67 Helena Alviar Garcia, 'The Legal Architecture of Populism' in Neuman (ed.) 2020, Ch. 5, 83.

68 See instead Sergei Guriev and Elias Pappaioannou, 'The Political Economy of Populism' (2022) 60(3) *Journal of Economic Literature* 753-832.

69 Bojan Bugaric, 'Could Populism Be Good for Constitutional Democracy?' (2019) 15(1) *Annual Review of Law and Social Science* 41-58.

70 Sergei Guriev and Elias Pappaioannou, 'The Political Economy of Populism' (2022) 60(3) *Journal of Economic Literature* 753-832.

71 Kenneth Roberts, 'Populism, Political Mobilizations, and Crises of Political Representation' in Carlos de la Torre (ed.) *The Promise and Perils of Populism* (Kentucky University Press, 2014).

72 Kirk Hawkins and Cristobal Rivera Kaltwasser, 'Introduction' in Hawkins et al. 2018, 2.

'left behind by technological change' and the global economy, amid growing inequality, people/voters who feel 'unease with their societies growing more diverse' and 'a sense that governments and elites ignore public concerns.'[73]

At this juncture, it is worth putting a placeholder in the reader's mind about the concept of populism and its analysis. As outlined above, most scholarship uses 'populism' in a pejorative sense. Such work proceeds from the assumption that populist politics is invariably associated with authoritarianism and is intrinsically antithetical to human rights, or at least to liberal conceptions of them. On such a view, populism and human rights are 'oil and water.'[74] Most scholarship thus rejects the idea that populism can help promote a healthy rejuvenation of inclusive, democratic, rights-based politics.[75] Yet it may be important to distinguish between the 'popular' and the 'populist,' or to make space for the scope for populist-driven or populist-based projects that might hold promise for greater human rights protection, fulfilment and enjoyment (if not only in 'net' terms). Populism is typically contrasted with constitutionalism, but (perhaps if one does not insist on defining it as necessarily having an anti-pluralist element) arguably has both authoritarian and emancipatory potential, and in empirical terms might have both positive and negative consequences for the health, or stimulation, of participatory democracy.[76] Populism can have positive human rights effects in particular settings.[77] Moreover, Neuman noted that we must ask whether 'populism' necessarily 'conflicts with' internationally recognised human rights or may also represent a legitimate exercise of such rights.[78]

We must be cautious with the idea of populism as a coherent global phenomenon. A leading study portrays it as 'spreading globally' in a 'swift and synchronised' way since about 2010.[79] Yet clearly the nature and scope of the populist threat to human rights varies considerably by geography, to the point where we might question the analytical value-add of the label altogether (as

73 Kenneth Roth, 'The dangerous rise of populism: global attacks on human rights values' (2017) 70th Anniversary Issue *Journal of International Affairs* 79-84, 80.

74 Marcelo Alegre, 'Populism and Human Rights: Oil and Water?' (unpublished paper, SELA 2016, University of Buenos Aires) https://law.yale.edu/sites/default/files/area/center/kamel/sela16_alegre_cv_eng.pdf.

75 For one summary, see Joseph Braun, 'Populism and Human Rights in Theory and Practice' Thesis (University of Nebraska-Lincoln, 2011).

76 Bojan Bugaric, 'Could Populism Be Good for Constitutional Democracy?' (2019) 15(1) *Annual Review of Law and Social Science* 41-58, 42.

77 For example, conservative Erdogan populism in Turkey may have shifted the culture so as to reduce discrimination against openly religious Turks: Jamie O'Connell, 'Representation, Paternalism and Populism' in Neuman (ed.) 2020, Ch. 6. See too Gerald Neuman, 'Populist threats to the international human rights system' in Neuman (ed.) 2020, 6-7.

78 Gerald Neuman, 'Preface' in Neuman (ed.) 2020, xi.

79 Sergei Guriev and Elias Pappaioannou, 'The Political Economy of Populism' (2022) 60(3) *Journal of Economic Literature* 753-832, 753-754.

we do in the first portion of Part III of this book). There is no single form of populism but rather a great variety of these, each with very different political origins, dynamics, and consequences.[80] In principle, a very different sort of populism is also possible: democratic and anti-establishment populism, which combines elements of liberal and democratic convictions.[81] We need to be cautious about erecting populism as not synonymous with democracy.[82] Indeed populism may just be 'democracy's way of saying 'listen harder!'[83] Meanwhile, 'the Establishment' can too easily roll out the term against disruptive actors whose views it dislikes.[84] We thus see human rights scholars describe or perhaps dismiss some populist narratives as 'low brow.'[85] Scholars or observers of populism deride (in the guise of analysis) supporters of Right-wing populists by describing them as ignorantly preferring 'nativist' values of a perceived or desired social homogeneity, yet typically in the name of human rights demand that the majority for diversity reasons respect the [native] desired social values of immigrant minorities. '"They" are ideological (the Right), but "We" have no ideological agenda and are merely committed to universal norms.' It is not hard to see why this sort of perceived dismissal and double standard might generate some febrile conditions for backlash.

As one scholar has cautioned, the concept is 'deeply ambiguous, promiscuously deployed, and chronically politicized.'[86] This is not a lone voice. Thus we should proceed bearing in mind that the currency and ubiquity of the term 'populism' has almost certainly come at the cost of analytical accuracy and contextual nuance.[87] We must return to this observation, and to the need to avoid assuming that populism is ubiquitous across all polities, and always the same or similar (mere sub-strains of a global 'pandemic') wherever it is found therein. Nevertheless, because this book is tracking the arguments of the 'populist challenge' literature, we proceed on the basis that 'populism' connotes the currently hegemonic brand of authoritarian-leaning illiberal

80 Bojan Bugaric, 'Could Populism Be Good for Constitutional Democracy?' (2019) 15(1) *Annual Review of Law and Social Science* 41-58.

81 Bojan Bugaric, 'Could Populism Be Good for Constitutional Democracy?' (2019) 15(1) *Annual Review of Law and Social Science* 41-58.

82 Duncan Johnson, 'In Defence of Democratic Populism' in Neuman (ed.) 2020, Ch 9.

83 Address by Jane Mansbridge, Princeton University, 11 May 2017, cited in Duncan Johnson, 'In Defence of Democratic Populism' in Neuman (ed.) 2020, 207.

84 See Gerald Neuman, 'Populist threats to the international human rights system' in Neuman (ed.) 2020, 4, esp. fn. 12.

85 Jeremy Waldron, 'Rule-of-Law Rights and Populist Impatience' in Neuman (ed.) 2020, 46.

86 Rogers Brubaker, 'Why populism?' (2017) 46(5) *Theory and Society* 357–385, 368.

87 Cesar Rodriguez-Garavito and Krizna Gomez (eds.), (Editors' introduction) in *Rising to the Populist Challenge: A New Playbook for Human Rights* (De Justitia, Bogota, 2018), 17, noting that the term has been applied to political figures as diverse as Donald Trump, Rafael Correa, Vladimir Putin, Nicolás Maduro, Marine Le Pen, Luiz Inácio Lula da Silva, Beppe Grillo, and Daniel Ortega.

anti-pluralist electoral populism. For now, we turn to what scholars and others see as the impact of populism on human rights in the last decade.

Backslide

Between the scholarly literature and institutional reporting, one is left in little doubt that the 2010s-plus era of populism has seen not just inaction on human rights commitments and protections but concerted efforts by many and various governments to undermine or retreat from these. For instance, on the Freedom House annual report, every year since 2006 more countries have shown deterioration than improvement in their overall human rights record. An annual rights index of over 160 countries produced by *The Economist* charts an overall annual decline since 2015. The World Justice Project's *Global Rule of Law Index* suggests declining scores in 'fundamental rights' in over 70 of the roughly 130 countries surveyed.[88]

The 'backslide' aspect of the literature explores this 'general erosion' both of rights protections and of wider societal rights culture and climate.[89] Our focus lies in another aspect of the populist challenge, below, rather than this perceived general or net backslide. Still, we ought to briefly outline the backslide phenomenon. In addition to steps by so-called populist administrations taken at the level of international human rights courts and institutions (to mute their various organs and processes, defund their operations, and so on),[90] most of this backslide on substantive rights protection and culture is at the national level. Some have offered attempted typologies of the sorts of measures against human rights organisations that governments have taken around the world over this time, in ways that are said not only to be more significant than in previous eras, but directly a feature of populist electoral campaigning and/or governance:[91]

- restrictions on foreign funding for human rights organisations;
- smear campaigns against human rights defenders and institutions;

88 Freedom House *Freedom in the World* 2022; The Economist *Democracy Index* 2021; World Justice Project *Global Rule of Law Index* 2021, all cited in Gareth Evans, 'The Future of Human Rights,' The Wallenstein Lecture, Advisory Council on International Affairs (AIV), The Hague, 1 November 2022.

89 See the events and processes canvassed by Gerald Neuman, 'Populist threats to the international human rights system' in Neuman (ed.) 2020, 7-12.

90 See, for example, Laurence Helfer, 'Populism and International Human Rights Law Institutions: A Survival Guide' in Neuman (ed.) 2020, Ch. 10.

91 Cesar Rodriguez-Garavito and Krizna Gomez (eds.), (Editors' introduction) in *Rising to the Populist Challenge: A New Playbook for Human Rights* (De Justitia, Bogota, 2018). See too, for example, the macro patterns described by Andrew Gilmore, 'The Backlash against Human Rights' (UN Assistant Secretary-General for Human Rights), Dublin, November 2017: https://www.ohchr.org/en/statements/2017/12/backlash-against-human-rights.

- killings, disappearances, arbitrary detentions and other violations of or restrictions on fundamental rights of those working in human rights organisations, the independent media and civil society more generally;
- laws and measures undermining or constraining freedom of association and freedom of expression;
- surveillance, disruption and other severe burdens on the operational capabilities of such organisations and individuals (as well as foreign experts under the international human rights treaty system);
- co-optation of sections of civil society into the state apparatus;
- laws promoting a populist-nationalist, revisionist view of history by criminalising criticism of the nation's history;
- laws or other measures to facilitate greater regime control of the media;
- the use of direct participation modes and personal presidential communication to 'the people' to circumvent separation of powers, as in some Latin American populism scenarios (Venezuela, Colombia).[92]

It should be observed that the 'backslide' might not invoke an overt backlash against human rights at all. A populist regime might, as in post-2012 Poland, systematically dismantle the legal environment for the protection and enjoyment of rights without explicit or rhetorical attacks on human rights or 'the movement' or its elites as such.[93] We return to this in Part III. For now, most scholarship accepts the narrative that there has been a net decline in civic and political space across the world and a net backslide in human rights in terms of levels and degrees of their promotion and protection. This is not just in terms of particular deliberate measures and actions by state actors that, in varying degrees of directness, are said to have worsened the extent and degree of enjoyment of human rights around the world. It is also in terms of the new prevalence of (populist) divisive and inflammatory political rhetoric that, it is said, has fostered a permissive climate – in society at large – for individuals and groups to escalate racial and other bias, harassment, discrimination, or targeting.

This is not the place to attempt to illustrate, catalogue, typologise or empirically measure such claims (or even, necessarily, their causal link with populism: but see below). As noted, the focus here is not on this 'backslide' in state activity in upholding or promoting particular human rights standards or mechanisms, as significant as this negative trend undoubtedly is. Instead, this book's focus is on a more 'meta' level: not the backslide on human rights standards and frameworks, but an explicit populist attack on human rights itself, as a legitimate legal-political language and practice. In other words, the

92 Helena Alviar Garcia, 'The Legal Architecture of Populism' in Neuman (ed.) 2020, Ch. 5.
93 Wojciech Sadurski, 'Populism and Human Rights in Poland' in Neuman (ed.) 2020, Ch. 4.

fundamental, existential risk that the 'populist challenge' literature perceives is not just in terms of the above-mentioned sorts of coercive measures and changed legal frameworks that affect the *efficacy* of human rights movements. It is also about populist political narratives that erode the very *legitimacy* of such movements and the overall human rights project and idea that they represent.[94] For argument's sake, we might call this phenomenon the 'populist backlash against human rights.'

Backlash

As observed in the introduction, in a 2018 national address elected then-Filipino president Manuel Duterte attacked local and foreign critics of his populist rhetoric around legitimising law enforcement actions that by-passed basic criminal justice due process rights.[95] When he said to such critics 'your concern is human rights; mine is human *lives*,'[96] Duterte was doing more than just defending an anti-crime strategy. He was seeking political advantage by positioning human rights protections and arguments made in rights terms – but also their proponents – as a principal feature of the societal problems that he had promised 'the people' that he would fix. Again, this is not just backsliding on rights protections, but a backlash involving expressly blaming rights and their defenders for society's ills. It is mostly in this sense, of an '*explicitly* anti-human rights agenda,'[97] that the 'populist challenge' literature sees this as fundamentally different from previous eras. That is, the argument that previously various leaders and governments may certainly have neglected, undermined, or violated human rights standards and frameworks, but did not necessarily seek to attack the legitimacy of the rights order or vernacular itself, but now they do so.

Thus a key plank of the 'populism and human rights' scholarship is that populist leaders and parties have not just fomented social division and stigmatisation, or overseen backsliding in the standard of substantive human rights protections and associated institutional independence and capacity. Instead, populists have (as these scholars tell it) gone beyond this and also downplayed,

94 Cesar Rodriguez-Garavito and Krizna Gomez (eds.), (Editors' introduction) in *Rising to the Populist Challenge: A New Playbook for Human Rights* (De Justitia, Bogota, 2018), 13, 22ff.

95 Third 'State of the Nation' Address, Manila, 24 July 2018, cited in Richard Heydarien, 'Penal Populism in Emerging Markets: Human Rights in an Age of Strongmen,' in Gerald Neuman (ed.) *Human Rights in a Time of Populism* (Cambridge University Press, 2020), Ch. 7, 148.

96 Third 'State of the Nation' Address, Manila, 24 July 2018, cited in Richard Heydarien, 'Penal Populism in Emerging Markets: Human Rights in an Age of Strongmen,' in Gerald Neuman (ed.) *Human Rights in a Time of Populism* (Cambridge University Press, 2020), Ch. 7, 148.

97 Phillip Alston, 'The populist challenge to human rights' (2017) 9(1) *Journal of Human Rights Practice*, 1–15, 1.

dismissed, and/or delegitimised the very concept of human rights themselves. On this account, the populist leader has sought to portray human rights (and those defending it) as elitist, overly litigious, bureaucratised, narrow-minded, minority-pandering, and out-of-touch obstructions to the legitimate frustrated will of the silent native majority masses. Taken to its logical conclusion, at stake is seen to be whether in a populist present and future the human rights project (or ideas or arguments or claims framed in human rights terms) will have any legal-political weight at all, given populism's 'outright rejection' or 'fundamental negation' of the culture, language, and modalities of human rights.[98] Thus some see the fate and future of the whole human rights project as being determined by whether and how the human rights 'movement' can respond to the populist challenge through the 2020s.[99]

After 2010, scholars were writing of how international human rights (and especially regional human rights legal mechanisms) faced increasing legitimacy problems. This was in the form of (or as a result of) a 'potentially disabling scepticism and critique, resentment and even resistance' from governments, including of states that 'pride themselves as promoters of human rights and democracy both at home and abroad.'[100] Likewise, in the area of international criminal justice, one could observe a host of attacks by state leaders, sometimes in a populist vein, on the legitimacy or credibility or effectiveness of institutions such as the International Criminal Court.[101] Supranational governance mechanisms have long generated state contestation, so what was seen as different was the political rhetoric not only challenging the legitimacy of human rights arguments and institutions but through populist techniques openly seeking domestic political (electoral) advantage by doing so. Thus, by the mid-2010s, scholars identified a 'growing backlash against one of the most distinctive projects of Modernity: human rights.'[102] A United

98 Darren O'Byrne, 'The Rise of Populism, the Demise of the Neoliberal and Neoconservative Globalist Projects, and the War on Human Rights' (2019) 9(2) *International Critical Thought* 254-268, 263, 267.

99 Andrew Fagan, 'The Gentrification of Human Rights' (2019) 41 *Human Rights Quarterly* 283, 285.

100 Johan Karlsson Schaffer, Andreas Føllesdal and Geir Ulfstein, 'International Human Rights and the Challenge of Legitimacy' in Andreas Føllesdal, Johan Karlsson Schaffer and Geir Ulfstein (eds.), *The Legitimacy of International Human Rights Regimes: Legal, Philosophical and Political Perspectives* (Cambridge University Press, 2013).

101 Diane Orentlicher, 'The Emerging Shape of Global Justice: Retrogression or Course Correction?' (2020) 35 *Maryland Journal of International Law* 61-72.

102 Andrew Fagan, 'Human Rights in a Time of Populism, by Gerald Neuman (ed.): Book Review' (2021) 43(2) *Human Rights Quarterly* 416-421, 416; see too Andrew Gilmore, 'The Backlash against Human Rights' (UN Assistant Secretary-General for Human Rights), Dublin, November 2017: https://www.ohchr.org/en/statements/2017/12/backlash-against-human-rights; John Tasioulas, 'Saving Human Rights from Human Rights Law' (2019) 52 Vanderbilt Journal of Transnational Law 1167; Erik Voeten, 'Populism and Backlashes against International Courts' (2020) 18(2) *Perspectives on Politics* 407-422;

Nations Assistant Secretary-General has argued that the 'actual backlash' against human rights 'seemed to kick in from 2012,'[103] but it is not necessary, or perhaps feasible, to give this 'backlash' a precise date. For some who focus only on Right-wing populism in Western democracies, a populist *war on human rights* is also markedly distinct from its neoconservative (Bush, Blair) predecessor (peaking with the invasion of Iraq) which fought *war in the name of human rights* rather than attacking the discourse of rights itself (but did as much damage to the rights project).[104] The populist backlash era is seen as far more fundamental a challenge because while neoconservatives or neoliberals were highly selective in using or ignoring rights discourse, here now the ideological battleground 'is the discourse of rights itself.'[105] On this argument, populists would reject human rights culture and discourse itself because it is a direct political threat (or opportunity for scapegoating). This is seen as contrasting with previous political forces who were not threatened by, and indeed have co-opted, the rights project. First, neoconservatives (who attempted to appropriate rights discourse in service of a 'values-based' Western force-backed agenda), and then neo-liberals (who are said to prefer to enjoy the freedoms of rights-based order but 'keep it at arm's length' to preserve the structural status quo).[106]

What, then, are said to be the features of a contemporary populist backlash against (not just backslide from) human rights? A senior UN human rights official summarised these supposedly distinctive 'backlash' patterns as different from the 'mere' backslide on human rights standards (previous section). These patterns are of new restrictions on civil society justified on sovereigntist grounds, especially laws and rhetoric on the foreign financing and cooperation of NGOs; reprisals against human rights defenders and obstructing, de-funding or undermining UN officials; scapegoating of minorities; and

---

Jolyon Ford, 'The Multilateral Human Rights System: Systemic Challenge or Healthy Contestation?' (2020) 35 *Maryland Journal of International Law* 90-103; and 'Backlash against a Rules-Based International Human Rights Order? An Australian Perspective' (2020) 38 *Australian Yearbook of International Law* 175-198. For a comprehensive study looking back at the 2010s era, see Sanja Dragic, *Post-Backlash Human Rights Law* (Brill, Amsterdam, 2022).

103 Andrew Gilmore, 'The Backlash against Human Rights' (UN Assistant Secretary-General for Human Rights), Dublin, November 2017: https://www.ohchr.org/en/statements/2017/12/backlash-against-human-rights.

104 Darren O'Byrne, 'The Rise of Populism, the Demise of the Neoliberal and Neoconservative Globalist Projects, and the War on Human Rights' (2019) 9(2) *International Critical Thought* 254-268, 265.

105 Darren O'Byrne, 'The Rise of Populism, the Demise of the Neoliberal and Neoconservative Globalist Projects, and the War on Human Rights' (2019) 9(2) *International Critical Thought* 254-268, 265.

106 Darren O'Byrne, 'The Rise of Populism, the Demise of the Neoliberal and Neoconservative Globalist Projects, and the War on Human Rights' (2019) 9(2) *International Critical Thought* 254-268, 265-6.

the tendency to depict human rights concerns as illegitimate interference in internal affairs, or the imposition of foreign ('Western') values.[107] Bilkova, meanwhile, sees patterns in how populist politicians use criticism of human rights for political purposes: the 'security' argument (human rights, notably due process for terrorism suspects, undermine vital national security goals); the 'legitimacy' argument (human rights have been hijacked by narrow interest groups and do not serve the public interest, at least of the majority); and – which is really much the same thing – the 'democracy argument' (human rights unreasonably privileges minorities' issues over those of the majority).[108] All of these are said to be a feature of this populist backlash, but at once one is struck by how these are not necessarily new or distinctive patterns and practices.

The gist of the populist discrediting of human rights would appear to be that human rights practice and discourse unduly focuses on minority or niche issues and/or obstructs the fuller experience of democracy as governance 'by and for and of' the people. Well before the mid-2010s wave of populism, Gearty captured this well:

> And what was so awful about democracy anyway? It was a simple idea, the government of a community by its representatives: only those who wanted to subvert it fuzzed it up with pompous talk of inalienable rights and spurious fear-mongering about the 'tyranny of the majority.[109]

The pre-Brexit vote period in the UK may represent a relatively high-water mark of explicit populist backlash against human rights and institutions (the *Human Rights Act* and the European Court of Human Rights). For example, Waldron chronicles what are said to be patterns of narrative whereby politicians attack the *Human Rights Act*, with its due process and fair trial rights, as a 'charter for criminals.'[110] Rights were portrayed there as alien non-indigenous innovations imposed by foreign bureaucracies, used by elite lawyers to help the undeserving take undue advantage of the migration and criminal justice and extradition law systems. So it is that by the mid-2010s, in the UK at least, one could read a newspaper headline like this:

107 Andrew Gilmore, 'The Backlash against Human Rights' (UN Assistant Secretary-General for Human Rights), Dublin, November 2017: https://www.ohchr.org/en/statements/2017/12/backlash-against-human-rights.

108 Veronica Bilkova, 'Populism and Human Rights' (2018) *Netherlands Yearbook of International Law* 143-174.

109 Conor Gearty, *Can Human Rights Survive?* (Cambridge University Press, 2006), 3.

110 Jeremy Waldron, 'Rule-of-Law Rights and Populist Impatience' in Neuman (ed.) 2020, 46.

> Tory Conference erupts in applause as [Prime Minister] attacks 'activist left-wing human rights lawyers.[111]

Human rights were part of what a preceding British prime minister (David Cameron) called 'deep problems in our society' including 'a growing sense that individual rights come before anything else.' Cameron's promise of a 'concerted fightback ... take on parts of the establishment' (the elite promoting these rights, or this balance of rights) would appear to fit the characterisation of (elite-led) populist backlash.[112] By such populist rhetoric, human rights came to have 'a bad name in the public sphere'[113] and play a role in the Brexit vote (due in part to conflating submission to the jurisdiction of the Strasbourg court with membership of the European Union).[114]

What *is* seen as distinctive about 'populism,' as explored earlier, is that is marked by anti-pluralism, anti-elitism, anti-institutionalism, and anti-minority majoritarianism. Given how human rights claims tend to be 'counter-majoritarian,'[115] the counter-populist literature notes how the populist treats human rights as an unreasonable, illegitimate impediment to the leaders' conception of the majority will, a 'needless obstacle to defending the nation from perceived threats and evils.'[116] The populist seeks political gain by portraying rights as overly narrow and limited, benefitting only 'the terrorist or asylum seeker at the expense of the safety, economic welfare and cultural preferences of the presumed majority.'[117] On this account, 'emblematic' of the populist's illiberal approach and at least part of the success of populist rhetoric consists in scapegoating human rights (and its defenders) for societal troubles, or at

111 Samuel Osborne, 'Tory Conference erupts in applause as PM attacks 'activist left-wing human rights lawyers'' *Independent* (London), 5 October 2016.

112 David Cameron, 'Human Rights in my Sights' *Sunday Express* (London, 21 August 2011), and Nicholas Watt, 'UK riots: David Cameron defends police cuts in Commons sitting,' *The Guardian*, 11 August 2011, both cited in Susan Marks, 'Four Human Rights Myths' LSE Law, Society and Economy Working Papers 10/2012, London School of Economics, 2-4.

113 Jeremy Waldron, 'Rule-of-Law Rights and Populist Impatience' in Neuman (ed.) 2020, 47-48.

114 See, for example, 'UK must leave ECHR, says Theresa May' *The Guardian* 26 April 2016 (in the context of the Strasbourg court's decisions on the extradition and deportation, respectively, of radical Muslim clerics Abu Hamza and Abu Qatada).

115 Kathryn Sikkink, 'A Cautionary Note about the Frame of Crisis and Peril in Human Rights Activism' in Cesar Rogriguez-Garavito and Krizna Gomez (eds.), (Editors' introduction) in *Rising to the Populist Challenge: A New Playbook for Human Rights* (De Justitia, Bogota, 2018), 171-184, 173.

116 Kenneth Roth, 'The dangerous rise of populism: global attacks on human rights values' (2017) 70th Anniversary Issue *Journal of International Affairs* 79-84, 80.

117 Kenneth Roth, 'The dangerous rise of populism: global attacks on human rights values' (2017) 70th Anniversary Issue *Journal of International Affairs* 79-84, 80.

least characterising human rights as deaf or hostile to the legitimate concerns of 'ordinary' citizens.[118]

In addition to the backslide effect of undermining and disarming international human rights treaty-based and other bodies and processes, the backlash narrative refers to populist rhetoric that makes explicit attacks on the legitimacy of these bodies. They are portrayed as 'part of the global elite, or the world government that threatens the nation; their decisions are said to favour the rights of criminals, terrorists, migrants, prisoners, and other enemies over the rights of the nation.'[119] The literature does give one reason to question whether enough examples are given to substantiate this as a pattern at scale, and beyond Europe and the US in particular, but for now this captures the gist of the backlash narrative. The sort of supra-national judicial review of the European Court of Human Rights is in direct tension with, and an obvious and effective target for, populist-sovereigntist thinking and both its anti-elitism and its 'narrative of blame.'[120] In the UK, notably, the populist attack on human rights (especially around the Brexit vote) has tended to be articulated as one against 'the overly bureaucratic European' interfering in domestic affairs.[121] For some, the main challenge of populism for the human rights movement is the ability of populist narratives of blame to alter gradually public normative conceptions about the judiciary and its role, de-legitimising courts and judges or legitimising anti-court behaviour and rhetoric, especially regional human rights courts which are 'foreign' in addition to being elitist and out-of-touch.[122] Populist leaders in a range of settings have skilfully exploited the professionalisation of civil society groups and their reliance on foreign funding in order to portray human rights advocates as part of the elite.[123] Moreover, this is a disloyal or non-national elite. The frequent claim of foreign-funded organisations as working against the people's interests and the country's national sovereignty falls squarely under this narrative. For instance, in democratic India, the Modi government routinely accuses human rights and environmental activists of working with vaguely defined foreign elements

118 Andrew Fagan, 'The Gentrification of Human Rights' (2019) 41 *Human Rights Quarterly* 283, 285.
119 Gerald Neuman, 'Human Rights responses to the Populist Challenge' in Neuman (ed.) 2020, 260.
120 Jan Petrov, 'The Populist Challenge to the European Court of Human Rights' (2020) 18(2) *International Journal of Constitutional Law*, 476–508.
121 Darren O'Byrne, 'The Rise of Populism, the Demise of the Neoliberal and Neoconservative Globalist Projects, and the War on Human Rights' (2019) 9(2) *International Critical Thought* 254-268, 264.
122 Jan Petrov, 'The Populist Challenge to the European Court of Human Rights' (2020) 18(2) *International Journal of Constitutional Law*, 476–508.
123 Cesar Rodriguez-Garavito and Krizna Gomez (eds.), (Editors' introduction) in *Rising to the Populist Challenge: a New Playbook for Human Rights* (De Justitia, Bogota, 2018), 19.

against the national interest of development, which brings connotations of treason and justifies heavy regulation.[124]

Populism's distinctive anti-pluralist positions are seen as hallmarks of the populist backlash. O'Byrne differs somewhat from other scholars by observing how the populist attack on human rights is sometimes a 'language game' of sorts.[125] That is, it is not necessarily always about human rights themselves, either literally or logically. Instead it is how human rights have come to be 'a signifier for a broader culture of inclusion that puts "the Other" [minorities, immigrants] on a par with everyone else,' and the populist's attack is only on the Other's rights, not necessarily on the whole idea of rights (and certainly not 'our' rights in the majority camp!).[126] Thus the populist attack is not against the protection of those rights that the majority would enjoy, but against an inclusive culture that 'dares to suggest others [minorities] might also be allowed the same privileges.'[127] In this way the 'cosmopolitan culture of human rights' and its focus on plurality and inclusion of the 'Other' becomes 'an easy target' in carefully manipulated populist messaging.[128]

Reflections

We must explore further the notion of the human rights project or movement as an 'easy target' for populists. Both the 'backslide' and 'backlash' narratives can come across as posited, in effect, on the notion that human rights was – until the advent of the 2010s populist – a legitimate, effective, coherent, and vital discourse (and set of institutions), now all under attack, scapegoating, and delegitimisation. This is something of a stylised simplification. However, it serves our purpose as we turn to explore questions at the heart of this book's intended contribution. Why and how have human rights over time become such an 'easy target' for the populist to gain political advantage? What is it about human rights or their practice that has made them so apparently vulnerable to populist delegitimisation narratives, such as the anti-elite

124 Cesar Rodriguez-Garavito and Krizna Gomez (eds.), (Editors' introduction) in *Rising to the Populist Challenge: a New Playbook for Human Rights* (De Justitia, Bogota, 2018), 19.

125 Darren O'Byrne, 'The Rise of Populism, the Demise of the Neoliberal and Neoconservative Globalist Projects, and the War on Human Rights' (2019) 9(2) *International Critical Thought* 254-268.

126 Darren O'Byrne, 'The Rise of Populism, the Demise of the Neoliberal and Neoconservative Globalist Projects, and the War on Human Rights' (2019) 9(2) *International Critical Thought* 254-268.

127 Darren O'Byrne, 'The Rise of Populism, the Demise of the Neoliberal and Neoconservative Globalist Projects, and the War on Human Rights' (2019) 9(2) *International Critical Thought* 254-268, 264.

128 Darren O'Byrne, 'The Rise of Populism, the Demise of the Neoliberal and Neoconservative Globalist Projects, and the War on Human Rights' (2019) 9(2) *International Critical Thought* 254-268, 264.

one? In what ways might the human rights movement even have contributed to the very challenge it sees as existential, either by developing certain traits that are easily dismissed or derided, or more systemically in terms of contributing (even if only by omission) to the conditions in which populism has popular traction at all?

For Human Rights Watch head Kenneth Roth, whose profile helped in generating the 'populist challenge' narrative, the best way to counter-populist trends and defend the human rights values 'that so many still cherish' is by a 'vigorous re-affirmation of human rights.'[129] Yet in saying 'values that so many still cherish,' Roth also said 'despite the problems they [human rights] face.'[130] Some of these problems may long predate the advent of 2010s+ populist politics, and some may even have fed into the rise of populism. It is these questions that the bulk of the literature overlooks or under-treats, and which we now turn to in Part II. Some of that analysis will support the argument that human rights might have become an easy political target in a populist context because its defenders (the 'movement') are fairly easy and obvious scapegoats. This might be because they are perceived, or can be portrayed, as an out-of-touch patronising legalistic professional elite class ignorant of the concerns of the 'ordinary person' and pandering unduly to undeserving minorities using rights-talk and judges (another unelected elite). As Fagan writes, the invocation or defence of human rights is associated (via populist rhetoric) with 'the elitist, self-assured attitudes of a socially and politically unrepresentative constituency of people.'[131] Yet if such a blame-apportioning approach or tactic appears to have traction with an appreciable class of people/voters, it should at least give pause for thought on the part of human rights scholars and activists.

In their analysis of the populist backlash, Rodriguez-Garavito and Gomez have argued that populist leaders not only benefit incidentally from the declining utility, in the context of the decline of Western power-centres, of naming-and-shaming strategies that hitherto connected localised Global South activists to major capitals and media outlets. The populist is also said to have learned to exploit existing 'fault lines and blind spots' of the modern human rights architecture and movement, and wield these traits against the movement for political advantage.[132] These traits include some of the patterns raised above, such as over-reliance on international funding, or an

129 Kenneth Roth, 'The dangerous rise of populism: global attacks on human rights values' (2017) 70th Anniversary Issue *Journal of International Affairs* 79-84, 83-84.

130 Phillip Alston, 'The populist challenge to human rights' (2017) 9(1) *Journal of Human Rights Practice*, 1–15, 2.

131 Andrew Fagan, 'The Gentrification of Human Rights' (2019) 41 *Human Rights Quarterly* 283, 285.

132 Cesar Rodriguez-Garavito and Krizna Gomez (eds.), (Editors' introduction) in *Rising to the Populist Challenge: A New Playbook for Human Rights* (De Justitia, Bogota, 2018), 12-15; 44.

over-concentration of agenda-setting power in Western-based international civil society relative to 'Global South' organisations. These faults or fault lines might also include characteristics that (given our earlier survey of what makes 'populism' distinctive) create ideal political fuel for populist politicking.

The first pattern or characteristic is a relative (perceived) neglect of poverty, economic inequality, economic justice themes and socio-economic rights (that is, relative to a perceived over-emphasis on civil and political rights and/or perceived 'niche' rights and social identity issues 'only' affecting minorities). On this narrative, the backlash is not against human rights necessarily but against the impact of neoliberal market policies as the hallmark of the liberal project with which human rights is associated, and which have 'directly undermined the credibility and legitimacy of liberal democracy' and, with it, the human rights project.[133] The second general characteristic is a tendency to fulfil the populist's caricature of out-of-touch elites with a 'legitimacy deficit' due to the human rights movement's 'inordinate dominance of law-centred discourses and strategies' and the 'disconnect between professionalized human rights NGOs, online activists and social movements.'[134]

The tendency to focus on the 'rhetorical content' of illiberal and anti-liberal populism 'obscures the need to delve deeper into the underlying material factors and conditions' that contributed to the conditions in which populism succeeded electorally and politically.[135] The counter-populist narrative is – even as it focuses on populism as the greatest threat to human rights – strangely dismissive of the phenomenon. Hence Fagan notes how populism is mostly construed as an 'entirely pathological force' that human rights defenders must 'resolutely battle' against, yet typically counter-populists do not attempt to delve into the wider social, political, and economic contexts out of which populism has re-emerged, or think critically about the appropriate response.[136] In addition to the questions above (about how human rights might have become vulnerable to the populist critique) are questions for scholars about the assumed baseline for assertions about the health or otherwise of the human rights project. This is because the 'populist [backlash] challenge' narrative can tend to convey the impression that human rights was flourishing before the advent of populist politics. We turn now to Part II to explore some of these questions.

133 Andrew Fagan, 'Human Rights in a Time of Populism 2021, by Gerald Neuman (ed.): Book Review' (2021) 43(2) *Human Rights Quarterly* 416-421, 420.

134 Cesar Rodriguez-Garavito and Krizna Gomez (eds.), (Editors' introduction) in *Rising to the Populist Challenge: A New Playbook for Human Rights* (De Justitia, Bogota, 2018), 12-15; 44.

135 Andrew Fagan, 'Human Rights in a Time of Populism 2021, by Gerald Neuman (ed.): Book Review' (2021) 43(2) *Human Rights Quarterly* 416-421, 420.

136 Andrew Fagan, 'Human Rights in a Time of Populism 2021, by Gerald Neuman (ed.): Book Review' (2021) 43(2) *Human Rights Quarterly* 416-421, 418, 420.

It will be necessary later in this book to unpack some questions about scholars' observations of backlash in respect of human rights. For instance, is the backlash necessarily against human rights norms and governance per se, or ('merely') against particular international and regional adjudication and other institutions and mechanisms?[137] How widespread is the backlash phenomenon, and is it a *populist* backlash, and what do studies of particular geographic or thematic contexts reveal about the limits of this general, worldwide 'populist backlash' motif? Has the backlash been effective in delegitimising rights, where and in what instances, and how would we know and measure such effects? What else, other than the populist backlash, might just as readily account for the problems faced by the human rights movement? In what respects can it be said that a/the backlash, mostly seen as state-led, is a *populist* one rather than a political-technocratic one? Is the backlash in some ways legitimate, and to what extent have the practices of human rights institutions or advocates contributed to or rendered them vulnerable to such attacks?

Nevertheless, on the assumption for now that there has been, since at least 2015, not only a backslide in substantive rights protections but a fairly widespread populist-led backlash against human rights itself, we turn now to Part II of this book. In effect, this picks up somewhat on the last of the above rhetorical research questions by addressing three particular questions:

- Does the impact of the deliberate populist backlash account for the perceived crisis in or existential challenge to human rights, or are there other (and pre-existing) explanations for this?
- Of these more enduring ('non-populist') challenges, to what extent are these a function of problems within human rights discourse or of the human rights movement itself, rather than purely external challenges?
- How might human rights – at least as advanced hitherto in its mainstream universalist institutional and rhetorical forms – have in some ways contributed to the populist backlash, or at least become vulnerable to (or disabled in responding to) populist backlash strategies of dismissal and delegitimisation?

137 See this distinction explained in Johan Karlsson Schaffer, Andreas Føllesdal and Geir Ulfstein, 'International Human Rights and the Challenge of Legitimacy' in Andreas Føllesdal, Johan Karlsson Schaffer and Geir Ulfstein (eds.), *The Legitimacy of International Human Rights Regimes: Legal, Philosophical and Political Perspectives* (Cambridge University Press, 2013).

II

PROBLEMS

Putting the 'populist challenge' narrative in perspective

For many scholars, as Part I showed, populism is *the* cause of a contemporary crisis in or for human rights or threat to their future.[1] Yet a key argument in this book is whether the 'populist challenge to human rights' literature, so framed, risks missing some objectively important factors relevant to the health, shape and prospects of the human rights project at this point in history, irrespective of the rise of populism. Part II now explores some conceivable arguments that – in relation specifically to the populist backlash – human rights, or at least the human rights 'movement,' might be 'part of the problem'[2] in driving or enabling populist anti-rights narratives, or at least in being ill-equipped or ill-prepared effectively to prevent or counter that rhetoric. The critiques and concerns set out in what follows are somewhat stylised for argument's sake: this short book does not purport to survey all extant critical perspectives on human rights. Moreover, these critiques do often overlap, interact, and compound each other in complex ways.

As a broad statement these concerns or critiques are of two kinds:

- *Structural features of the modern human rights project and of rights argumentation.* Here, we are interested to explore whether and to what extent

1 See too James Loeffler and Mila Versteeg, 'The Future of Human Rights Scholarship' (2018) 81 *Law and Contemporary Problems* i.

2 David Kennedy, 'The International Human Rights Regime: Part of the Problem?' (2002) 14 *Harvard Human Rights Journal* 101-126; and see *The Dark Sides of Virtue* (Princeton University Press, 2004); also 'The International Human Rights Regime: Still Part of the Problem?' in Rob Dickenson et al. (eds.) *Examining Critical Perspectives on Human Rights* (Cambridge University Press 2012).

DOI: 10.4324/9781003311140-3

it might be said that these features contributed – even in just a background sense – to fertile conditions in which the backlash took off and/or in which populist strategies (including explicit ones to scapegoat human rights) could attract not insignificant popular support.
- *Particular institutional features and patterns of international, transnational, or localised human rights practice.* Here, we are interested to explore whether and to what extent it might be said that these patterns of practice and rhetoric made it difficult (or even counter-productive) – in the face of populist backslide or backlash trends – to invoke human rights arguments and mechanisms to counter the populists.

We need to explore these two lines of enquiry further than the 'populist challenge' literature outlined in Part I has done. The premise in that literature is 'look what the populist backslide has done to human rights protections, look what the populist backlash has done to the legitimacy and relevance of rights arguments, vocabularies, actors and institutions.' This part asks instead 'in what ways did human rights, as practised, potentially contribute to populism itself, and to the explicit populist backlash against human rights, or become so vulnerable to populist strategies?' This is why unpacking the 'backlash' concept – and distinguishing it from unjustified, unexpected, unilateral outright attack – seems worthwhile (Part III).

In what follows, it might pay to bear a particular set of reflections in mind. Are many of these critiques in substance criticisms of human rights (and the 'movement') as such, or of a much wider modernity phenomena-set of liberalism, constitutionalism, capitalism, globalisation, and democratisation? Indeed is the distinction, the 'or' in this question, untenable because the modern human rights project is so bound up in these 'isms' (the so-called 'liberal world order') that one cannot analyse 'human rights' (and populism) without engaging with this much broader canvass? If so, what subject-matter expertise is apt? This short book's scope does not extend to unpacking all of this. Yet it is worth stopping often – when down in the weeds of the 'populism + human rights' literature – to question one assumption in particular. This is the assumption that human rights were as successful and ubiquitous, as their critics suppose, in becoming the dominant frame for contestation or for advancing versions of 'the social good.' This is significant because implicit in many of these critiques is that it was the *success* of the human rights project (i.e., one particular conception and institutional manifestation of what 'human rights' could have meant) – and not just the many *failures* that critics point to – that has been a key driver of conditions in which populist messages have found traction. Gearty once cautioned that it is exactly at moments of apparent triumph (on the part of the human rights project) that dangers can be found 'lurking in the margins' which, if left unnoticed, could well 'soon spread and damage the whole.'[3] Challenges to the integrity and even the very existence of human rights might thus be a function of its supposed ubiquity and success as a vocabulary of governance and social contestation and politics.[4] If populism is seen as a reaction to some perceived external imposition that is preventing a truer nation-building experience, proponents of human rights might at least reflect on how the 'success' of the idea and/or movement have contributed to that perception. This is so even if we should be circumspect around claims about the ubiquity, penetration and traction of human rights in the 'pre-populist' (pre-2010s) period.

COUCHING THE 'POPULIST ERA' IN SOME HISTORICAL PERSPECTIVE

The thesis of the populist backlash literature is that this is a new, fundamental, and existential crisis for human rights. Populism, on this account, carries the risk of human rights – as 'a movement, a mode of activism, and a language of claim, aspiration and justification'[5] – losing legitimacy and relevance altogether. A proper assessment of this claim requires asking (which that literature, with some exceptions, does not) whether other factors account for the perceived problems facing human rights. Indeed, it requires addressing the accuracy of and baseline for the 'crisis' diagnosis, including by asking whether the legitimacy and relevance of human rights were *already* questionable before the mid-2010s 'onset' of populism.

Much of the broader human rights literature charts (or rather, asserts) a relative decline in the salience, utility and/or significance of human rights at least a decade before the advent of the so-called 2010s+ populist era. This decline is positioned as relative to the triumphal 'age of rights,' human rights as 'the supreme cause'[6] of humanity, through the 1990s and peaking as the 21st century set in. This period has been summed up as 'more and more of the peoples of the world embracing this language as a way of organising political debate and of informing their relations with the world.'[7] Human rights was *the* 'idea of our time ... the only political moral idea that has received universal

3 Conor Gearty, *Can Human Rights Survive?* (Cambridge University Press, 2006), 9.

4 Conor Gearty, *Can Human Rights Survive?* (Cambridge University Press, 2006), 140.

5 Susan Marks, 'Four Human Rights Myths' LSE Law, Society and Economy Working Papers 10/2012, London School of Economics, 6.

6 Samuel Moyn, 'The Future of Human Rights' (2014) 11(20) *SUR: International Journal on Human Rights* 57-66, 57.

7 Conor Gearty, *Can Human Rights Survive?* (Cambridge University Press, 2006), 8.

acceptance,'[8] a 'universal ideology, an international standard for legitimacy of sovereign power, common vernacular of justice.'[9] Thus:

> [n]o other jurisprudence or legal-political-moral idea before then had so unequivocally tilted the balance of power towards the citizen and away from the state ... Even dictators feigned respect for human rights. By the 1990s, human rights ideas had taken a foothold in civil society sectors in virtually every country. Human rights became the ubiquitous language of the last half of the twentieth century. The euphoria was palpable.[10]

Human rights were powerful and effective, on this account. For decades – from 1960s–1970s decolonisation, to post-Soviet Europe, to the Arab Spring – framing an issue as a 'human rights' one carried certain power and effect in politics and international relations. True, across this period human rights were routinely and sometimes massively violated. Yet it was difficult to deny that the human rights lexicon at least offered a powerful rhetorical device for those challenging injustice, oppression, or exclusion. By employing a human rights framework on any particular issue, one gained access not just to recognised standards and established institutions, but to a whole powerful political language with 'sacred' status.[11]

Yet from at least 2000 onwards, scholars were asking whether the 'age of rights' was already passing. Certainly they were doing so after the excesses of the 'global war on terror' and the damage that the 2003 invasion of Iraq in particular (and Abu Ghraib, etc.) did to the credibility of the human rights and democratisation projects (whose values it invoked). Some diagnosed or predicted the 'end'[12] or 'end times'[13] or 'twilight'[14] of human rights, or pondered entering a 'post human rights era'[15] or needing a 'post human rights agenda.'[16] On this argument, the 'balloon of human rights has certainly

8 Louis Henkin, *The Age of Rights* (Columbia University Press, 1990) xvii.

9 David Kennedy, 'The International Human Rights Regime: Still Part of the Problem?' in Rob Dickenson et al (eds.) *Examining Critical Perspectives on Human Rights* (Cambridge University Press 2012), 20.

10 Mukua Mutua, 'Is the Age of Human Rights Over?' in Sophia McClennen and Alexandra Schulthesis Moore (eds.) *The Routledge Companion to Literature and Human Rights* (Routledge, 2016), Ch. 42, 450-458, 454.

11 Michael Ignatieff, *Human Rights as Politics and Idolatry* (Princeton University Press, 2001), 53.

12 Costas Douzinas, *The End of Human Rights* (Oxford University Press, 2000).

13 Stephen Hopgood, *The End-times of Human Rights* (Cornell University Press, 2013).

14 Eric Posner, *The Twilight of Human Rights* (Oxford University Press, 2014).

15 Danielle Celermajer, 'Are we entering a post human rights era?' (2005) 14(1) *Human Rights Defender* 2-5.

16 Ingrid Wuerth, 'International Law in the Age of Trump: A Post-Human Rights Agenda' *Lawfare* Blog, 14 November 2016; www.lawfareblog.com/international-law-age-trump-post-human-rights-agenda.

been popped' and their 'age is over,'[17] they are 'on the road to nowhere.'[18] Human rights are 'no longer the way forward' but merely enjoyed a historical 'moment' that was a 'status quo project for a stable time'[19] (the decade post-1989): human rights are just 'so 1990s.'[20] At the very least, as Gearty wrote in the mid-2000s (in a similar vein to many others), the idea of human rights risked being 'destroyed forever' or at best 'subverted out of all present recognition'[21] such were the seriousness of the challenges to its relevance and legitimacy and power to transform. More recently, the 'political tide' is said to be against human rights amid 'deep disenchantment' in the human rights project or enterprise, where intellectual support for this 'contested, distorted, dismissed' idea is 'crumbling.'[22]

On these accounts, human rights had, at the very least, become a 'less compelling'[23] frame or idiom to use in political discourse well before the populist backlash. Thus by 2016 Mutua could argue that the 'dimming' or 'fading' or 'eclipse' in the power of human rights (to mobilise action or 'provoke deep-seated moral and legal outrage') was not just a temporary lull in an otherwise still-seductive project: the rights era was 'truly over.'[24] Human rights had gone from being 'a phenomenal success – perhaps more than any other moral language of our time' – to losing their ability to 'coalesce action.'[25] A more recent scholarly collection called *Human Rights Futures* suggested that human rights face a future of 'ineffectiveness, ambivalence, failure and irrelevance' if 'innovative steps' are not taken, yet the assumption in some of this work is that this future has already arrived. Notably, populism is not specified as one of the threats that human rights was not well positioned to counter.[26]

17 Mutua 2016, 455.
18 Stephen Hopgood, 'Human Rights on the Road to Nowhere' in Stephen Hopgood, Jack Snyder and Leslie Vinjamuri (eds.) *Human Rights Futures* (Cambridge University Press, 2018), Ch. 12.
19 David Kennedy, 'The International Human Rights Regime: Still Part of the Problem?' in Rob Dickenson et al (eds.) *Examining Critical Perspectives on Human Rights* (Cambridge University Press 2012), 22.
20 Marti Koskienemmi, 'Human Rights: so 90s,' address, Oxford Martin School, March 2014.
21 Conor Gearty, *Can Human Rights Survive?* (Cambridge University Press, 2006), 1.
22 Grainne de Burca, *Reframing Human Rights in a Turbulent Era* (Oxford University Press, 2021), 9.
23 David Kennedy, 'The International Human Rights Regime: Still Part of the Problem?' in Rob Dickenson et al (eds.) *Examining Critical Perspectives on Human Rights* (Cambridge University Press 2012), 22.
24 Mukua Mutua, 'Is the Age of Human Rights Over?' in Sophia McClennen and Alexandra Schulthesis Moore (eds.) *The Routledge Companion to Literature and Human Rights* (Routledge, 2016), Ch. 42, 450-458, 450-1.
25 Mutua 2016, 456.
26 Stephen Hopgood, Jack Snyder and Leslie Vinjamuri (eds.), 'Editors' Introduction' in *Human Rights Futures* (Cambridge University Press, 2018), 2.

If the human rights project is 'indeed, in real trouble,'[27] it is not obvious that populism is the source of that risk. Or at least we need to re-examine the 'populist challenge' narrative to ask what else might be at play and to point out the need to account for the thesis that human rights was hardly a thriving, undamaged project before the populist era. Fagan argues that human rights have become a 'socially exclusive, politically unpopular credo for a diminishing number of supporters, with ever diminishing influence.'[28] If this is so, we do need to ask whether this was the work of populist strategising or whether the rights project had somehow already become something to which many 'ordinary' people had become at best indifferent, or cynical, or at worst (and in backlash-fuelling ways) actually hostile.

Waldron has asked 'what conception of human rights can be retrieved from populist hostility?'[29] Yet this does rather imply that it is populism, not some other combination of factors (including how human rights have been framed and practised), that has undermined the 'age of rights.' For our purposes, we need not dwell too much further now on such grand sweeping characterisations of eras and epochs. What we *do* need to ask is whether there might be explanations for the claimed 'crisis' in the legitimacy and relevance of human rights *other than* the calculating scapegoating schemes and delegitimisation strategies of populist backlash politicians. Again, this is because the 'populist challenge' narrative arguably does not do enough to consider whether other factors account for the state and status of human rights. These include factors that make the backlash more explicable, even if not excusable. Of course, we also need (in Part III) to question the empirical basis and assumptive baseline upon which the 'crisis' diagnosis (or any other diagnosis) – too frequently made in the literature to attempt to catalogue – is made in the first place. With this in mind, what are some enduring features of human rights, as practised or perceived, that might in some ways feed into or even fuel the 'populist challenge' picture, or at least put it into historical and other perspectives? Might some of these critiques render the situation more complex than the 'populist challenge' thesis, or impression, of one-directional attack on the legitimacy or utility or credibility of human rights? Such problems are considered here as plausible alternative explanations for the perceived challenges to the future of human rights (i.e., alternative to the 'populist backslide/backlash' challenge). With some exceptions, there is not necessarily any evidence that particular populist politicians in particular localities have explicitly dismissed or criticised rights on these grounds, let alone successfully.

27 Andrew Fagan, 'The Gentrification of Human Rights' (2019) 41 *Human Rights Quarterly* 283, 284.

28 Andrew Fagan, 'The Gentrification of Human Rights' (2019) 41 *Human Rights Quarterly* 283, 285.

29 Jeremy Waldron, 'Rule-of-Law Rights and Populist Impatience' in Neuman (ed.) 2020, 45.

Before surveying these critiques, one highly significant point must be made about putting the 'populist challenge' thesis in perspective. Arguably, the 'populist challenge' too easily paints a global picture, both of human rights as a monolith, and of populism itself (as if it were climate change with global impact). True, we can see patterns and sometimes uncannily similar copycat or shared playbook of populist political styles or strategies. And the idea of human rights might conceivably be significantly affected by political discourse that is confined (for example) to only some geographies or themes. Yet Part I showed that it is hardly the case that every or even most countries are experiencing a contemporary populist political scene. Part I also flagged that within those that are commonly said to be affected, the patterns and prevalence and impact of populism must surely vary greatly, especially in terms of how explicit the anti-rights backlash is, and whether it has any traction or effect. We can leave this point here, but these questions alone surely ought to put scholars on notice that debate about the 'populist challenge' can risk proceeding on the basis that it has a far greater prevalence and significance than it might have in fact. Part III returns to this.

ENDURING CRITIQUES OR DRAWBACKS OF THE HUMAN RIGHTS PROJECT

'Distortive'

It is conceivably arguable that even if we could all agree on the basis and nature of human rights and that there was nothing unavoidably problematic or paradoxical about them conceptually, nevertheless, they are distortive or have become distorted in some of the ways outlined below. That is, something about the process by which and form in which the modern-day (1970s+) human rights phenomenon came to be practised and institutionalised as an important legal-political motif created conditions which, over time, have problematised the human rights idea and ideal and/or exposed it to criticism or dismissal, including by populists.

A 'displacement' critique

One fundamental criticism of the modern human rights story (underpinning or closely related to the others that follow) is that it has been successful to the point where it has displaced other frames or vocabularies or modes of principles-based politics. So ubiquitous, and so useful to so many disparate state and other actors, that is has even displaced what it is possible to imagine as a possible alternative or supplementary form or language of emancipatory, participatory, protective, or remedial politics. The displacement critique is potentially particularly powerful when seen alongside the view (also below) that, over time, human rights became very narrowly conceived. This would be the view that by being hegemonic but simultaneously narrow or selective, human rights occupied all the political and policy space for talking about values such as freedom, equality, or dignity and yet provided no real forum or framework for engaging with economic insecurity and economic inequality issues. As it happens, perceived neglect of those concerns is seen as a key feature of the message of many contemporary populists.

This critique is that as human rights became a dominant governance paradigm, actors at all sorts of levels needed to be able to translate their concerns, claims, or interests into rights-talk (and often, legally recognisable rights). This process both distorts or diminishes the 'real' nature of their demands. It also has another effect: it creates antagonism across the body politic: 'my' rights balanced against yours, closing off a culture of compromise and opportunities for dialogue. This is the Kennedy argument that universalistic human rights are 'hegemonic,' they occupy or colonise 'the field of emancipatory possibility' in ways that take away attention, energy, legitimacy, or resourcing from other strategies, and crowd out other ways of seeing or framing or articulating social harm and its remediation.[30] These 'other ways' might hold greater legitimacy or traction to contest particular issues in non-rights terms in particular contexts. Kennedy's critique of the hegemonic effects of rights-talk was that it operates to displace other 'lost vocabularies' that might be equally universal or (in strategy terms) effective, such as 'duty' or 'responsibility' or 'collective commitment.'[31] The transformation of political questions into legal questions, and then into questions of legal rights, has made other forms of collective emancipatory politics less available.[32]

Moyn articulates a version of Kennedy's critique, that human rights had this hegemonic effect as they became powerful (because 'other visions imploded').[33] Gearty too has asked why is it that human rights came to colonise 'so much ethical territory, to the exclusion of other moral notions that have done useful work in their day':[34] 'where once we had ideas like 'socialism,' 'social justice,' and 'fairness,' nowadays increasingly 'human rights' is being called upon to do all the moral work.'[35] Others wonder whether privileging human rights language was a 'wrong turn' and a range of other vocabularies or concepts might have offered 'more progress.'[36]

30 Kennedy, 'Dark Sides' (2004), 9-10.
31 Kennedy, 'Dark Sides' (2004), 9-10.
32 Kennedy, 'Dark Sides' (2004), 29, 33.
33 Samuel Moyn, *The Last Utopia* (Harvard University Press, 2010), 5.
34 Conor Gearty, *Can Human Rights Survive?* (Cambridge University Press, 2006), 9.
35 Conor Gearty, *Can Human Rights Survive?* (Cambridge University Press, 2006), 9.
36 Stephen Hopgood, Jack Snyder and Leslie Vinjamuri (eds.), 'Editors' Introduction' in *Human Rights Futures* (Cambridge University Press, 2018), 21-22.

Fagan's version of this displacement argument is a clear extension of Kennedy's. It is that we have come to equate 'human rights' with the pursuit of social justice, whereas it is either only one mode of that pursuit or actually has very little to say about structural social injustice: the 'sheer degree of faith' placed in human rights has 'hegemonically restricted our collective engagement' (with structural causes of poverty, inequality, etc.).[37] It has 'more often than not restricted the political imagination' by displacing other vocabularies of justice or social justice and reducing everything to 'a series of [legal?] provisions' that in fact do not just ignore but reinforce structural causes of injustice.[38]

This hegemony is also problematic then, on this critique, because rights frame issues (and their resolution) both too narrowly and too generally.[39] Too narrowly, in only having a 'minimalist' approach to proposals to transform the world.[40] Too narrowly also because the focus is on harms done by governments rather than powerful private or non-state actors and systems, and overwhelmingly on rights as enshrined and remedied in law, especially public law. Human rights thus privilege reason over faith, public over private, law over politics or economics. It sees emancipation too narrowly as what governments do to individuals, as participatory (not economic or distributive), as legal not political, and problems that are hard to frame in terms of individual or group rights get overlooked and under-resourced.[41] On the other hand, human rights are too generalised because we are left with abstract normative concepts that do not necessarily facilitate a discussion about human inter-relationships and values and needs, while also creating a tendency to dictate what is 'good' for people everywhere in general and prescriptive ways.[42] As noted, the dominance of rights-talk also forces parties to articulate their claims or concerns in rights vocabulary or risk being ignored. Forcing everyone to framing their preferences or needs as rights-holders tends to make social interaction adversarial, discouraging alliances and compromise and shared solutions.[43] Moyn

37 Andrew Fagan, 'The Gentrification of Human Rights' (2019) 41 *Human Rights Quarterly* 283, 305.

38 Andrew Fagan, 'The Gentrification of Human Rights' (2019) 41 *Human Rights Quarterly* 283, 305.

39 Kennedy, 'Dark Sides' (2004), 10-17.

40 Samuel Moyn, 'The Future of Human Rights' (2014) 11(20) *SUR: International Journal on Human Rights* 57-66, 57.

41 David Kennedy, 'The International Human Rights Regime: Still Part of the Problem?' in Rob Dickenson et al (eds.) *Examining Critical Perspectives on Human Rights* (Cambridge University Press 2012), 24.

42 David Kennedy, 'The International Human Rights Regime: Still Part of the Problem?' in Rob Dickenson et al (eds.) *Examining Critical Perspectives on Human Rights* (Cambridge University Press 2012), 24.

43 David Kennedy, 'The International Human Rights Regime: Still Part of the Problem?' in Rob Dickenson et al (eds.) *Examining Critical Perspectives on Human Rights* (Cambridge University Press 2012), 24.

later echoed Kennedy's view, arguing that rights-talk with its absolutist ('mine versus yours') effect deprives us of alternatives, in a socio-political community, to struggling against each other for victory.[44]

We may need to return to the last portion of this critique, since it not only rests on some rather utopian ideas about how peaceful and productive societal dialogue would be without rights-talk but also implies a curious denial of agency and strategic judgement to 'local' activists choosing when and how to invoke rights (or legal strategies) and when not. The displacement thesis also ultimately assumes that human rights were powerful, ubiquitous, hegemonic, and exclusive. Critical scholars provide no real evidence for this other than their own repeated statements that this displacement took this place. Still, in trying to contextualise the idea that it is populism that has so undermined human rights, we should be slow to discount this thesis. Thus, for now, it is conceivable that one part of the perceived problem with human rights is this hegemonic tendency or effect, and (supposedly) a resulting mass popular alienation from rights-talk *irrespective of whether populists delegitimise rights for having that hegemonic, alienating effect.* Kennedy's example is intuitively powerful, even if empirically impossible to substantiate: that anti-poverty campaigners are forced to debate in terms of 'ultimately impossible legal quandaries – rights of whom, against whom, remediable how – and [are drawn] into institutional projects of codification and reporting familiar from other human rights efforts' even though other ways to campaign might be available.[45] If so, this might help account for a disconnection between needs or preferences and the means available to properly express these without framing them as 'rights' with all that this entails. If human rights are simultaneously hegemonic (displacing other frames) and narrow (not really accommodating various structural socio-economic concerns), this might account for popular disillusionment with human rights and for them becoming less compelling in shaping behaviour and debate. This effect might have occurred even without a populist strategy to delegitimise rights for their distortive, displacing tendency. Or, if there was such a strategy, it might explain why (especially if we accept the 'triumphant rights era' description) human rights may have decreasing traction with the population: 'you keep saying how important and universal human rights are, but they have not really changed our lives.' This brings us to the next critique.

A 'disappointment' critique

Directly related to the alleged dominance, especially after 1989, of human rights as a legal-political vocabulary is a rather unsurprising corollary. This

44 Samuel Moyn, 'The Future of Human Rights' (2014) 11(20) *SUR: International Journal on Human Rights* 57-66, 58.

45 Kennedy, 'Dark Sides' (2004), 9-10.

is perhaps the most standard 'lay person' critique of human rights: that it over-promises or 'promises more than it can deliver.'[46] That the gap between normative declaration and practical effectiveness or yield (empowerment, enforcement, or remediation) has undermined their credibility and power: the human rights movement 'overpromised, but underperformed, to stem human privation and suffering.'[47] It is a 'foreign emancipatory friend who does not materialize' when things get tough.[48] It came to suffer, over time, from a 'sense of the disjunct' between the universality and promise of human rights and the actual scope for giving these rights effect,[49] what Koskeniemmi called the 'anti-climax.'[50] So it is said how the movement is itself deeply frustrated with the inability to deliver,[51] and perhaps 'bit off more than it could chew,'[52] or at least over-stated its significance.[53] It might paradoxically be a victim of its success: disappointment with the inability of the human rights project, which relies on the power of its transformative promise, to deliver meaningful mitigatory protections against the externalities of economic and cultural globalisation. If so, the decline of human rights – if it has occurred or will occur – may result not from populist backlash necessarily, but from the realisation that rights do not necessarily deliver yield or guarantee priority claims, so that there might also be 'a search for some other kind of non-negotiable "absolutes".'[54]

The disappointment (and the narrower 'enforcement gap') critique is such a familiar line of criticism that the literature around the failings of human rights, especially in 'enforcement' terms, is quite unmanageably large. Nevertheless, if the context is how human rights fares in the face of populist messaging, this general and familiar critique is certainly not negligible. Indeed, if this perception has currency, it may not be particularly relevant (in the populism context, i.e., the public's opinion) whether or not technically there are strong counter-arguments to the 'effectiveness' (disappointment) critique, and even

46 Kennedy, 'Dark Sides' (2004), 21.
47 Mutua 2016, 155.
48 Kennedy, 'Dark Sides' (2004), 23.
49 See, for example, Steve Stern and Scott Strauss (eds) *The human rights paradox: universality and its discontents* (2014).
50 2014.
51 Ron Dudai, 'Human Rights in the Populist Era: Mourn then (Re)Organize' (2017) 9 *Journal of Human Rights Practice* 16.
52 David Kennedy, 'The International Human Rights Regime: Still Part of the Problem?' in Rob Dickenson et al. (eds.) *Examining Critical Perspectives on Human Rights* (Cambridge University Press 2012), 22.
53 See, for example, Andrew Fagan, *Human Rights: Confronting Myths and Misunderstandings* (Edward Elgar, Cheltenham, 2009): the basis and legitimate scope of human rights has long been over-stated, which has damaged and trivialised the doctrine.
54 Martti Koskenniemi, 'Human Rights Mainstreaming as a Strategy for Institutional Power' (2010) 1(1) *Humanity* 47, 47–8.

if we can question whether it is fair to erect very high standards of 'success' or 'delivery' in judging what human rights has achieved. For some critical scholars, human rights have been a 'grievous illusion' and indeed for such scholars this accounts for 'despair and scepticism' within socially progressive movements around the future of human rights.[55]

Mutua writes of the 'messianic germ' in human rights.[56] It is not surprising that disappointment is bound to follow, based on this thesis. People's experience of human rights is that they are (that is, scholars assert that they are seen as) 'partial, subjective, selective' but that this disappointment is the inevitable 'wages of speaking in universal terms in a plural world.'[57] As Mutua observes, creeds and ideologies that overpromise – and inevitably underperform – are destined to suffer public fatigue.[58] Deflation and disappointment resulting from the perceived unmet promises or expectations about the emancipatory impact of rights might undermine popular support for human rights arguments and frameworks without necessarily requiring a populist explicitly to point this out. In this sense, the 'populist challenge' narrative may not adequately account for the diminished popular status or traction of rights-based appeals or arguments, or at least (by focusing on the messenger and not the message) obscure why explicit denunciation or delegitimisation of rights is effective in mass politics. A cousin of disappointment, in this context, is hypocrisy. When one combines unmet expectations from the liberal-democratic-market model with human rights hypocrisy and double-standards by leading Western democracies (violations while preaching respect for human rights or manipulating the rights agenda in international forums to advance national interests), it might not be surprising that the power of human rights might be diminished.[59] It is certainly not surprising that a populist might take advantage of such inconvenient truths. Again, the challenge to human rights is perhaps not then 'the populist backlash' as such (which is just picking up on the 'disappointment' signal) but the deflating effect of experiencing over time the limited transformational power of universal rights relative to the promise seen in them.

In this overarching 'disappointment' critique, then, are the 'standard' complaints about inadequate or uneven implementation or enforcement of globally proclaimed rights, the 'vague and conflicting norms, their uncertain

55 Ratna Kapur, 'On *Gender, Alterity and Human Rights: Freedom in a Fishbowl*' (2019) 122 *Feminist Review* 167-171, 169.

56 Mutua 2016, 451.

57 David Kennedy, 'The International Human Rights Regime: Still Part of the Problem?' in Rob Dickenson et al. (eds.) *Examining Critical Perspectives on Human Rights* (Cambridge University Press 2012), 26.

58 Mutua 2016, 451.

59 Mutua 2016, 452-3.

status, the broad justifications and excuses.'[60] These are all important in trying to contextualise the scale or distinctiveness of the 'populist challenge' to the overall human rights project. Yet in terms of how the new era of populism may have found that project already an 'easy target' before the backsliding and backlashing, such familiar critiques might be of less interest than another question. This is whether the human rights idea and movement themselves (as they have come to be practised) are 'causing harm' to the processes of trying to achieve and universalise the values and benefits to which rights relate.[61] That might be so if, over time and by being expressly associated with neoliberal economics and militaristic foreign policies, the human rights movement finds itself in the 'uncomfortable position of legitimating more injustice than it eliminates.'[62] One way in which this might happen, and a function of the 'displacement' thesis, is where the human rights project is perceived as only relevant to, or only giving attention to, niche problems that are widely seen (or can be shown by populist rhetoric to be) 'peripheral to a broadly conceived program of social justice.'[63] This brings us to the next line of critique.

'Disconnected'

A sense that the human rights project has become disconnected from many people's experiences, or has alienated their support, might be one plausible explanation for why the populist backlash is not a fundamental challenge to human rights (because they were in decline or diminished legitimacy and relevance anyway). Alternatively, or in addition, this disconnect or alienation might be a plausible explanation for why the populist backlash against rights-talk, rights institutions, and rights defenders might have some popular traction. The 'populist challenge' narrative might obscure this.

A 'developmental (economic)' critique

In his mid-2000s ('pre'-populism ...) lectures entitled 'Can Human Rights Survive?' Conor Gearty argued that:

> The single greatest mockery of our subject is the extent to which the gulf in resources between rich and poor has continued to deepen even while we

60 Kennedy, 'Dark Sides' (2004), 8, 21.
61 Kennedy, 'Dark Sides' (2004), 8.
62 Kennedy, 'Dark Sides' (2004), 21.
63 Kennedy, 'Dark Sides' (2004), 8, 21.

> in the developed world have been celebrating more and more our commitment to global human rights.[64]

Over two decades ago, Kennedy argued that human rights foregrounds problems of '*participation* and *procedure*' rather than '*distribution*' and so is unlikely ever to transform key structural features of the economy.[65] For this reason, human rights was bound over time to lose connection with 'bread and butter' issues (incidentally, often the fuel of populist rhetoric). The movement, frameworks, and institutional systems of human rights obscure structural socio-economic injustice,[66] the deeper-level inequalities, and deprivations 'hidden in plain sight' in most societies.[67] By confining their focus and criticism to the identification of (mostly state-based) violations and the denunciation of abuses, human rights began 'leaving unchallenged the conditions in which those abuses had become possible.'[68] This is a function, on this account, of the human rights project being inextricably bound up in a particular liberal-capitalist status quo political project. Especially but perhaps not only in more affluent and developed economies, human rights fails to identify and engage with fundamental forms of social and economic injustice 'precisely because it is itself a product of these systemic and structural forces.'[69]

This is what Susan Marks has called the myth of 'pure suffering,' that violations are a governance failure analysed in a narrow sense, when in fact any particular violation is properly to be understood as part of a problem implicating wider systemic or structural processes, dynamics, and institutions.[70] For her, human rights practice tends to involve forms of engagement that by their nature and in advance already rule out 'collective political … potentially transformative' agency:

> The project is to keep calm and carry on … human rights too paper over the cracks that are the context for indignity and unfreedom. Human rights too sweep the systemic basis of inequality under the carpet.[71]

64 Conor Gearty, *Can Human Rights Survive?* (Cambridge University Press, 2006), 150. Over a decade later, Moyn gave fuller expression to this point: Samuel Moyn, *Not Enough: Human Rights in an Unequal World* (Harvard University Press/Belknap, 2018).
65 Kennedy, 'Dark Sides' (2004), 9-10.
66 Susan Marks, 'Human Rights and Root Causes' (2011) 74 *The Modern Law Review* 57.
67 Marks, 'Four Myths,' 17.
68 Marks, 'Four Myths,' 12-13.
69 Andrew Fagan, 'The Gentrification of Human Rights' (2019) 41 *Human Rights Quarterly* 283, 296.
70 Marks, 'Four Myths,' 12-13.
71 Marks, 'Four Myths,' 16.

The human rights project is vulnerable to this critique, that its framing and thinking do not assist with the most pressing challenges of the day: the 'structural violence' of the 'war on the poor' in terms of health, lifestyle, and socio-economic inequalities.[72] Moyn, who has been influential in the critique of rights, argues that the human rights movement has made an 'obsession' of pursuing civil and political rights against authoritarian states rather than engaging in a larger campaign of 'economic welfare and inequality.'[73] Human rights as framed and institutionalised are just 'not enough' for tackling these deeper enduring economic equality issues.[74] Likewise, Salomon argues that to speak of 'international law and human rights' is often to evoke thoughts of countering terrorism, justifying humanitarian intervention, or enforcing international criminal justice; yet 'what remains overlooked is that the machinery of international law when it comes to human rights applies, in multifarious and significant ways, to matters of world poverty, inequality and development.'[75] Alston argues that mainstream human rights advocacy addresses economic and social rights issues 'in a tokenistic manner at best, and the issue of inequality almost not at all.'[76] Others argue that human rights has 'nothing to say' on key issues such tax, labour markets, trade, and prices and seems 'toothless and ill-equipped to deal with the root causes of socio-economic inequalities in contemporary societies.'[77]

Fagan has a somewhat different take, one highly relevant to putting the 'populist backlash' narrative in some context, including this arguable disconnect between the global rights lexicon and many people's lived experiences. For him, 'gentrification' (by which he appears to mean both the professionalisation of the human rights movement and middle-class affluence and social stability in liberal democracies) 'restricts the ability of human rights to engage robustly with rising deprivation, inequality, and marginalization' within those societies.[78] Fagan's focus is the 'precariat,' living in chronic insecurity (jobs, immigration, etc.) within affluent societies (and of course

72 P Farmer, *Pathologies of Power: Health, Human Rights, and the New War on the Poor* (University of California Press, Berkeley, 2004).

73 Samuel Moyn, 'The Future of Human Rights' (2014) 11(20) *SUR: International Journal on Human Rights* 57-66, 62.

74 Samuel Moyn, *Not Enough: Human Rights in an Unequal World* (Harvard University Press/Belknap, 2018.

75 Margot Salomon, 'The Future of Human Rights' for the Special Issue 'International Law, Human Rights and the Global Economy: Innovations and Expectations for the 21st Century' (2012) 3(4) *Global Policy* 455-457.

76 Phillip Alston, 'The populist challenge to human rights' (2017) 9(1) *Journal of Human Rights Practice*, 1–15, 6, 9.

77 Luca Bonadiman and Ukri Soirila, 'Human Rights, Populism, and the Political Economy of the World' (2019) 37(4) *Nordic Journal of Human Rights* 301-328, 315-318.

78 Andrew Fagan, 'The Gentrification of Human Rights' (2019) 41 *Human Rights Quarterly* 283, 283-4, 287.

in unequal but less net affluent societies).[79] Fagan uses, as an illustration, the UK human rights community's general (non-)response to the Grenfell fire disaster in London's state social housing, asking why this was not capable of being framed in human rights terms. The 'gentrification' argument appears to have two prongs. First, that the rights movement has gentrified (focusing on niche identity and cultural issues, and due process concerns) and this 'class' neglects socio-economic issues of concern to the rump majority (an omission exploited by populists) such that 'human rights' have an ever-reducing influence. Second, that there is less of a 'care factor' in more affluent and liberal societies; the urgency and traction of conventional human rights discourse is just not there due to material advantage and comfort, or perhaps complacency. Hopgood likewise argues the middle class have less need for human rights and can access opportunities through their status, explaining how rights might have become less compelling or urgent a cause.[80] On this argument, relative inequalities in more affluent liberal societies are not seen as sufficiently (or any longer) 'morally compelling' or severe to 'justify describing them as human rights violations.' Because the human rights frame (on this argument) does not 'see' structural inequality and socio-economic deprivation as a rights issue (the grand struggles of history are behind us, etc.), the gentrified elite focus elsewhere. That is, on 'the more personal, lifestyle-type concerns,' and the work of the human rights framework is that it ensures these pursuits are possible and (by ignoring structural advantage and disadvantage) are possible for everyone.[81]

This line of thinking underpins criticism of the rights project having little traction in economic development debates[82] or observations that countries of the 'Global South' preferred a discourse around development out of frustration with the perceived lack of focus of the rights project on material well-being and development.[83] This also underpins calls for human rights to reclaim thematic categories such as 'development, inequality and poverty,' 'global public goods,' 'world economy, trade and finance,' along with cli-

79 Andrew Fagan, 'The Gentrification of Human Rights' (2019) 41 *Human Rights Quarterly* 283, 297, citing Guy Standing, *The Precariat: the New Dangerous Class* (Bloomsbury, London, 2011).

80 Stephen Hopgood, 'Human Rights on the Road to Nowhere' in Stephen Hopgood, Jack Snyder and Leslie Vinjamuri (eds.) *Human Rights Futures* (Cambridge University Press, 2018), Ch. 12.

81 Andrew Fagan, 'The Gentrification of Human Rights' (2019) 41 *Human Rights Quarterly* 283, 297.

82 Morten Broberg and Hans-Otto Sano, 'Strengths and weaknesses in a human rights-based approach to international development,' (2018) 22(5) *The International Journal of Human Rights*, 664-680.

83 Luca Bonadiman and Ukri Soirila, 'Human Rights, Populism, and the Political Economy of the World' (2019) 37(4) *Nordic Journal of Human Rights* 301-328, 313.

mate change and environmental degradation, and 'demonstrate how they are (also) matters of "international law and human rights."'[84] The (perceived) failure of the human rights project to focus sufficiently (and deliver) on socio-economic rights and inequality is a key diagnosis of the decreasing relevance or legitimacy of rights and a recurrent theme in forward-looking analyses of the future of human rights.[85] And when Amnesty International raised the alarm about the populist backlash against human rights, it also noted that 'the inequality and neglect underlying popular anger and frustration arose at least in part from the failure of states to fulfil people's economic, social and cultural rights.'[86] Indeed, this is one area where some of the more thoughtful 'populist backlash' literature *has* engaged in a greater extent of introspection about how the human rights movement is not well placed credibly to engage on the 'bread and butter' issues that populists respond to and/or feed on. Alston, Rodriguez-Garavito, and others have called for socio-economic rights and economic marginalisation and inequality to become a far more important, explicit, and authentic part of the overall rights agenda:[87] human rights proponents 'need to start looking at budgets, at tax policy, and at fiscal policies in general … issues of redistribution.' [88]

A 2016 expert report to the UN Human Rights Council argued that the 'second-class status' of social and economic rights – and the view that they are 'toothless and ineffectual' with no yield in terms of social justice progress – had led to a 'loss of credibility in the eyes of rights holders.' This would have

> deeply negative consequences for the potential of the human rights movement to gain the widespread support that it needs in order to establish its credibility in the eyes of the literally billions of people whose fundamental needs continue to be of only minor relevance to the core human rights

84 Margot Salomon, 'The Future of Human Rights' for the Special Issue 'International Law, Human Rights and the Global Economy: Innovations and Expectations for the 21st Century' (2012) 3(4) *Global Policy* 455-457.

85 Sherif Elsayed-Ali, 'The Future of Human Rights' 'Next Strategy' Series (Amnesty International, 2019) https://nextstrategy.amnesty.org/2019/08/09/the-future-of-human-rights/.

86 *Amnesty International report 2016–2017: The state of the world's human rights* (London, 2017), 14.

87 Phillip Alston, 'The populist challenge to human rights' (2017) 9(1) *Journal of Human Rights Practice*, 1–15, 6, 9; Cesar Rodriguez-Garavito, 'The Future of Human Rights: from Gatekeeping to Symbiosis' (2014) 11(20) *SUR: International Journal on Human Rights* 499-510, 506; Luca Bonadiman and Ukri Soirila, 'Human Rights, Populism, and the Political Economy of the World' (2019) 37(4) *Nordic Journal of Human Rights* 301-328.

88 Phillip Alston, 'The populist challenge to human rights' (2017) 9(1) *Journal of Human Rights Practice*, 1–15, 9. See too Gerald Neuman, 'Human Rights responses to the Populist Challenge' in Neuman (ed.) 2020, 259-260, on the need to 'rebalance' international human rights to address the neglect of socio-economic issues.

> agenda. The fact that the movement is subject to powerful challenges at the global level is due in significant part to the perception that its overriding preoccupations do little or nothing to address the most abiding and pressing challenges confronted by a large part of humanity.[89]

Alston (author, in another capacity, of the above report) rightly qualified the 'populist challenge' argument (that the source of the threat is populists, rather than other factors we are now considering) by specifically referring to post-globalisation socio-economic exclusion and inequality in these terms:

> [T]he reality is that the majority in society feel that they have no stake in the human rights enterprise, and that human rights groups really are just working for 'asylum seekers', 'felons', 'terrorists', and the like. This societal majority seems far less likely today than it might have been in the past to be supportive of the rights of the most disadvantaged merely out of some disappearing ethos of solidarity.[90]

Clearly, this 'disconnection' phenomenon – itself related both to disappointment with the overpromise of the rights project and the perceived inability or unwillingness of that project to really grapple with key structural issues in society – has some potential insights to offer in terms of situation the populist backlash against human rights in some greater context. It must be said that some of this critique can be seen as deeply contradictory, simultaneously positioning rights as useless and potentially powerful ('rights-talk obscures or has nothing to say on deep structural issues … but we must deploy rights more deliberately towards socio-economic and inequality issues'). It is also somewhat ironic how this line of argument places enormous expectations on what rights can do (transform and restructure the entire political economy of society) yet castigates the rights project for not delivering on promises. Moreover, the critique can seem a bit unfair or inaccurate since, technically speaking, the global socio-economic rights framework has a *lot* to say on these issues (although this may be beside the point if the public perception is that it does not). Meanwhile, we must always be wary of arguments that some political cultures prefer non-rights discourse (e.g., the language of development) given how convenient such a narrative is to autocratic and unresponsive regimes and power-holders within societies.

89 'Report of the Special Rapporteur on extreme poverty and human rights' (UN Human Rights Council, 26 April 2016), A/HRC/32/31, 9 (para [18] and [19]).

90 Phillip Alston, 'The populist challenge to human rights' (2017) 9(1) *Journal of Human Rights Practice*, 1–15, 6.

We return to some of this in Part III. For now, nevertheless, there *is* arguably something from this critique for the backlash literature to reflect on in the context of popular uptake of populist messaging, which (when done well) speaks to people's insecurities within their daily lives. This is whether human rights 'offer effective enough answers to some of the anxieties and preoccupations people confront in their daily lives.'[91] If not, this may help account for current circumstances in ways that merely decrying the populist backlash overlooks. Indeed, people may feel more than merely disconnected with the rights project. Whatever the effect of populist politicking, the human rights movement (etc.) might actually have been alienating key constituencies, which is our next critique.

An 'over-reach (alienation)' critique

Elsewhere we explore how implicit in the concept of 'backlash' is a somewhat legitimate or at least explicable pushback against perceived undue over-reach or over-bearing behaviour. Claims and arguments framed in human rights terms (and especially when sought through judicial enforcement) can be 'bad politics' in some circumstances,[92] exposing perhaps the weakness of the claim or alienating a range of important actors. Has the human rights movement generally (here, including the judiciary) engaged systematically at scale in claims, norm-development, or enforcement activities that are perceived to stretch the rights frame too far, exceed a real or perceived mandate, or orient the rights machine towards issues seen as peripheral or divisive? If so, this might be one explanation for its problems, or vulnerability to critique, or indeed populist backlash. Kennedy's well-known critique of the movement accused its proponents and analysts of having no real sense of a 'cost-benefit' approach to where rights-talk was effective and legitimate and where either not so or counter-productively problematic.[93]

At least in the shadow of 'backlash,' there is considerable intuitive force to arguments about the risk of over-reach, of exceeding mandates, of not including important groups on the 'journey,' of alienating state and non-state actors. In addition to a principled unease, one might have with an argument that effectively says 'do not push your rights too far,' whether such an 'over-reach' critique has any empirical basis is quite another thing from its intuitive merit. In particular, it would require heavily context-specific, non-generalisable cost-benefit analyses, as well as nuanced understanding of costs or benefits

91 Luca Bonadiman and Ukri Soirila, 'Human Rights, Populism, and the Political Economy of the World' (2019) 37(4) *Nordic Journal of Human Rights* 301-328, 311.

92 Kennedy, 'Dark Sides' (2004), 31.

93 Kennedy, 'Dark Sides' (2004), 31.

to whom). Nevertheless, we can proceed on the basis that over-reach and/or alienation are one possible set of factors accounting both for challenges to the rights project independent of any populist backlash (and potentially obscured by excessive focus on the populists), and for any popular traction that the explicit populist attack on human rights might have. Briefly, the critique might be said to have four aspects. First, the overall alienation from the rights project described above (in terms of its perceived limited impact on or engagement with 'bread and butter' socio-economic issues). If higher-profile international rights NGOs prioritise issues such as the death penalty, freedom of religious belief, or a range of gender or LGBT identity rights issues, some would argue, this might only alienate or dismay those whose day-to-day priorities might lie in social justice demands (access to food, shelter, medicine, healthcare).[94] For Hopgood, one of three 'deeper underlying shifts' that herald the end times of human rights lies in over-reach on universalist claims, leading to 'pushback against human rights on principle, particularly in cases of religious belief.'[95] Immigration/migration issues have certainly helped fuel populist sentiment in Europe and the US. Neuman argues that human rights advocates might have contributed to this backlash by making very broad (i.e., unfounded) claims about state and societal 'duties' to receive migrants.[96] Such claims might be contestable empirically or on principle, yet merely dismissing them carries a risk of missing important feedback on how rights discourse is being received in various circles.

Second, strategies of 'reckless activism'[97] (or perhaps more accurately a lack of strategy or of cost-benefit thinking) – pushing weak, still-developing, highly niche, or highly divisive agendas – might have alienated sections of the public and/or both governmental and corporate decision-makers, or put weak institutions into very difficult political-policy spaces, inviting the executive to curtail then their influence. As one recent study argued, some ambitious human rights litigation may 'aggravate' or unduly test liberal democracy in some more newly democratised states.[98] Wuerth argues that the West

94 Stephen Hopgood, 'Challenges to the Global Human Rights System' (2014) 11(20) *SUR: International Journal on Human Rights* 67-75, 69.

95 Stephen Hopgood, 'Challenges to the Global Human Rights System' (2014) 11(20) *SUR: International Journal on Human Rights* 67-75, 69.

96 Gerald Neuman, 'Human Rights responses to the Populist Challenge' in Neuman (ed.) 2020, 266.

97 Joseph Raz, 'Human Rights in the Emerging World Order' (2010) 1 *Transnational Legal Theory* 31, 47.

98 Lisa Conant, 'Canaries in the Mine? European legal mobilization and its implications for democracy' (Paper presented at the Law and Society Association conference, Lisbon, Portugal, 13-16 July 2022, author copy).

over-reached by pursuing human rights objectives through international law and, in so doing, weakened the wider corpus of international law.[99]

Third is the risk that regional human rights courts and international treaty bodies might have engaged in over-reach and 'overstepped the authority that states once delegated to them,' by 'expanding their jurisdiction and engaging in dynamic, evolutive interpretation' of their mandates.[100] This 'judicial over-reach' narrative was arguably a key factor in UK Brexit-era populist political attacks on the decisions of the European Court of Human Rights in areas of counter-terrorism and national security. Yet one struggles in the counter-populist literature to detect any sense that the force and appeal of this argument might require some reflection on whether there is some reasonable basis to the over-reach critique (as opposed to it just being a feature of supposedly irrational right-wing attacks on precious, infallible rights courts). Neuman wonders whether the reasoning of some bodies is 'too absolute' and might gift to populist critics an easy target by explicitly disregarding important state interests.[101] In reflections on the populist era, no less than Judge of the International Court of Justice the late James Crawford – a staunch defender of international law and human rights – observed that sometimes backlash can be an *appropriate* response, for example to institutional mandate over-reach or to 'norm fatigue' from proliferating instruments and measures.[102] Orentlicher has observed that the sense of dismay at the backlash against international law-making and institution-building came after a 'heady' and 'giddy' period of global institution-building in the 1990s and 2000s, notably in the area of criminal justice with high-profile temporary and permanent international criminal tribunals and courts.[103] This is not so much an over-reach argument as a reminder that what can seem 'populist backlash' might also be entirely

99 Ingrid Wuerth, 'International Law in the Age of Trump: A Post-Human Rights Agenda' *Lawfare* Blog, 14 November 2016; www.lawfareblog.com/international-law-age-trump-post-human-rights-agenda.

100 Johan Karlsson Schaffer, Andreas Føllesdal and Geir Ulfstein, 'International Human Rights and the Challenge of Legitimacy' in Andreas Føllesdal, Johan Karlsson Schaffer and Geir Ulfstein (eds.), *The Legitimacy of International Human Rights Regimes: Legal, Philosophical and Political Perspectives* (Cambridge University Press, 2013). Full discussion of the extensive literature on judicial over-reach, especially in the Strasbourg system context, is beyond this book's scope.

101 Gerald Neuman, 'Human Rights responses to the Populist Challenge' in Neuman (ed.) 2020, 266.

102 James Crawford, 'The Current Political Discourse Concerning International Law' (2018) 81(1) *The Modern Law Review* 1, 6. Later he observes that international law is (must be) flexible and that withdrawal from institutions or instrument regimes 'is not always to be condemned': 22.

103 Diane Orentlicher, 'The Emerging Shape of Global Justice: Retrogression or Course Correction?' (2020) 35 *Maryland Journal of International Law* 61-72, 61-62.

unsurprising corrective or rebalancing after an intensive period of institution-making and norm-creation.

The idea of 'fatigue' is apt to a fourth possible version of the over-reach/alienation critique. This might be that activities to try and bring a rights frame to bear on a whole proliferation of fields over-extends their normative basis or, in some other perceived way, weakens their currency and persuasiveness. They become about everything and so nothing. Thus it is argued that not everything can be 'squeezed into the human rights tent'[104] or that rights language is just too diluted or contaminated and suffers from a kind of 'familiarity and vagueness that makes almost any demand for equal treatment, justice or freedom expressible in rights language, whether or not such a demand is truly justified.'[105] Indeed some have tied this pattern to the populist backlash, arguing that the continuous process of trying to fit human rights into other frameworks, such as development or climate change, has 'caused their inflation and dilution' and this 'lack of coherence' 'might have made it easier for conservative and populist movements to hijack human rights language and causes.'[106] In the context of the populist backlash, Neuman cautions against further proliferation in human rights, arguing that continual expansion in recognition (or specious assertion, more accurately) of new rights in more fields of life may widen the 'theory versus practice' gap (or state recognition versus activist assertion gap), discrediting human rights through over-reach.[107]

We should accept of course that the 'alienation' critique has a range of potential responses, raising as it does complex issues of strategy and communication (and responsiveness to donors and others) for higher-profile rights organisations locally and globally. Still, it remains arguable that how organisations respond (in the above 'cost-benefit' sense) to such choices may have bearing on how deep and widespread popular support is for the human rights motif. If so, this involves us at least moving beyond a counter-populist approach of merely decrying populism, so as to explore both sides of the dilemma. Thus one scholar's question of whether, for instance, a 'cutting-edge focus' on LGBT rights might increase the salience and effectiveness of human rights or rather generate a degree of resistance or aversion and/or doom potential alliances with other social movements that have considerable

104 Conor Gearty, *Can Human Rights Survive?* (Cambridge University Press, 2006), 15, 144.

105 Stephen Hopgood, 'Challenges to the Global Human Rights System' (2014) 11(20) *SUR: International Journal on Human Rights* 67-75, 70.

106 Luca Bonadiman and Ukri Soirila, 'Human Rights, Populism, and the Political Economy of the World' (2019) 37(4) *Nordic Journal of Human Rights* 301-328, 305, 307-9

107 Gerald Neuman, 'Human Rights responses to the Populist Challenge' in Neuman (ed.) 2020, 254, 259.

local legitimacy, such as religious groupings.[108] Are these uncomfortable questions for the human rights movement, or necessary ones in the context of populism and the wider zeitgeist of counter-globalisation in cultural and other terms? Even for a committed activist such as Morales, the difficult truth is that sometimes human rights are politically 'dangerous': pushing a human rights line or policy might be dangerous *to the wider cause of human rights.*[109] This might be especially so in a populist era.

In this vein, there is perhaps a fifth dimension to the alienation critique. Kennedy would argue that rights-talk can force an artificial choice for individuals and groups (he means in emerging economies) between 'tradition' and 'modernity.' This is a function, really, of the hegemonic 'displacement' effect outlined above. The argument is that the effect of universalistic human rights is to delegitimise or downplay localised forms of political discourse. This can serve to strengthen reactionary (potentially but not necessarily populist) 'traditionalists' who can dismiss or ridicule human rights in terms that may be appealing to those left feeling insecure by the cultural and economic uncertainty of modernisation processes.[110] Now this critique does seem simplistic or exaggerated in terms of what role rights-talk might play in processes of societal change globally. Yet in the context of a 'populism' discussion, for now it is worth recording the argument that one reason rights might have either lost their appeal, or indeed contributed to popular backlash, is that the rights project forces people to choose between binary visions of traditional versus modern society. This alienates them from the rights project. It follows that either human rights are less compelling in such contexts, or less readily defended when backsliding (populist or other) occurs, or more easily scapegoated. But if there is any merit to this critique, the point is that this may be a function of how rights have come to operate or can only ever operate. It is not just a function of very clever manipulations by populist leaders. Arguably, a focus on populism as *the* threat to human rights risks obscuring opportunities to reflect on these issues.

A 'communitarian' critique

Did populism undermine the power and traction of human rights, or did human rights (as practised, preached or pursued) either help feed populist narratives or at least find itself without the legitimacy, credibility, or popularity needed to provide a counter-narrative to populism? It is potentially highly

108 Stephen Hopgood, 'Challenges to the Global Human Rights System' (2014) 11(20) *SUR: International Journal on Human Rights* 67-75, 69.

109 Daniel Morales, 'Revelation out of Rupture: Building Human Rights from the Bottom up' (2020) 35 *Maryland Journal of International Law,* 127-133, 131.

110 Kennedy, 'Dark Sides' (2004), 21.

relevant to such a question that one significant and enduring critique of the rights project – well before the 2010s+ 'populist era' – is that it was always or certainly became (or became perceived as) overly centred on individuals' claims versus the state or community, rather than other framings of mutual, communal, or group interests. Both as classically conceived and in terms of the message perhaps received by people around the world, 'human rights' is about individualistic entitlements or claims 'where in moral terms society comes second' to the individual.[111] Fairly or not, it is seen as handicapped by 'naïve individualism'[112] and as promoting or defending a self-centred and not communal approach to society, one focused on entitlements rather than responsibility to the collective.[113] In combination with accusations of human rights being a culturally specific (Western liberal) artefact, much ink has been spilled on how the rights project, so framed, was inevitably going to struggle for legitimacy in cultures where the individual–communal balance might be perceived somewhat differently. In this sense of potentially producing cultural dissonance and backlash, the 'communitarian' critique is related to the 'alienation' critique above. It is not only the populist backlash context, then, that has long seen calls for the development of a more communal conception of human rights.[114] Indeed, the contemporary focus on climate change, in particular, is further fuelling arguments that 'group rights' are no different to individual ones in being ill-suited binary or balancing frames for considering collective responses.

The 'communitarian' school of thought is exemplified in the work of Etzioni. He has advanced this argument since 1993, but in 2018 made a particular pitch for its relevance in a work entitled *Law and Society in a Populist Age*.[115] The gist of the position that Etzioni represents would suggest that the ideology of human rights has lost popular traction and moreover ceded space to populist politics (or exposed itself to attack therefrom). This is principally, on this view, because of its excessive focus, firstly, on individuals' rights versus 'the community' and 'the common good,' and secondly, on rights held

111 Stephen Hopgood, 'Human Rights on the Road to Nowhere' in Stephen Hopgood, Jack Snyder and Leslie Vinjamuri (eds.) *Human Rights Futures* (Cambridge University Press, 2018), Ch. 12.

112 Andrew Fagan, 'The Gentrification of Human Rights' (2019) 41 *Human Rights Quarterly* 283, 288.

113 See, for example, succinct descriptions of this critique in Jeremy Waldron, *Nonsense upon Stilts: Bentham, Burke and Marx on the Rights of Man* (Methuen, 1987); or Cass Sunstein, 'Rights and Their Critics' (1995) 70(4) *Notre Dame Law Review* 727.

114 Kathryn McNeilly, 'What should human rights in the future look like?' *The Conversation* 3 October 2017.

115 Amitai Etzioni, *The Spirit of Community: Rights, Responsibilities, and the Communitarian Agenda* (Crown, New York, 1993); and *Law and Society in a Populist Age* (Bristol University Press, 2018).

by individuals or groups as claims against society, as opposed to appropriate emphasis on the commensurate *responsibilities* of individuals or groups towards those societies.

On this argument, human rights (although proponents like Etzioni often use 'liberalism' interchangeably) is a 'morally incomplete' language that cannot 'address the populism that is rising in many democratic polities.'[116] For Etzioni, human rights has lost both legitimacy and cultural relevance by its neglect of responsibilities and favouring the individual over the group, and so must be 'complemented by considerations of community and the common good' and develop a 'more comprehensive moral language ... of communitarian conceptions' if it is effectively to counter populism.[117] Whatever one makes of Etzioni's own prescriptions (that the tension between liberal and communitarian conceptions requires a compromise 'liberal communitarian' approach to counter populism),[118] and even without traversing the whole 'cultural relativism' debate in human rights, the point here arguably remains. The point remains even if we filter out the fact that critiques of individuals' rights and the promotion of 'human responsibilities' alternatives can be extremely convenient for paranoid repressive autocratic regimes or for reactionary patriarchal authorities within some cultural traditions. It remains even if one ponders whether the shared experience of the COVID-19 pandemic and shared consciousness of the climatic catastrophe might be shifting the relative emphasis – in varying societies around the world – from the individual to the communal. The point is that fixing too readily on populist politicians and strategies as the threat to human rights can distract us from features of rights practice or design that are highly relevant to the populism phenomenon. The perception of an insufficient emphasis on responsibilities (versus rights) or on the collective (versus the individual) is one that human rights struggles to escape from, and populist leaders can make something of this in delegitimising or downplaying human rights.

In considering the 'displacement' effect above, we have already seen the argument that people co-existing in society who might have found other ways to reconcile incompatible preferences were instead forced into corners and inflexible bargaining positions by having to articulate their claims as (individualistic) rights in order to have them taken seriously. This is Kennedy's argument that human rights promote individualistic thinking that 'blunts' the experience or articulation of a shared life in a community or 'collective political life.'[119] Even where there is a focus on groups' rights, the focus

116 Etzioni 2018, 3-26.
117 Etzioni 2018, 3-26.
118 Etzioni 2018, 3-26.
119 Kennedy, 'Dark Sides' (2004), 15-17.

becomes on one's rights-holding status or identity and, together with the binary absolutism of rights/no rights, may create oppositional or exclusive ways of thinking about (let alone negotiating with) those that are not rights-holders in the same way.[120] But this is a very sophisticated analysis: for the 'average' person, for the most part, the issue is somewhat simpler and perhaps just more an impressionistic sense that the rights project promotes irresponsible individualism and is somehow harmful (or at least not that valuable) to the collective. It is not hard to see that blaming populists for leading a backlash on human rights might blind one to whatever level of validity there may be, 'in the streets' and notably among voters, for this sort of conception.

'Delegitimised'

With its critique of the (alleged/perceived) individualistic focus of human rights, this line of argument is very closely related to the next line of criticism: that human rights could or can never escape its particular historical genesis in Western liberal political philosophy and politico-cultural traditions. This has profound effects for the legitimacy of rights-based approaches and strategies and language in hard cases in non-Western societies. We can outline this critique briefly given its ubiquity and persistence, while supplementing it with a broader critique that whatever their historical origins, human rights have been captured or co-opted by particular powerful public and private interests. The brevity of treatment is certainly not to downplay the likely resonance, in an era of populism, of claims that rights are 'foreign impositions' or 'instruments of capitalism.' It is so as to spend more time on two very closely inter-related critiques of the human rights movement and paradigm ('over-legalisation' and 'professionalisation') that also go to the heart of questions of legitimacy and that 'speak' directly to the anti-elitism that is said to be so distinctive about populism as a phenomenon.

A 'liberalism (and imperialism)' critique

A proper assessment of the populist challenge to human rights must account for the enduring narrative that in any event (even without the populist-led backlash), the reach and resonance of human rights remain limited by their contingent relationship to Western liberalism. This is the well-trodden argument that the supposedly universal rights tradition and norm-system is actually the product of a particular (historical and cultural) moment and place: 'post-Enlightenment, rationalist, secular, Western, modern and capitalist.'[121]

120 Kennedy, 'Dark Sides' (2004), 15-17.
121 Kennedy, 'Dark Sides' (2004), 18.

Thus the literature, even before one opens the highly influential critical 'Third World' scholarship,[122] is replete with statements such as how human rights always struggles with its European pedigree and the suspicion that claims – or some claims – are not just culturally biased but 'represent an attempt to impose "the ideas of the West"' across the globe.[123] Human rights became synonymous with freedom, but (it is argued) with a particular and narrow liberal conception of freedom, within its own 'fishbowl,'[124] inherently limited its appeal, utility, or appropriateness in a diverse world.

Leading critics in this vein argue that this fundamental challenge to the legitimacy and appeal of human rights has never successfully been answered.[125] There are really two aspects to this. One is this specific contingent cultural heritage, which purports to express as universal norms and mindsets and values that are culturally and contextually specific. On such a view, despite being adopted as a counter-authoritarian language by activists in the Global South, the human rights movement remains a 'cultural possession' of the West and has not been able effectively to 'blunt the charge of normative, philosophical, and cultural exclusivity,' and this has 'contributed to its decline.'[126] Not even the sincerity of those who wield this critique in well-meaning ways in support of dignity and freedom, nor the obvious disingenuousness in the self-preserving deployment of this accusation by autocrats and reactionaries in the non-Western world, has affected the traction that this critique has.[127]

The other is a more sinister idea, about how easily powerful state and corporate and other interests have captured or co-opted the rights frame to serve their interests, while presenting human rights as universal. So for many scholars – but ominously in a post-Iraq, post-9/11, post-globalisation populist era, for many voters and others – human rights are or were a 'mechanism of Western imperialism.'[128] Human rights were or very much remain, on this account, merely a tool and discourse for imperial domination of states on the global

122 A An-Na'im and F Deng (eds.) *Human Rights in Africa: Cross-cultural Perspectives* (Brookings Institution Press, Washington DC, 1990); Mukua Mutua, 'Savages, Victims, and Saviors: The Metaphor of Human Rights' (2001) 42 *Harvard International Law Journal* 201; and *Human Rights: A Political and Cultural Critique* (University of Pennsylvania Press, Philadelphia 2002).

123 Joseph Raz, 'Human Rights in the Emerging World Order' (2010) 1 *Transnational Legal Theory* 31, 44.

124 Ratna Kapur, *Gender, Alterity and Human Rights: Freedom in a Fishbowl* (Edgar Elgar, 2018).

125 Mutua 2016, 452.

126 Mutua 2016, 452. For brevity, we engage with Mutua as broadly representative, intellectually, of this critical tradition.

127 Mutua 2016, 453.

128 Mutua 2016, 452.

periphery.[129] So human rights were a 'Western crusade of the white middle and upper classes in Europe and the United States' no different from the colonial mission of their forefathers, using human rights (rather than Christianity) to 'deliver primitive peoples into the Age of Europe.'[130] For scholars like Kapur, human rights has been 'irrefutably hegemonic: a governance project primarily concerned with ordering the lives of non-European peoples and subaltern subjects' and 'creating the conditions for the exponential flourishing of the neo-liberal market.'[131] Human rights comprises 'tactics and vehicles of governance and domination.'[132] Universal human rights is, on this critique, such a successful idea that even though (as above) they do not really challenge or transform the status quo in the political economy, they are appropriated and used to legitimise imperial and capitalistic projects around the world. They were at some point captured by those who would use human rights 'to mask other, more brutal projects, such as colonial-style militarism.'[133] Rights-talk can cover for particular interests 'clothed in the language of the universal.'[134] By being rolled explicitly into foreign policy agendas, human rights get used to justify, defend, and legitimate war-making and various acts of repression.[135] This underpins the critique that the human rights movement consistently underestimates the usefulness of the human rights vocabulary and machinery for people whose political projects are repressive or aggressive.[136]

Thus Douzinas, in his 2000 diagnosis of (but also call for) the 'end' of human rights, observed how human rights had become stagnant and instrumentalised in the process of being 'institutionalised by self-interested structures of world power.'[137] The explicitly human rights-based foreign policy positions of Western states in the 1990s (such as was invoked to justify NATO's bombing of Serbia over the Kosovo crisis) turned human rights from 'a discourse of rebellion and dissent into that of state legitimacy.'[138] Yet if states gained legitimacy from invoking the rights project in such cases, they did so at the expense of the very legitimacy on which they sought to rely.

129 Nicola Perugini and Neve Gordon, *The Human Right to Dominate* (Oxford University Press 2015).
130 Mutua 2016, 455.
131 Ratna Kapur, 'On *Gender, Alterity and Human Rights: Freedom in a Fishbowl*' (2019) 122 *Feminist Review* 167-171, 168.
132 Ratna Kapur, 'On *Gender, Alterity and Human Rights: Freedom in a Fishbowl*' (2019) 122 *Feminist Review* 167-171, 168.
133 Conor Gearty, *Can Human Rights Survive?* (Cambridge University Press, 2006), 13, 60.
134 David Kennedy, 'The International Human Rights Regime: Still Part of the Problem?' in Rob Dickenson et al (eds.) *Examining Critical Perspectives on Human Rights* (Cambridge University Press 2012), 22.
135 Kennedy, 'Dark Sides' (2004), 29, 33.
136 Kennedy, 'Dark Sides' (2004), 21.
137 Costas Douzinas, *The End of Human Rights* (Oxford University Press, 2000), 3-4.
138 Costas Douzinas, *The End of Human Rights* (Oxford University Press, 2000), 7.

It does not take another book to observe the damage to the credibility of human rights done by invoking them – from Kosovo to Iraq to post-9/11 to Libya – in support of an explicitly rights-based foreign policy and counter-terrorism policy. If such ventures killed the goose that laid the golden egg of legitimacy-in-the-name-of-rights, one surely has to see the populist challenge in perspective. If so, populists did not discredit and delegitimise rights: Tony Blair and company have already done so. Even without the overlay of military adventures, critical scholars have shown us how rights as institutionalised in the global treaty system can legitimate the regimes that participate in those frameworks, while also narrowing our focus onto only their particular specified violations in ways that can normalise the residual (not currently categorised as violations) activities of the repressive or unresponsive state.[139]

Overall, this line of argument posits that this susceptibility to capture or co-optation might be inevitable in rights: the paradox that their success in dominating discourse is also partly attributable to their 'ambivalent porosity.'[140] Human rights became a globalised phenomenon, but this was partly because they are so open-textured that the same terms and norms are open to appropriation and deployment by all manner of different actors. Koskeniemmi argues that even if human rights were once (for a brief decade, it would seem, after 1989) a powerful claim to protection, resources, and participation, this passed. By a Weberian logic of inevitable bureaucratisation, they became a governance vocabulary open to any party to defend whatever interests.[141] On this critique, not only did they become a regime, a practice of governance (more than an idea or movement for contesting power),[142] they now suffer from 'a certain degree of embeddedness within the very system they should challenge.'[143]

Importantly in a 'populism' context where tropes of powerful private capitalist interests abound, one consequence of this susceptibility to appropriation and embeddedness in a non-threatening governance discourse is that whatever their historical origin and even without the imperial militaristic

139 David Kennedy, 'The International Human Rights Regime: Still Part of the Problem?' in Rob Dickenson et al (eds.) *Examining Critical Perspectives on Human Rights* (Cambridge University Press 2012), 22.

140 Kennedy, 'Dark Sides' (2004), 8.

141 Marti Koskienemmi, 'Human Rights: so 90s,' address, Oxford Martin School, March 2014.

142 David Kennedy, 'The International Human Rights Regime: Still Part of the Problem?' in Rob Dickenson et al (eds.) *Examining Critical Perspectives on Human Rights* (Cambridge University Press 2012), 19.

143 Luca Bonadiman and Ukri Soirila, 'Human Rights, Populism, and the Political Economy of the World' (2019) 37(4) *Nordic Journal of Human Rights* 301-328, 313.

association, rights (and indeed international law more generally)[144] are discredited by their association with neoliberal market economics and private capital. Too many scholars to mention have observed the 'amenable relationship' between human rights and capitalism, which on this view has co-opted and muted the more revolutionary aspects of human rights or those aspects that would question the 'structural and systemic drivers of injustice.'[145] So, for example, we see the argument that human rights may have at times 'looked like a handmaiden to neoliberalism,' because capitalist forces 'have a self-interest in advancing human rights frameworks.'[146] Human rights became, for Mutua, the 'moral argument for the liberal project,' an ideology that 'refines – and culminates in – political democracy, the rule of law, individual rights, constitutionalism, and free markets.'[147]

For Fagan, the counter-populist human rights scholarship overlooks a significant issue: the 'connection' between capitalism (or 'neoliberalism') and the populist challenge to human rights: that the impact of neoliberal market policies (the liberal project with which human rights is associated) have 'directly undermined the credibility and legitimacy of liberal democracy.'[148] This raises the question (Part III) of whether the target of populism is human rights or a much broader political trend or status quo. If so, whether the human rights project is so intertwined with that order that its vocabularies and institutions (if not, perhaps, its underlying values) cannot be separated from the bigger historical phenomenon with which it is associated and against which there is backlash. Nevertheless, for now we might explore how, if human rights are increasingly discredited or disregarded as a legitimate and effective framework, one partly related explanation for this is how the motif does not really touch on corporate and market power or has been easily co-opted by these.[149] This critique is an extension of the 'distortion' argument above, that the narrowness of the human rights agenda hitherto has discredited it because it either does not really address non-state private power or actively facilitates its domination. Thus we see critiques such as that the movement has focused on engaging in somewhat ideological battles in the public sphere, 'neglect-

144 See, for example, Ntina Tzouvala, *Capitalism as Civilisation: a History of International Law* (Cambridge University Press, 2020).

145 Andrew Fagan, 'The Gentrification of Human Rights' (2019) 41 *Human Rights Quarterly* 283, 288.

146 Mark Heywood, 'South Africa's Journey from Socialism to Human Rights: The True Confessions of an Errant Socialist' (2019) *Journal of Human Rights Practice* 305.

147 Mutua 2016, 451.

148 Andrew Fagan, 'Human Rights in a Time of Populism 2021, by Gerald Neuman (ed.): Book Review' (2021) 43(2) *Human Rights Quarterly* 416-421, 420.

149 Upendra Baxi, *The Future of Human Rights* (Oxford University Press, 2008). See too David Kinley, *Civilizing Globalization: Human Rights and the Global Economy* (Cambridge University Press 2009).

ing those more technical aspects that have allowed to erect and establish unprecedented forms of private power on a global scale.'[150] Thus Anghie saw human rights and international law as merely a facilitator of the expansion of global business activity.[151] Baxi meanwhile cautioned of an 'appropriation by capital of human rights logic and rhetoric'[152] in service of smoothing the rougher edges of global capitalism in a self-legitimating fashion, the 'corporate colonisation'[153] of human rights. Thus too arguments such as Whyte's, that hegemonic versions of human rights have been turned into 'the morals of the market,' that is, into an effective tool for refuting socialist and postcolonial demands for greater economic equality by not engaging with those structural issues. At the same time, this project upholds 'a neoliberal right to equality [as] a right of everyone to preserve their unequal wealth and power' in the face of political demands for redistribution.[154]

It is a very difficult and fraught academic process to attempt to make connections between some of these critical perspectives and the street-level phenomenon of populism, in pursuit of some greater clarity on how the former put the latter in perspective, or even help explain the success of the latter. Some accounts of the populist challenge observe that human rights cannot effectively counter populism until it finds 'a different narrative to disentangle human rights' from its complicity with neoliberalism and capitalism more generally.[155] Indeed, taken to its conclusion, that argument would be that any 'crisis' of human rights might be less about the effect of populism than this entanglement or complicity with dominant economic paradigms and the structural and distributional inequality problems that they perpetuate.[156] For present purposes, it is enough to stand back and acknowledge that if human rights faces a legitimacy and credibility challenge in the 2020s, this is something with a much more complex aetiology than simply what populist leaders have 'done' to the otherwise unproblematic phenomenon of human rights.

150 Luca Bonadiman and Ukri Soirila, 'Human Rights, Populism, and the Political Economy of the World' (2019) 37(4) *Nordic Journal of Human Rights* 301-328, 321.

151 Antony Anghie, *Imperialism, Sovereignty and the Making of International Law* (Cambridge University Press, 2005) 269-71.

152 Upendra Baxi, *The Future of Human Rights* (Oxford University Press, 2006), 263.

153 Anna Grear, 'Challenging Corporate 'Humanity': Legal Disembodiment, Embodiment and Human Rights' (2007) 7(3) *Human Rights Law Review* 511; Anna Grear, *Redirecting Human Rights: Facing the Challenge of Corporate Legal Humanity* (Palgrave Macmillan, 2010); also Christopher Harding, Uta Kohl and Naomi Salmon, *Human Rights in the Market Place: The Exploitation of Rights Protection by Economic Actors* (Ashgate, 2008).

154 Jessica Whyte, *The Morals of the Market: Human Rights and the Rise of Neoliberalism* (Verso 2019).

155 Luca Bonadiman and Ukri Soirila, 'Human Rights, Populism, and the Political Economy of the World' (2019) 37(4) *Nordic Journal of Human Rights* 301-328, 322.

156 Luca Bonadiman and Ukri Soirila, 'Human Rights, Populism, and the Political Economy of the World' (2019) 37(4) *Nordic Journal of Human Rights* 301-328, 302.

A 'legalisation' critique

A persistent critique of how human rights practice has come to be shaped is that universal rights are too enmeshed in the confines of law and legal frameworks, while the human rights movement (at all levels) is too preoccupied with lawyering. Much of this revolves around Amartya Sen's argument about the limits of law in advancing human rights.[157] This is the argument that over-legalisation of the language, strategies, tactics, and very conceptualisation of human rights – the tendency to reduce one's view of them to a set of protections as captured in international treaties or national laws – obscures the moral and ethical claims that flow from recognising and valuing the inherent dignity of every human being. That is, viewing human rights claims exclusively or excessively through the lens of legal rules may reduce their social efficacy, since a good deal of their power lies in their rhetorical force and the moral vision they embody, whether or not they have been translated into actionable legal rules.[158] For Douzinas, human rights were captured not just by states but by the liberal project, transformed from their existence as substantive subjective natural law norms into particular institutional features of a positivist legal order: by their connection to law and their reduction into legalised rights claims then became 'merely rights.'[159] Thus Tasioulas has written of the need to 'save human rights from human rights law.'[160] This argument is that international human rights law has blurred the distinction between human rights (with particular obligations and consequences) and universal human interests or values more generally, and the movement suffers from an 'insufficiently critical promotion of the legalization and judicialization of human rights.'[161]

It is in this context that scholars describe a 'crisis of legalism.'[162] They decry the perceived over-legalisation of the international human rights project,[163] 'fetishizing' the judiciary,[164] the 'inordinate dominance of law-centred

157 Amartya Sen, 'Human Rights and the Limits of Law' (2006) 27(6) *Cardozo Law Review* 2913–2927.

158 Cesar Rogriguez-Garavito, 'The Future of Human Rights: from Gatekeeping to Symbiosis' (2014) 11(20) *SUR: International Journal on Human Rights* 499-510, 501-2, citing Amartya Sen.

159 Costas Douzinas, *The End of Human Rights* (Oxford University Press, 2000), 4.

160 John Tasioulas, 'Saving Human Rights from Human Rights Law' (2019) 52 Vanderbilt Journal of Transnational Law 1167.

161 John Tasioulas, 'Saving Human Rights from Human Rights Law' (2019) 52 Vanderbilt Journal of Transnational Law 1167.

162 Conor Gearty, *Can Human Rights Survive?* (Cambridge University Press, 2006), Ch. 3.

163 Michael Ignatieff, *The Ordinary Virtues: Moral Order in a Divided World* (Harvard University Press, 2017).

164 Kennedy, 'Dark Sides' (2004), 21.

discourses and strategies,'[165] and the tendency to adopt the implementation and use of legal frameworks as the main objective of rights practice as an end in itself (instead of as a means to advancing people's rights *per se*).[166] Kennedy's critique was that the focus on formalising rights as laws and on mechanisms for their implementation not only becomes an end in itself but leads to us forcing all of human experience into the exercise of particular legal entitlements (or non-entitlements) and on framing claims in ways that can be 'seen' and recognised by law.[167] Earlier we noted how the 'distortive' or 'displacement' thesis informs many other critics of rights practice. Here, this displacement argument would be that the transformation of political questions into legal questions, and then into questions of legal rights, distorts and diminishes the nature of these claims and also crowds out other strategies, rendering 'other forms of collective emancipatory politics less available.'[168] The absoluteness of rules makes compromise more difficult. The emphasis on law 'demobilizes other actors and other vocabularies,'[169] while the gap between law-on-the-books or legal institutions and the rest of 'real' life undermines the law's promise to bring about emancipation.[170]

For Gearty, this issue was at the heart of his mid-2000s essays collection, titled *Can Human Rights Survive?*[171] How, he asked, did we come to rely on such an inherently conservative part of society – the law, legal profession, judiciary – to 'carry our radical project through to completion ... which great social movement has ever before put the lawyers in its front-line?'[172] This line of critique has a strong constituency among critical scholars. How, Gearty asked, does one keep rights issues and claims 'part of the maelstrom of the politics that has given rise to them' rather than narrowed, distorted, and 'quarantined in the reactionary ... realms of the law'?[173] He saw the key question for the whole future of human rights as being how

165 Cesar Rodriguez-Garavito and Krizna Gomez (eds.), (Editors' introduction) in *Rising to the Populist Challenge: a New Playbook for Human Rights* (De Justitia, Bogota, 2018), 12-13, 36.

166 Cesar Rogriguez-Garavito, 'The Future of Human Rights: from Gatekeeping to Symbiosis' (2014) 11(20) *SUR: International Journal on Human Rights* 499-510, 501-2. This legal 'ends versus means' distinction is a recurring theme of Conor Gearty's *Can Human Rights Survive?* (Cambridge University Press, 2006).

167 Kennedy, 'Dark Sides' (2004), 9-10, 17.

168 Kennedy, 'Dark Sides' (2004), 29, 33.

169 Kennedy, 'Dark Sides' (2004), 21.

170 Kennedy, 'Dark Sides' (2004), 21.

171 Conor Gearty, *Can Human Rights Survive?* (Cambridge University Press, 2006), 12.

172 Conor Gearty, *Can Human Rights Survive?* (Cambridge University Press, 2006), 12.

173 Conor Gearty, *Can Human Rights Survive?* (Cambridge University Press, 2006), 12.

> [H]uman rights can be embedded in society as a set of realistic and achievable political goals and not just as a guide to good behaviour in individual cases. A curious feature of the human rights movement has been that the answer to this question has largely been seen to lie with legal codification rather than with direct and sustained political action.[174]

Such a line of questioning picks up on the critical perspective that while human rights holds out the promise of a legal vocabulary for achieving justice above or outside 'the clash of politics,'[175] something which is neither possible nor desirable.[176] The 'false promise of certainty offered by a supra-political reading of human rights by judges' is, in this view, only a short-term fix that results in both the legalisation of politics and a politicisation of law.[177] Human rights norms are presented as norms to be enforced by judges rather than as 'mobilizational' political things.[178] Kelly argues that resorting to litigated rights as the main instrument or vector of human rights development and protection results in 'an underdeveloped and meagre' and over-judicialised human rights culture.[179] For Kennedy, the human rights movement (albeit perhaps more acutely in the international arena than in domestic contexts) suggests that 'rights' bring emancipation, whereas it is people making difficult political decisions that do so.[180] Human rights has erred in framing itself as preceding or being above politics, creating a false promise of emancipation through legally framed rights, whereas rights can only be achieved and maintained through political contestation.[181] The framing in legal terms or forms (as rights) of what are effectively political decisions is said to undermine the 'radical power' and emancipatory potential of human rights, while also depriving political communities of 'the opportunity properly and critically to comment or engage with them.'[182] Human rights issues are political and must operate in the realm of politics. One can see how this critique might play, eventually, into a sense of human rights being distorted but also disconnected from communities that seek to access its language and protection. Some attribute the populist backlash directly (but without particular explana-

174 Conor Gearty, *Can Human Rights Survive?* (Cambridge University Press, 2006), 61.
175 Kennedy, 'Dark Sides' (2004), 21.
176 Kennedy, 'Dark Sides' (2004), 21.
177 Conor Gearty, *Can Human Rights Survive?* (Cambridge University Press, 2006), 80.
178 Samuel Moyn, 'The Future of Human Rights' (2014) 11(20) *SUR: International Journal on Human Rights* 57-66, 61-63.
179 James Kelly, 'Legislative Capacity and Human Rights in the Age of Populism: Two Challenges for Legislated Rights' (2020) 21(1) *Jerusalem Review of Legal Studies*, 94–111.
180 Kennedy, 'Dark Sides' (2004), 21.
181 Conor Gearty, *Can Human Rights Survive?* (Cambridge University Press, 2006), 72.
182 Conor Gearty, *Can Human Rights Survive?* (Cambridge University Press, 2006), 69-70, 84.

tion of aetiology) to the 'excessive centrality' of law, lawyers, and 'legalistic strategies':[183] human rights advocates 'need to engage in moral arguments not just technical legal rights ones.'[184]

Gearty's argument achieved greater prominence through Moyn's outright adoption of it in *The Last Utopia* (2010).[185] Moyn's argument is that human rights became prominent by promising an alternative to political contest and struggle (a higher claim above politics), the last utopia where others failed.[186] For Moyn, the partial success of human rights came from it 'selecting' legal modes and forms, so avoiding politics and all its 'hard choices, compromising bargains and dirty hands.'[187] Yet, he argued, this condemned the rights project to failure because human rights do not really descend into the messy reality of power politics and so make 'little practical difference, amounting to an ornament on a tragic world that they do not transform.'[188] Human rights need to leave the 'safety' of legalism and legalistic artefacts and be prepared to descend into 'programmatic contest for power' and the grubby trade-offs of socio-political life in order to remain relevant.[189] Neuman's nod to Kennedy and Moyn is to argue that the best response to the populist challenge is to facilitate open political contestation at the national level, 'where the contest of ideas must be won.'[190]

What is the upshot of this critique for present purposes? If the human rights project and movement have become too 'legalised' or law-based, this might conceivably be relevant on the two levels we are considering. First, that we need to be cautious of the 'populist challenge' narrative as it may obscure other factors that have weakened or discredited human rights irrespective of any populist agenda or attacks. Second, that to understand properly the future of human rights given the populism phenomenon, scholars and the movement need to reflect on how patterns in human rights practice might have exposed the project to populist attack and/or compromised its ability to respond effectively and credibly and to develop a compelling counter-narrative. It must be said that even if excessive legalisation has retarded the fuller expression and flourishing of the human rights project, there is no particular evidence that

183 Duncan Johnson, 'In Defence of Democratic Populism' in Neuman (ed.) 2020, 208, 2013.

184 Duncan Johnson, 'In Defence of Democratic Populism' in Neuman (ed.) 2020, 208.

185 Samuel Moyn, *The Last Utopia* (Harvard University Press, 2010), 217.

186 See, e.g., Samuel Moyn, *The Last Utopia: Human Rights in History* (Harvard University Press, 2012).

187 Samuel Moyn, *The Last Utopia* (Harvard University Press, 2010), 217.

188 Samuel Moyn, 'The Future of Human Rights' (2014) 11(20) *SUR: International Journal on Human Rights* 57-66, 61.

189 Samuel Moyn, 'The Future of Human Rights' (2014) 11(20) *SUR: International Journal on Human Rights* 57-66, 57.

190 Gerald Neuman, 'Human Rights responses to the Populist Challenge' in Neuman (ed.) 2020, 256.

populist politicians have articulated this critique as such. It is, by and large, a scholarly one. Yet we turn now to explore how this 'legalisation' critique is bound up with a critique of professionalisation and elitism in the human rights movement in ways that might be said to be very relevant to assessing the populist challenge to human rights.

The link between 'legalisation' and professionalisation of the field and a problematic air of elitism was articulated well before the populist backlash. In 2002, Kennedy warned against the movement's (real or perceived) over-reliance on 'enlightened, professional elites' which might result in 'alienating people from the vocabulary of their own governance.'[191] Some years earlier, Douzinas had criticised how 'official thinking' on human rights had become entrusted with, among others, 'rich international lawyers' in New York and Geneva, accentuating the over-legalisation of human rights.[192] Whether or not this is a fair assessment, it is really not difficult to see how the manipulation of such an idea might play into a populist backlash calculated to disable and delegitimise the human rights project. Indeed, this connection has been made explicit in a handful of recent critical analyses of populism and human rights. For Kelly (writing in 2020), the legalisation-judicialisation trend is problematic because it perpetuates a culture for 'the few, not the many' because access to judicial rights protection and litigation cost-resources are not fairly distributed across society.[193] The answer to populism in constitutional democracies, others argue, lies in reclaiming popular engagement with human rights 'for the many, not the few' by re-focusing on legislative action through representative institutions (and away from court-based litigation strategies).[194] For Fagan too (2021), writing expressly in the context of populism, the combination of legalisation and professionalisation of human rights has been problematic: the defence and promotion of human rights 'cannot be left entirely to lawyers and other members of a professional elite.'[195] They must also be advanced through social movements 'which one should not need a college degree to participate in.'[196] This brings us to the inter-related critique of elit-

191 Kennedy, 'Dark Sides' (2004), 21.

192 Costas Douzinas, *The End of Human Rights* (Oxford University Press, 2000), 7.

193 James Kelly, 'Legislative Capacity and Human Rights in the Age of Populism: Two Challenges for Legislated Rights' (2020) 21(1) *Jerusalem Review of Legal Studies*, 94–111.

194 Gregoire Weber et al (eds.) *Legislated Rights: securing Human Rights Through Legislation* (Cambridge University Press, 2018); these arguments are probably 'unduly optimistic' in an age of elected populist majorities: see James Kelly, 'Legislative Capacity and Human Rights in the Age of Populism: Two Challenges for Legislated Rights' (2020) 21(1) *Jerusalem Review of Legal Studies*, 94-111.

195 Andrew Fagan, 'Human Rights in a Time of Populism 2021, by Gerald Neuman (ed.): Book Review' (2021) 43(2) *Human Rights Quarterly* 416-421, 420.

196 Andrew Fagan, 'Human Rights in a Time of Populism 2021, by Gerald Neuman (ed.): Book Review' (2021) 43(2) *Human Rights Quarterly* 416-421, 420.

ism in the human rights movement. Again, the point of canvassing such critiques is that they predate the 'populist challenge' narrative and may (perhaps cumulatively) equally account for the state and status of human rights in the 2020s. Moreover, they might be problems that the populist backlash narrative obscures or need to engage with if effective responses to the backlash are to be arrived at.

A 'professionalisation' (elitism) critique

One dilemma for human rights, well before the populist backlash, has been that its effective institutionalisation, bureaucratisation, and integration into governance systems has also (it is argued) stymied its radical potential while creating a distance and dissonance with 'ordinary people.' Human rights has become an elaborate international practice,[197] a 'regime of governance' or 'expert language' translating political demands into mere 'administrative goals' to be negotiated, measured, and monitored by 'a sophisticated but self-referential international bureaucracy.'[198] If so, the human rights bureaucracy is itself 'part of the problem'[199] with contemporary human rights irrespective of any backlash. On this account, professionalisation 'strengthens lawyers at the expense of priests, engineers, politicians, soothsayers, and citizens who might otherwise play a more central role in emancipatory efforts.'[200] This process has separated advocates and subjects, pulls local elites away from their base, reduces them to 'local informants,' or distracts them with the international process, 'the [local human rights] elites turning their attentions like sunflowers to Geneva, to New York, to the Center … to the work of resolutions and reports.' [201]

Human rights claims and interventions thus get turned into technical matters, 'embedding human rights in the culture of expertise'[202] but creating a troubling distance with the experiences of rights-holders themselves. Thus scholars argue that human rights advocates used to 'speak truth to power' but now 'to the dismay of some activists' are associated 'with those very elites that

197 Charles Beitz, *The Idea of Human Rights* (Oxford University Press, 2009). See too Martti Koskenniemi, 'Human Rights Mainstreaming as a Strategy for Institutional Power' (2010) 1(1) *Humanity* 47.

198 Luca Bonadiman and Ukri Soirila, 'Human Rights, Populism, and the Political Economy of the World' (2019) 37(4) *Nordic Journal of Human Rights* 301-328, 311.

199 Kennedy, 'Dark Sides' (2004), 27.

200 Kennedy, 'Dark Sides' (2004), 27.

201 Kennedy, 'Dark Sides' (2004), 27.

202 Luca Bonadiman and Ukri Soirila, 'Human Rights, Populism, and the Political Economy of the World' (2019) 37(4) *Nordic Journal of Human Rights* 301-328, 326.

have become target of relentless criticism.'[203] Indeed the movement is typically accused of 'excluding more localised and grassroots forms of human rights activism.'[204] For Snyder, for example, the human rights project is too focused on large international organisations that do not or cannot represent 'local' views, impose top-down approaches, and perpetuate this distance between the global human rights elite and local activists.[205] Professionalisation of the movement is said to have driven a 'growing disconnect between formal organizations and the myriad other actors who use the language and the values of human rights.'[206] Some scholars attempt to give this an empirical basis by interpreting surveys about human rights among various populations as suggesting that the concept is seen, among 'the global masses,' as not just Western but elitist and remote.[207] Perceived human rights elitisim and professionalism (versus local experience and suffering) are 'perennial'[208] issues that predate the 'populist era.'

We need not necessarily accept the argument that this distance – the vastly different experiences of elite human rights practitioners and local activists or just rights-holders – creates 'false solidarity'[209] or even self-regarding 'professional narcissism guising itself as empathy.'[210] Even without going so far, there remains the criticism that the distance (in wealth, mobility, access to information, and impact) between globally active human rights professionals and the people they purport to represent.[211] It does not take much to see how this is relevant when we put 'populism (anti-elitism)' and 'human rights' into the same sentence. Indeed, on its face alone, there must be some insight to be gained from this critique of how the rights movement became this way or even just became perceived to operate this way. The backlash narrative's

203 Luca Bonadiman and Ukri Soirila, 'Human Rights, Populism, and the Political Economy of the World' (2019) 37(4) *Nordic Journal of Human Rights* 301-328, 311.

204 Luca Bonadiman and Ukri Soirila, 'Human Rights, Populism, and the Political Economy of the World' (2019) 37(4) *Nordic Journal of Human Rights* 301-328, 302.

205 Jack Snyder, 'Empowering Human Rights through Mass Movements' in Stephen Hopgood, Jack Snyder and Leslie Vinjamuri (eds.) *Human Rights Futures* (Cambridge University Press, 2018), Ch. 4, 94-97. Of course, 'elites' is a complex idea since many 'local' activists might be seen, in their own local context, as elites in that particular society.

206 Cesar Rodriguez-Garavito and Krizna Gomez (eds.), (Editors' introduction) in *Rising to the Populist Challenge: a New Playbook for Human Rights* (De Justitia, Bogota, 2018), 13.

207 Shannon Kindornay, 'Mainstreaming the Human Rights Based Approach into the Post-2015 Framework,' in Julia Kozma, Ana Müller-Funk, and Manfred Nowak (eds.), *Advancing the Protection of Human Rights* (Neuer Wissenschaftlicher Verlag, Vienna, 2014), 261-274.

208 Beth Simmons, 'The Future of the Human Rights Movement' (2014) 28(2) *Ethics and International Affairs* 183-196.

209 Kennedy, 'Dark Sides' (2004), 27.

210 Kennedy, 'Dark Sides' (2004), 29.

211 Kennedy, 'Dark Sides' (2004), 29.

focus on 'what populists have done to human rights' might obscure this self-reflection. This is more than just a critique about barriers to entry to 'the movement' and the alienation of activists who lack technical legal knowledge or networks.[212] It may be more something akin to the broader narrative, well beyond human rights, of the effect of a 'tyranny of experts.'[213] If it is an accurate picture of human rights practice and practitioners, it might not be specific to this field, but part of a far wider post-globalisation zeitgeist of diminished trust in, deference to, and tolerance of perceived networks of elite governance. For instance, Posner's (largely US-oriented) assessment of a populist backlash driving a crisis of 'liberal internationalism' and international law has – at its heart – a thesis about public distrust in technocratic rule-by-elites.[214] If international law is seen as 'rule by technocracy,' its vulnerability in an era of populism is that it is perceived as both 'establishment' and 'technocratic' (aloof), while having an insidious corrosive effect on national sovereignty.[215] Populism then is a backlash against the 'malign influence' of technocratic elites who are 'thought to be more loyal to foreigners or to themselves than to the public.'[216]

While Douzinas lamented the state co-optation and foreign policy instrumentalisation of the human rights agenda from the 1990s, as well as the gentrification or professional elitism of human rights,[217] he also observed that the 'grassroots' level of human rights activity also increased dramatically during this time. This sort of contradictory observation is one reason to be cautious with the 'elitist' critique, which tends to treat the human rights project as a zero-sum object that is either top-down and elite-dominated, or (should be more) driven bottom-up by virtuous community-based actors. As Part III will argue, the truth is probably that where human rights claims and strategies are useful, they are used by a whole range of diverse actors and were not necessarily appropriated by elites in New York or Geneva such that 'grassroots' actors could not avail themselves of the symbolic capital and power of human rights. Nevertheless, it is arguable that populist leaders have skilfully exploited

212 Cesar Rogriguez-Garavito, 'The Future of Human Rights: from Gatekeeping to Symbiosis' (2014) 11(20) *SUR: International Journal on Human Rights* 499-510, 501-2.

213 William Easterly, *The Tyranny of Experts: Economists, Dictators, and the Forgotten Rights of the Poor* (Basic Books, 2013).

214 Eric Posner, 'Liberal Internationalism and the Populist Backlash' (2020) 49 *Arizona State Law Journal* 795.

215 Eric Posner, 'Liberal Internationalism and the Populist Backlash' (2020) 49 *Arizona State Law Journal* 795, 796. For one (internally US-oriented) argument that international law is highly elitist and disconnected from everyday Americans, see John McGinnis and Ilya Somin, *Should International Law Be Part of Our Law?* (2007) (59) *Stanford Law Review* 1175.

216 Eric Posner, 'Liberal Internationalism and the Populist Backlash' (2020) 49 *Arizona State Law Journal* 795, 801, 819.

217 Costas Douzinas, *The End of Human Rights* (Oxford University Press, 2000).

the professionalisation of civil society (and their reliance on foreign funding too) in order to portray human rights advocates as part of the elite.[218] On this account, 'emblematic' of the populist's illiberal approach and at least part of the success of populist rhetoric consists in scapegoating human rights (and its defenders) for societal troubles or at least characterising human rights as deaf or hostile to the legitimate concerns of 'ordinary' citizens.[219] Moreover, human rights are an easy political target because its defenders (the 'movement') are fairly easy and obvious scapegoats: an out-of-touch patronising professional class ignorant of the concerns of the 'ordinary person' and pandering unduly to undeserving minorities using rights-talk and judges (another unelected elite). As Fagan writes, the invocation or defence of human rights is associated (via populist rhetoric) with 'the elitist, self-assured attitudes of a socially and politically unrepresentative constituency of people.'[220]

There has been some high-level acknowledgement by a senior UN human rights official of the counter-productive nature of some rights strategies in the face of populist or other backlash, particularly where these are compromised by perceived association with a global technocratic elite disconnected from people's legitimate concerns and lived experiences.[221] That official argued that while UN-related and other human rights machineries must support civil society actors, they 'need to do so in an intelligent way, otherwise it can play into the rhetoric of various regimes':

> The human rights movement, through a variety of means ... has to show how human rights benefit those who consider themselves *ordinary people*. Human rights is not just about protecting prisoners, LGBTI, persons with disabilities, migrants and refugees. Crucial though it clearly is to keep all those categories at the forefront of our concerns, we also need to show people that human rights is vital for everyone, and that it's not just a niche topic for beleaguered minorities and *out-of-touch liberals* [emphasis added].[222]

218 Cesar Rodriguez-Garavito and Krizna Gomez (eds.), (Editors' introduction) in *Rising to the Populist Challenge: a New Playbook for Human Rights* (De Justitia, Bogota, 2018), 19.

219 Andrew Fagan, 'The Gentrification of Human Rights' (2019) 41 *Human Rights Quarterly* 283, 285.

220 Andrew Fagan, 'The Gentrification of Human Rights' (2019) 41 *Human Rights Quarterly* 283, 285.

221 Independently of the 'populist backlash' thesis, see too generally Charles Beitz, *The Idea of Human Rights* (Oxford University Press, 2009) on why human rights language and modes or argument generate resistance and evoke a 'disabling skepticism' and why the 'practice' of human rights can be problematic and counter-productive.

222 Andrew Gilmore, 'The Backlash against Human Rights' (UN Assistant Secretary-General for Human Rights), Dublin, November 2017: https://www.ohchr.org/en/statements/2017/12/backlash-against-human-rights. See too Phillip Alston, 'The populist challenge to human rights' (2017) 9(1) *Journal of Human Rights Practice*, 1–15, 6.

This argument is valuable as it brings us closer to this book's purpose of provoking greater self-reflection than merely (if rightly) mourning or denouncing what populists have 'done' to human rights. Some authors argue that the response to the populist challenge is not to 'double down' on the existing human rights project, because it either has no impact against populist politics or may even be part of what feeds populism.[223] On this view, the strategy of merely 'doubling down' (albeit with some adjustments such as 'better communication') does not follow from the 'populist challenge' diagnosis that we are facing something fundamentally different to anything that has come before. Moreover, such an approach avoids confronting 'uncomfortable' questions about how human rights may have contributed to the discontent (etc.) in which populists thrive. Any 'doubling down' may just be compounding 'errors and mistakes.'[224]

This part of the book has tried to survey some factors that might account for the vulnerability of human rights to populist attacks and to situate the populist challenge thesis in a broader context that shows how significant the project's problems arguably were before any 'backlash' arrived or was generated. Economic inequality is the focus for scholars of where human rights has 'failed,' but a range of other omissions might sit alongside this. More enduringly, the failure to regulate the governance and remedial gap for adverse human rights impacts in the face of accumulations and concentrations of private and corporate power. More recently, the inability to offer any meaningful check on technology's societal impact[225] might undermine its status as the hegemonic values-based frame for global discourse and contestation. Yet just setting such ideas out must surely raise the question of whether critical scholars – even as they tell us how ineffectual rights are – simultaneously hold entirely unreal expectations for what 'human rights' (or any other discourse or system, 'democracy,' or whatever one chooses) could do or could ever have done. De Burca (who rejects the critical scholarship) summarises its thesis succinctly. This is that human rights are 'flawed, inadequate, hegemonic, confining, apolitical, peripheral, pointless,' a project that is elitist and expert-driven, that 'defuses' protest and mass mobilisation, and 'de-fangs' politics (or at least impedes distributive politics) through an 'excessively narrow and purist' discipline mainly for legally focused advocates.[226] If any of this is valid, it creates

223 Luca Bonadiman and Ukri Soirila, 'Human Rights, Populism, and the Political Economy of the World' (2019) 37(4) *Nordic Journal of Human Rights* 301-328, 301.

224 Luca Bonadiman and Ukri Soirila, 'Human Rights, Populism, and the Political Economy of the World' (2019) 37(4) *Nordic Journal of Human Rights* 301-328, 307.

225 Alexandra Huneeus, 'Human Rights and the Future of Being Human' (2018) 112 AJIL Unbound 324-328.

226 Grainne de Burca, *Reframing Human Rights in a Turbulent Era* (Oxford University Press, 2021), 226-229.

some imperative for reflection on whether populists and the backlash they are leading are the course of the legitimacy crisis in human rights. De Burca is right that critical scholarship can tend to understate the achievements of human rights, exaggerate the movement's dysfunction, and mischaracterise the movement generally.[227] Moreover, the 'end times' critique, diagnosing or calling for the end of the human rights era, is probably simultaneously 'thought-provoking and inexact.'[228] There are many potential ways to respond to critiques either of the inefficacy of human rights (for example, shifting our yardstick of progress or expectation) or, relevantly for our purposes, its credibility given its Western origins and liberal associations (for example, Global South, anti-colonial and post-colonial scholars, activists, jurists, and others have made significant contributions to the universal rights project).[229] However, the point of surveying critical approaches was not to counter them (ripe as they might in many cases be) but to reinforce the need to see the 'populist challenge' narrative in greater perspective.

In categorising how populists use criticism of human rights in political ways (i.e., fettering national security and unduly benefiting minorities or narrow interest groups), Bilkova argues that these narratives are 'overly simplified or incomplete' or 'go against some of the basic premises on which the whole system of human rights is based.'[230] Yet this is precisely the point: it is not that relevant how inaccurate or unfair criticism or delegitimisation of human rights may be. The question is whether it is an effective strategy. The purpose of this part has also been to show that there are good reasons still to reflect on 'self-inflicted' aspects of the human rights movement and to avoid a 'populist challenge' narrative that focuses on populists (the messengers) rather than popular grievance or failings of the human rights movement (the message). Reflecting on populism and human rights, Fagan worries that the human rights movement does not respond well to criticism and, being tone-deaf, that its 'standard response' – to double down on asserting the importance of rights – 'may only serve to hasten its decline.'[231] Rightly, he argues that the 'on-going crisis of human rights is not merely a consequence of demagogues stoking their supporters' prejudices and hostilities.' The human rights community has also 'contributed to the very conditions which now pose a threat

227 Grainne de Burca, *Reframing Human Rights in a Turbulent Era* (Oxford University Press, 2021), 191.

228 Cesar Rodriguez-Garavito and Krizna Gomez (eds.), (Editors' introduction) in *Rising to the Populist Challenge: a New Playbook for Human Rights* (De Justitia, Bogota, 2018), 12.

229 See, for example, Kathryn Sikkink, *Evidence for Hope: Making Human Rights Work in the 21st Century* (Princeton University Press, 2017).

230 Veronica Bilkova, 'Populism and Human Rights' (2018) *Netherlands Yearbook of International Law* 143-174.

231 Andrew Fagan, 'The Gentrification of Human Rights' (2019) 41 *Human Rights Quarterly* 283, 285.

to the community and its doctrine.'[232] Fagan worries that an 'overly righteous dismissal' by human rights advocates of the populist message (i.e., as merely filled with prejudice) along with the movement's inability to self-reflect on why that message resonates is poor strategy in pragmatic electoral politics terms and also prevents the human rights community from engaging in important self-critical analysis and change.[233]

For Posner, part of the problem in countering populism are the 'cosmopolitan' intellectual and governance elite whom he derides for merely dismissing populist nationalism as 'primitive and morally indefensible.'[234] Posner's view is that this is a dangerous form of blindness. It leads, he argues, to us all seriously under-estimating the nationalist-populist-sovereigntist appeal. Scholarly and administrative elites simply do not understand, it follows, how perceptions come to form about triumphalist over-reach by international legal and governance elites.[235] By naively and condescendingly dismissing the populist backlash against the liberal order outright – a bunch of 'mere deplorables' – there is a missed opportunity to undertake the hard patient work of developing compelling counter-narratives or explaining the supposed benefits of international law and governance, including human rights. If, as Alston argued, the reality is that 'the majority in society feel that they have no stake in the human rights enterprise' – which is really just working 'for "asylum seekers", "felons", "terrorists", and the like'[236] – what is the movement's response? This brings us to Part III of this book.

232 Andrew Fagan, 'The Gentrification of Human Rights' (2019) 41 *Human Rights Quarterly* 283, 287.

233 Andrew Fagan, 'The Gentrification of Human Rights' (2019) 41 *Human Rights Quarterly* 283, 286-287.

234 Eric Posner, 'Liberal Internationalism and the Populist Backlash' (2020) 49 *Arizona State Law Journal* 795, 801.

235 Eric Posner, 'Liberal Internationalism and the Populist Backlash' (2020) 49 *Arizona State Law Journal* 795, 801.

236 Phillip Alston, 'The populist challenge to human rights' (2017) 9(1) *Journal of Human Rights Practice*, 1–15.

III

PROGRESS?

Evaluating proposals to counter populism and revitalise human rights

Part I explored the 'populist challenge' thesis in relation to both a claimed general backslide on human rights standards (across the world) and a claimed particular deliberate backlash aimed at undermining the human rights idea and movement for domestic political advantage. Part II challenged this. It explored whether, taken at face value, the 'populist challenge' thesis might obscure the variety of ways in which human rights, as practised and preached, might have been facing significant challenges before and irrespective of any populist backlash, and indeed might have at least lacked credible and effective responses to populism, or at most contributed to populism's rise. Now, in Part III, we draw on such insights in order to evaluate proposals to counter populism and 'revive' human rights.

Reframing

'Populist backlash' as blindness

It is not necessary here to define 'backlash' or to resolve whether it implies merely unusually robust resistance or reformism, or rather a definitive fulsome negation and rejection of either an institution or a whole normative system.[1] Nevertheless, we do need to unpack the concept and its use in

1 Erik Voeten, 'Populism and Backlashes against International Courts' (2020) 18(2) *Perspectives on Politics* 407-422. For a definition in the human rights context, see Sanja Dragic, *Post-Backlash Human Rights Law* (Brill, Amsterdam, 2022). See too Leslie Vinjamuri, 'Human rights backlash' in Stephen Hopgood, Jack Snyder, and Leslie Vinjamuri (eds.), *Human Rights Futures* (Cambridge University Press, 2018), Ch 5. This volume does not refer to populist

DOI: 10.4324/9781003311140-4

the 'populist challenge' thesis. Scholars have used the term 'backlash' to describe state resistance against aspects or features of the international human rights system (especially the European Court of Human Rights but also the Inter-American Court of Human Rights and its African counterpart, and the International Criminal Court). However, this is only a subset of a much broader set of international legal and governance institutions (especially dispute resolution bodies, from trade and investment, to peace and security, to public health) against which a state-led 'backlash' has been observed in recent years. That is, the populist backlash on human rights is part of a much broader literature tracking what are seen as populist–nationalist, sovereignty-invoking political attacks on and undermining of international institutions, and the mostly treaty-based law that underpins them.[2]

Arguably, this convenient shorthand term can otherwise obscure more than it reveals or indeed produce a form of analytical partial blindness. In particular, it might drive a focus on (or indeed dismissal of) the populist 'doer' who supposedly drives anti-rights rhetoric and so obscure attention to their message or audience. Below are some questions that a future research agenda around the populist backlash might ask, and to which the literature to date arguably has not given sufficient attention:

- How central and explicit have 'human rights' (norms, institutions, vocabulary) actually been to the populist's playbook? Part I revealed that notwithstanding the backlash motif, the 'populist challenge' literature has not really marshalled overwhelming evidence of the explicit use of anti-rights rhetoric as a political tool. Is there something of a 'straw man' to the backlash thesis: how much evidence is there, from what sufficient diversity

backlash as such, but to 'where states have pushed back against human rights encroaching on their autonomy by creating alternate value systems or reinterpreting the demands of rights' (Editors' Introduction, 18). For a discussion of mere 'pushback' versus extraordinary 'backlash' see Mikael Rask Madsen et al., 'Backlash Against International Courts: Explaining the Forms and Patterns of Resistance to International Courts' (2018) 14 *International Journal of Law in Context* 197.

2 See, for example, 'The Backlash against International Law,' Special Issue of the 2020 (Vol. 38) *Australian Yearbook of International Law* and 2020 Symposium (Vol. 35) *Maryland Journal of International Law*. See too James Crawford, 'The Current Political Discourse Concerning International Law' (2018) 81(1) *The Modern Law Review* 1; David Caron and Esmé Shirlow, 'Dissecting Backlash: The Unarticulated Causes of Backlash and its Unintended Consequences' in Andreas Follesdal and Geir Ulfstein (ed), *The Judicialization of International Law: A Mixed Blessing*? (Oxford University Press, 2018) (engaging with Cass Sunstein, 'Backlash's Travels' (2007) 42 *Harvard Civil Rights – Civil Liberties Law Review* 435); Erik Voeten, 'Populism and Backlashes against International Courts' (2020) 18(2) *Perspectives on Politics* 407-422; Eric Posner, 'Liberal Internationalism and the Populist Backlash' (2020) 49 *Arizona State Law Journal* 795.

of countries, that anti-rights/rights-mechanisms rhetoric was indeed so central to the wider populist message? How explicitly do actors whom we might label or typologise as 'populist' in fact attribute blame to (or actively generate or exploit negative sentiment against) human rights or its defenders?

- Even if there is a pattern at scale, is this delegitimisation strategy necessarily effective, does it resonate with audiences and in which situations and settings, with what more precise effects on the state and status of human rights?[3] Has the populist backlash in fact been effective in delegitimising (etc.) human rights? Where and how would we be able to know this with any confidence? In what ways, and particular contexts, might the backlash have backfired, in terms of re-energising rather than sidelining human rights as a form and toolkit of political mobilisation? Is it too soon or too empirically challenging to know or measure this with any certainty?
- To what extent, if and when and where it *is* raised expressly in populist rhetoric, is the human rights project just an incidental target in a much wider political process of de-globalisation and backlash against the prevailing neo-liberal order and/or perceived problems of elite governance more generally? In this sense, is it useful for human rights scholars to study 'populism and human rights': is this too narrow a frame, or does it attribute too much impact or significance to the place of the human rights project in the wider status quo?

Concepts such as 'backlash' may obscure that what counts as 'progress' or 'backsliding' is likely to be deeply contestable and contested. The 'backlash' concept or device may also foster 'all or nothing' thinking: a monolithic system or movement uniformly affected by a monolithic (here, populist) tide that affects all human rights actors and issues everywhere in the same way. Yet, backlash against one human rights grouping, institution or concept might be accompanied by the advancement of the human rights project elsewhere or in other respects or other geographies. It might stimulate pushback against the backlash or compromise positions that represent a net gain in human rights promotion and protection terms.[4] Moreover, there can conceivably be a backlash (populist or other) against a normative system or order without that necessarily implying a fundamental or total rejection of that order. And a system might purportedly be attacked or discredited but with no particular or enduring effect or in a way that generates anti-backlash pushback and so revitalises

3 Cf. Gerald Neuman, 'Populist threats to the international human rights system' in Gerald Neuman (ed.) *Human Rights in a Time of Populism* (Cambridge University Press, 2020), 4.
4 These arguments are also explored in Jolyon Ford, 'The Multilateral Human Rights System: Systemic Challenge or Healthy Contestation?' (2020) 35 *Maryland Journal of International Law* 90-103, 103.

the system. The backlash might be perceived as legitimate and enlightening, and result in responsive shifts for example in judicial or institutional practices. The 'backlash' may be just an over-due corrective, requiring the institution (etc.) to be humble, patient, and responsive. An empirical and contextualised study would be needed on such things. Much will depend on such complex empiricism and cause–effect assumptions. So, much also depends on one's perspective and framing: backlash events or effects may seem more alarming if one starts from the position that the human rights system was legitimate and flourishing before the backlash. Unpacking this assumption was at the heart of Part II of this book.

We have seen (Part I) that we need to be cautious to the point of being sceptical about 'populism' as a pejorative concept or label. In the same way, we need to be cautious (where the counter-populist literature might not have been) with the concept of 'backlash.' Like 'populism' (and especially in combination), it is also used in a pejorative way that may close off analysis artificially and prematurely. Both the international law and human rights backlash literatures conceive of 'backlash' as a one-way, unprovoked, unjustified cynical political strategy that harms otherwise perfectly legitimate, effective, and useful institutions and systems. Populist backlash is then something that 'happens to' those institutions and norms, which are passive, blameless, and undeserving victims. Yet, the concept of 'backlash' arguably connotes a legitimate, perhaps not unexpected, grievance response, especially to something that is over-reaching or over-bearing.[5] It implies a reaction that is not just foreseeable, predictable, or explicable (for example, to overreach of authority or over-exertion of pressure or under-inclusion of participation) but one in which there is something understandable, legitimate, or justified about the response. Otherwise, we would speak in terms of an outright unprovoked *attack on* something rather than a *backlash against* that thing. Indeed, in decrying world leaders' attacks on international law and withdrawal from international regimes and commitments, we saw in Part II how Crawford observed that sometimes backlash can be an appropriate (not just understandable) response to mandate overreach or proliferating instruments and measures.[6]

If this line of analysis has any merit, is this something that human rights proponents might reflect on and learn from, rather than only decry the phenomenon of 'backlash' while also dismissing it as 'populist'? Indeed, it might

5 Jolyon Ford, 'The Multilateral Human Rights System: Systemic Challenge or Healthy Contestation?' (2020) 35 *Maryland Journal of International Law* 90-103.

6 James Crawford, 'The Current Political Discourse Concerning International Law' (2018) 81(1) *The Modern Law Review* 1, 6; also that withdrawal from institutions or instrument regimes 'is not always to be condemned': 22.

be fruitful to think of how, perhaps paradoxically,[7] the international legal order (of which human rights is one high-profile part) might be partly responsible for the conditions that may help drive the populist backlash or might have contributed to structural or perception problems that render populist messaging appealing or exposed itself to negative strategies. For instance, if populist critiques of free trade or foreign investment agreements are effective, the answer is not just to decry such critiques as 'populist backlash' but to understand how and with which constituencies such regimes might generate backlash. Those legal regimes are not simply subjected to this external populist force 'out-of-the-blue,' or we would not call it a backlash. The more appropriate and strategic response is to explore where those involved in the treaty-based promotion of freer international trade or investment might have failed to acknowledge or address popular economic insecurities or persuade populations of the benefits of such regimes. Not to do so is to play right into the hands of those who would portray out-of-touch governance and legal elites advancing 'globalist' agendas on the basis that their value to communities is self-evident and any disagreement or discomfort can only be a sign of deplorable narrow-mindedness and provincialism. Likewise here, it is not enough to decry the populist challenge to human rights without asking how the human rights project and its main proponents might have generated backlash or fed populist unease – generally and in particular polities – rather than human rights and its 'movement' being the victim of unjustified cynical attacks. As Part II explored, it is entirely viable to argue that the human rights idea and system was not in great health in terms of popular credibility and legitimacy before the 2010s. It is also possible to argue that things other than populism (including the movement's own strategies and structural features) may have contributed to or enabled this situation.[8] Is it possible, too, that the populist challenge is not necessarily an entirely negative phenomenon, or it may be too soon to tell, or at least it requires a closer look?

The backlash thesis has not resulted in blindness across the board. Neuman did pose the question of whether the human rights system has 'contributed unintentionally to the rise of populism by provoking backlash … and whether the spread of populism points in other ways to lessons that human rights advocates and institutions should learn.'[9] At the end of Part II, we noted high-level acknowledgment by a senior UN human rights official of the

7 Peter Danchin, Jeremy Farrall, Shruti Rana, and Imogen Saunders, 'The Pandemic Paradox in International Law' (2020) 114 (4) *American Journal of International Law* 598-607.

8 That is, rather than thinking in terms of 'populism causes violations,' thinking in terms of 'do violations [unfulfilled socio-economic rights] cause populism?' See Gerald Neuman, 'Preface' in Neuman (ed.) 2020, xv.

9 Gerald Neuman, 'Preface' in Neuman (ed.) 2020, xi.

potentially counterproductive nature of some rights strategies in the face of populist backlash. His argument is worth laying out more fully:

> 'We need to better understand what we are up against. And by changing our rhetoric to show that we understand, without compromising our values, why people are now turning towards xenophobic populists. This is crucial. Populists are always inimical to human rights because it appears that they have a need to pinpoint scapegoats ... to blame for society's ills. Wringing our hands isn't enough. We all have to show better understanding of why the populists succeeding in attracting people, and we need to come up with and propose credible alternatives to address the insecurities that currently leads people to the populists...
>
> ... The human rights movement, through a variety of means ... has to show how human rights benefit those who consider themselves ordinary people ... to show people that human rights is vital for everyone, and that it's not just a niche topic for beleaguered minorities and out-of-touch liberals.'[10]

Likewise, Rodriguez-Garavito and Gomez have summarised some of the ways – beyond the 'inordinate dominance of law-centred discourses and strategies' and insufficient attention to economic inequality – in which human rights as practised might have come to expose itself to populist strategies. These include over-reliance on international funding, or an over-concentration of agenda-setting power in international non-governmental organisations (NGOs) relative to 'Global South organisations' including such that the latter's priority issues supposedly receive less focus. In addition, a disconnect among professionalised human rights NGOs, online activists, and social movements, and 'difficulties in developing persuasive human rights narratives that meaningfully engage with the majority of the population.'[11]

It may be that scholars in the intellectual global elite need to think twice about a framing that suggests a regrettable 'backlash' phenomenon driven by certain forces, without examining our own roles in a system that may be viewed (rightly or not) variously as patronising, unresponsive, over-promising, or empty-gestured.[12] This is not just to remind us that what is dismissed as 'populist' may also be 'popular' at least in majoritarian terms. It is to remind

10 Andrew Gilmore, 'The Backlash against Human Rights' (UN Assistant Secretary-General for Human Rights), Dublin, November 2017: https://www.ohchr.org/en/statements/2017/12/backlash-against-human-rights. See too Phillip Alston, 'The populist challenge to human rights' (2017) 9(1) *Journal of Human Rights Practice*, 1–15, 6.

11 Rodriguez-Garavito and Gomez, 12-13.

12 Jolyon Ford, 'The Multilateral Human Rights System: Systemic Challenge or Healthy Contestation?' (2020) 35 *Maryland Journal of International Law* 90-103, 103.

us that we must not just decry attacks on human rights, international law, and the idea of a rules-based and values-based global order. We must also seek to understand how those in influential governance and other positions might have lost the public's support, in particular places and on particular issues, in explaining, more digestibly and persuasively, the supposedly 'universal' and 'self-evident' benefits of this order.[13] Most scholars can be said to be complicit at some level in this elitist exercise, since we appear to proceed on an assumption that further international legal integration of the world (generally, economic and trade integration but also human rights integration) is both inevitable and beneficial, and that it enjoys the support of most ordinary people.[14]

Gearty characterises this dismissive attitude towards those who question or critique rights as viewing others as 'a bunch of castaways from true, rights-based civilisation.'[15] No wonder there is a backlash to writing off those with concerns or contrary views. This elite is the 'cosmopolitans' whom Posner derides for dismissing nationalism as 'primitive and morally indefensible' without exploring why it resonates.[16] By being dismissive in this way, one is seriously under-estimating the nationalist–populist–sovereigntist appeal. One is unlikely to begin to understand how perceptions come to form about triumphalist overreach by international legal elites.[17] By dismissing outright the messenger ('populist') and the audience ('mere deplorables'), one may miss the message. If so, the human rights movement might naively not undertake the hard patient work of developing compelling counter-narratives, or explaining in an ongoing and non-patronising way the supposed benefits of the rules-based international order incorporating universal rights protections.

The importance of values and concepts such as the rule of law is not self-evident and needs to be articulated or translated (without condescension) in terms that resonate with people, including as voters.[18] Hence, Alston's prescription, in the face of populism, that the human rights movement needs to 'devote more time and effort to being persuasive and convincing,' rather than simply annunciating principles 'as though they were self-evidently correct and

13 Jolyon Ford, 'The Multilateral Human Rights System: Systemic Challenge or Healthy Contestation?' (2020) 35 *Maryland Journal of International Law* 90-103, 103.
14 Eric Posner, 'Liberal Internationalism and the Populist Backlash' (2020) 49 *Arizona State Law Journal* 795, 796.
15 Conor Gearty, *Can Human Rights Survive?* (Cambridge University Press, 2006), 1.
16 Eric Posner, 'Liberal Internationalism and the Populist Backlash' (2020) 49 *Arizona State Law Journal* 795, 801.
17 Eric Posner, 'Liberal Internationalism and the Populist Backlash' (2020) 49 *Arizona State Law Journal* 795, 801.
18 Ian McDougall, 'Populism and the Rule of Law' Lexis-Nexis 'Insights,' 10 June 2021.

applicable.'[19] Critiques such as that human rights 'over-protect' criminal elements – whether valid or not in jurisprudential terms – might nevertheless be genuinely held views, and we ought not disregard such views without at least some reflection.[20] Voeten likewise notes that just because rhetoric (in his study, of opposition to international courts) is 'populist' does not mean that some or even all of the critiques are invalid: opposition to some international courts or their activities may have some 'substantive roots.'[21] Thus, pro-rights groups should 'listen to the grievances of populists' and not assume the infallibility of their own position (or indeed of human rights).[22] Scholars should avoid putting themselves in a position where they are effectively saying that critiques of rights are illegitimate because they are 'populist.'[23]

An immigration/refugee rights example might be apt. It sometimes appears difficult for those committed to human rights to face squarely the argument that the rise of nationalist–populist sentiment (and political parties) in Europe might in part be a function of immigration policies, pursuant to perceived human rights obligations or value commitments, that may have been perceived by large parts of the population as simply going too far. Angela Merkel's decision to welcome those fleeing the Syria conflict, and the way in which this quite clearly drove popular support for the right-wing anti-immigration party in Germany, is perhaps the most stark example of this. There at the heart of the 'populism and human rights' debate is an inconvenient (possible) truth that is seldom articulated:[24] that the perceived overreach of human rights arguments helped generate fuel for populist–nationalist strategies. This is then no longer about 'what populists have done to human rights,' but how the use of human rights principles has done something to foster a climate in which populism has more traction. This is why unpacking 'backlash' as a concept is interesting, because unlike the idea of an attack on human rights, 'backlash' suggests feedback, or some degree of legitimacy in the actor/s pushing back against overreach with which they were not comfortable. One does not need to take a position on the merits, in international law, of various migration/asylum trends, to argue that one fairly sure way to expose human rights to populist attack in future is to push arguments for

19 Phillip Alston, 'The populist challenge to human rights' (2017) 9(1) *Journal of Human Rights Practice*, 1–15, 11.

20 Gerald Neuman, 'Human Rights responses to the Populist Challenge' in Neuman (ed.) 2020, 261.

21 Erik Voeten, 'Populism and Backlashes against International Courts' (2020) 18(2) *Perspectives on Politics* 407-422.

22 Gerald Neuman, 'Human Rights responses to the Populist Challenge' in Neuman (ed.) 2020, 270.

23 Duncan Johnson, 'In Defence of Democratic Populism' in Neuman (ed.) 2020, 195.

24 An exception is Daniel Morales, 'Revelation out of Rupture: Building Human Rights from the Bottom up' (2020) 35 *Maryland Journal of International Law*, 127-133.

more open immigration on the basis of human rights without making a far more concerted and deliberate effort to convince much of the public why such policies are important to *them*, and why such protections belong to a wider class of due process protections that guard against the abuse of state power against *anyone*. In principle in the United States, where right-wing populists are marked by a deep distrust of over-reaching federal or governmental power, such arguments might actually anticipate a degree of traction. However, the mere assertion of 'human rights,' without more, seems unlikely to do so.

As one committed to the normative ideas of a right to (seek) asylum under international law, Morales is a rare example of a human rights scholar asking hard, uncomfortable questions about 'populism and human rights' rather than merely condemning the 'populism' part. For him, the difficult truth is that sometimes human rights are politically 'dangerous,' or pushing a human rights line or policy might be dangerous *to the wider cause of human rights.*[25] This is an argument that following rights-based policies to their conclusion especially in the area of immigration policy in Europe and the United States might provoke a populist backlash that ironically drives the very sort of politics that is inimical to the human rights project flourishing. Neuman likewise argues that human rights advocates might have contributed to this backlash by making very broad (i.e. unfounded) claims about state and societal 'duties' to receive migrants.[26] It is a confronting and contestable idea that to preserve human rights one might not push human rights, that one might be hesitant to invoke them too strongly just when they appear needed. Yet, it is an idea that will not go away by putting it where some intellectuals would, in the 'too hard' ('politically correct'?) basket. This is where the Kennedy/Gearty/Moyn 'return human rights to the domain of politics, not law' critique has some power, if only because of the need to persuade people of the merits of rights-based approaches, not simply assert their moral superiority (with the implicit or explicit insinuation that those unsure or opposed to these positions lack morality). In the Germany–Syria refugees, for example, while it may also not be obvious as a matter of international law, it may simply not be self-evident to the average German voter that people arriving in their country via a series of safe countries that are more proximate to the conflict have any legal 'right' to enter, stay, and assimilate. If they have such a right, that is not the end of the question in an age of populism: the public needs to be persuaded that this right is part of a fabric of internationally recognised rights that matter for all. If not, the argument must perhaps be put 'merely' in moral terms lest it

25 Daniel Morales, 'Revelation out of Rupture: Building Human Rights from the Bottom up' (2020) 35 *Maryland Journal of International Law*, 127-133, 131.

26 Gerald Neuman, 'Human Rights responses to the Populist Challenge' in Neuman (ed.) 2020, 266.

overreach itself when framed in human rights terms (with the insinuation of a legal basis for those claims) without a more clear and compelling explanation of why this is so.

'Populist backlash' as distraction

For some, the response to the populist challenge in the 2020s is largely determinative of the fate and future of the whole human rights project.[27] For others, populism is a distraction (as the main problem facing the human rights movement) and the 'actual challenge' is nationalism, such that one solution for the human rights movement is to 'shift its focus' to that issue.[28] This unconvincing populism/nationalism distinction does not advance our understanding in any way. Yet, there certainly is a set of arguments to be made that the focus on populism can be unhelpful or misleading, and operate as a distraction. Even if we accept that there has been a popular backlash against human rights, Part II discussed a range of factors – not reducible to 'populism' – that might have contributed to this. Moreover, it explored whether it is other factors or weaknesses in the human rights project that have brought it to where it is today. Is 'populism' the problem, or a distraction from patterns that either are enduring (within human rights as it exists) or not necessarily populist (just plain authoritarianism)? Combined with the problems with 'populism' as a useful label, this distraction risk partly explains the title of one chapter in a 2020 collection of essays: 'Enough about Populism!'[29]

Koskeniemmi has argued that we need to unpack what comprises the populist backlash against human rights before we can ask what response is needed.[30] Ron Dudai also argues that the focus on populism might be misleading.[31] For instance, on its face, it is relatively easy to assert that populism has been successful in Europe in eroding the legitimacy of human rights, and

27 Andrew Fagan, 'The Gentrification of Human Rights' (2019) 41 *Human Rights Quarterly* 283, 285.

28 Luca Bonadiman and Ukri Soirila, 'Human Rights, Populism, and the Political Economy of the World' (2019) 37(4) *Nordic Journal of Human Rights* 301-328, 308.

29 Luigi Lonardo, 'Enough about populism' in Jure Vidmar (ed.), *European Populism and Human Rights* (Brill Nijhoff 2020), Chapter 5 (92-114).

30 Martti Koskenniemi, 'Rocking the Human Rights Boat: Reflections by a Fellow Passenger' in Nehal Bhuta, Florian Hoffmann, Sarah Knuckey, Frédéric Mégret, and Margaret Satterthwaite (eds.), *The Struggle for Human Rights Essays in Honour of Phillip Alston* (Oxford University Press, 2021).

31 Ron Dudai, 'Human Rights in the Populist Era: Mourn then (Re)Organize' (2017) 9 *Journal of Human Rights Practice* 16, 17. See too Luca Bonadiman and Ukri Soirila, 'Human Rights, Populism, and the Political Economy of the World' (2019) 37(4) *Nordic Journal of Human Rights* 301-328, 305, 307-9.

of particular institutions (especially regional courts).[32] Yet, for Orentlicher, for example – writing in a special issue on populism and international law – it may be misleading to focus on populism as the source or driver of the challenges faced in the last decade by institutions such as the International Criminal Court.[33] The 'setbacks' experienced in international criminal justice have, on this view, 'fundamentally different' and prior origins from the 'populist attack' framing. Those setbacks and legitimacy challenges are not really attributable to populism, even if populist leaders are deeply antithetical to institutions such as the International Criminal Court (ICC) and have not hesitated to attack these.[34] Instead, the ICC's weaknesses and setbacks may have other plausible explanations none of which is fundamentally or necessarily populist. Many of these may have pre-dated the populist era and motif (for example, overreach and poor performance by the ICC prosecutor and overreach in the exertion of universal jurisdiction by some European states; the perceived excessive focus on African cases, and so on).

For example, the June 2018 US withdrawal from the UN Human Rights Council could be framed as a highly populist move by the Trump administration (and an existential disengagement crisis for this human rights institutional order). Yet, if we foreground the 'populist' aspect too heavily, we might obscure the scope for seeing how it is also possible to frame that event as a form of principled contestation to a dysfunctional overly ritualistic body that brought human rights into disrepute. That 'populist' move might, in theory, have stimulated action and counter-action that might, in aggregate, strengthen the legitimacy and effectiveness of some institutions of the global human rights order.[35] Meanwhile, Lacey has questioned assumptions that the resurgence of populism in Europe and North America has placed the rule of law under pressure, questioning whether many of the events and trends are best understood as associated with populism, whether any such association is just contingent, and indeed whether populism inevitably threatens the rule of law.[36]

Duterte is held up as the elected populist who scapegoated human rights for political ends while also inciting and endorsing serious violations, particularly extrajudicial killings by police. He undoubtedly did so, while criticising human

32 See for example Jan Petrov, 'The Populist Challenge to the European Court of Human Rights' (2020) 18(2) *International Journal of Constitutional Law*, 476–508.

33 Diane Orentlicher, 'The Emerging Shape of Global Justice: Retrogression or Course Correction?' (2020) 35 *Maryland Journal of International Law* 61-72.

34 Diane Orentlicher, 'The Emerging Shape of Global Justice: Retrogression or Course Correction?' (2020) 35 *Maryland Journal of International Law* 61-72, 64.

35 Jolyon Ford, 'The Multilateral Human Rights System: Systemic Challenge or Healthy Contestation?' (2020) 35 *Maryland Journal of International Law* 90-103, 95, 103.

36 Nicola Lacey, 'Populism and the Rule of Law' (2019) 15 *Annual Review of Law and Social Sciences* 79-96.

rights advocates as obstructing national safety and progress, condemning and promising to disband the national human rights commission, and mocking the-then United Nations Special Rapporteur on Extrajudicial Killings.[37] Yet, the counter-populist narrative does tend to assume that Duterte was undoing what was, until then, a very strong culture of public support for human rights. This approach may not do enough to factor in studies that suggest (in this particular country's context) not only a somewhat entrenched political culture of populism[38] but also a widespread endemic culture of belief in the Philippines about the legitimacy of power and authority and its primacy over individual rights or liberties.[39] More broadly, human rights-based condemnation of someone like Duterte can obscure the socio-economic and political context in which his message came into national prominence. His majority popular support can be understood as resulting from popular perceptions of the failure of successive liberal democratic Filipino regimes to 'address basic social ills,' a form of 'democratic disillusionment' and social dislocation overlaid with an openness to try a greater degree of illiberalism.[40] Such an example reminds us that deploying labels such as 'populism' cannot be a substitute for properly contextualised study that is self-conscious about the state of human rights before the presumed backlash.

Another way in which the focus on populism might distract us is that it might not account for the distinction, in the Introduction, between rights as a vocabulary of politics and resistance (which might remain powerful) and rights systems as institutionalised, which might be severely weakened in some contexts. Also, attacks on the institutional machineries of the human rights system may seek particular reforms and are not necessarily attacks on the validity or applicability or legitimacy of the underlying values and principles.[41] Dragic has argued persuasively that a key factor in preserving (or rebuilding?) the legitimacy of human rights is to avoid conflating 'human rights' with particular institutions that protect or administer them (much as people distinguish attacks on religious institutions and their administration from attacks

37 See generally Richard Heydarian, *The rise of Duterte: A populist revolt against elite democracy* (Springer, Singapore, 2017), and Paul Kenny, *Populism in Southeast Asia* (Cambridge University Press, 2019).

38 Alfred McCoy, 'Philippine populism: local violence and global context in the rise of a Filipino strongman' (2017) 15(3-4) *Surveillance & Society*, 514–522.

39 for example, Sheila Maxwell, 'Perceived threat of crime, authoritarianism, and the rise of a populist president in the Philippines' (2018) 43(3) *International Journal of Comparative and Applied Criminal Justice*, 207-218.

40 Ronald Pernia, 'Human Rights in a Time of Populism: Philippines under Duterte' (2019) 19(3) *Asia-Pacific Social Science Review* 56–71, 59.

41 Jolyon Ford, 'The Multilateral Human Rights System: Systemic Challenge or Healthy Contestation?' (2020) 35 *Maryland Journal of International Law* 90-103.

on the religion that these institutionalise).[42] Waldron argues that the idea of human rights itself (perhaps unlike activists or even 'the movement') is too abstract to be the 'sustained object of political suspicion,' and that popular antipathy to human rights is not necessarily evenly spread.[43]

Amid concerns about states seeing human rights institutions as illegitimate, or now populists portraying them as such, there is not necessarily a lot of empirical evidence about levels of perceived legitimacy.[44] Meanwhile, although in their rhetoric populist leaders or governments present international law as, at most, a 'mere law of coordination,'[45] in their practice they are highly instrumental towards it, cherry-picking and selective in their engagement and endorsement, or disengagement and discrediting, and they do not necessarily expressly reject human rights.[46] A government or group (populist or otherwise) can be concerned about the organisation and activities of transnational institutions without necessarily rejecting 'transnational values.'[47] If the legitimacy of international institutions was indicated only by the absence of resistance and criticism, this could be just as worrying: such non-engagement (rather than disengagement) could indicate low-quality compliance or the fact that the institutions are politically unthreatening and irrelevant. In this sense, contestation (even robust contestation) is not necessarily alarming (let alone populist) backlash. Such contestation is 'hard-wired into human rights both as a political and legal concept.'[48]

The examples given by authors who perceive a significant distinctive challenge to the international human rights system, including from administrations of liberal democratic states, are not necessarily persuasive.[49] States

42 Sanja Dragic, *Post-Backlash Human Rights Law* (Brill, Amsterdam, 2022).

43 Jeremy Waldron, 'Rule-of-Law Rights and Populist Impatience' in Neuman (ed.) 2020, 43.

44 Johan Karlsson Schaffer, Andreas Føllesdal and Geir Ulfstein, 'International Human Rights and the Challenge of Legitimacy' in Andreas Føllesdal, Johan Karlsson Schaffer, and Geir Ulfstein (eds.), *The Legitimacy of International Human Rights Regimes: Legal, Philosophical and Political Perspectives* (Cambridge University Press, 2013), 16: 'Expressions of legitimacy may often be more difficult to gauge and measure than expressions of illegitimacy.'

45 Heike Krieger, 'Populist Governments and International Law' (2019) 30(3) *European Journal of International Law* 971-996.

46 Heike Krieger, 'Populist Governments and International Law' (2019) 30(3) *European Journal of International Law* 971-996; exactly the same point is made by Veronica Bilkova, 'Populism and Human Rights' (2018) *Netherlands Yearbook of International Law* 143-174.

47 Darren O'Byrne, 'The Rise of Populism, the Demise of the Neoliberal and Neoconservative Globalist Projects, and the War on Human Rights' (2019) 9(2) *International Critical Thought* 254-268, 265.

48 Johan Karlsson Schaffer, Andreas Føllesdal, and Geir Ulfstein, 'International Human Rights and the Challenge of Legitimacy' in Andreas Føllesdal, Johan Karlsson Schaffer and Geir Ulfstein (eds.), *The Legitimacy of International Human Rights Regimes: Legal, Philosophical and Political Perspectives* (Cambridge University Press, 2013), 15.

49 For instance, Johan Karlsson Schaffer, Andreas Føllesdal and Geir Ulfstein, 'International Human Rights and the Challenge of Legitimacy' in Andreas Føllesdal, Johan Karlsson

reacting strongly to critical reports or adverse judgements are neither new to nor potentially fatal for the international rights order. When such authors say that liberal states are not just articulating criticisms but 'even resisting' institutional activities, their 'prominent cases of contestation' (on one view) demonstrate nothing remarkable; human rights concepts and practices and litigation outcomes challenge and contest governmental action – of course this generates resistance, whether framed as 'backlash' or not. The point here is that while such instances should generate reflection on the legitimacy of judicial and other institutional human rights activities – particularly to avoid overreach, unduly expansive judicial jurisprudential approaches, or exceeding of mandates – they do not necessarily herald systemic crisis for the human rights idea or project, or even its institutional manifestations.[50] Moreover, to point to state reactions to regional human rights courts (and most examples are European) as signs of a wider legitimacy crisis in human rights perhaps only serves to reinforce the need not just for more diverse studies geographically but also for wider reflection on critical scholars' voices. That is, reflection on arguments about how 'the movement' has perhaps come to rely too heavily on judicial enforcement of legislated rights rather than a more diverse set of strategies that do not rely on litigation as a 'lazy' form of what ought to be overt political forms of contestation.

Populism might not be the problem, or might distract us from the problem. For Hopgood, the greatest challenge to human rights is not actions by state actors whether populist or not, but public apathy, 'people around the world simply not considering them to be as important as their advocates would have us believe.'[51] We may need to distinguish more clearly between populist leaders and parties (manipulating or responding to populations), and 'the people.' In relation to a backlash thesis, in terms of the latter set of actors, it is possible that human rights does not necessarily generate a visceral reaction or lashing out. It may simply be that large parts of populations do not perceive the human rights frame or movement to offer anything, or anymore. If so, to quote singer-songwriter Taylor Swift, the supposed 'backlash' is 'not hate [of

Schaffer and Geir Ulfstein (eds.), *The Legitimacy of International Human Rights Regimes: Legal, Philosophical and Political Perspectives* (Cambridge University Press, 2013).

50 The authors used here to exemplify such scholarship do concede this: Johan Karlsson Schaffer, Andreas Føllesdal, and Geir Ulfstein, 'International Human Rights and the Challenge of Legitimacy' in Andreas Føllesdal, Johan Karlsson Schaffer, and Geir Ulfstein (eds.), *The Legitimacy of International Human Rights Regimes: Legal, Philosophical and Political Perspectives* (Cambridge University Press, 2013), 17 (it would be 'premature' to assume that governments' strong reactions to institutional outcomes necessarily indicate deeper crises of legitimacy about human rights more generally, or even about those institutions).

51 Stephen Hopgood, 'What is the greatest challenge to human rights?' *The Conversation* 23 October 2018; https://theconversation.com/what-is-the-greatest-challenge-to-the-future-of-human-rights-we-the-people-are-105428:

human rights], it is just indifference.'[52] The damage that populist messaging has done to human rights is considerable even if one does not start from the premise that human rights were in great shape before the 2010s. However, if the greater risk (at least in some democracies) is apathy, study of the populist moment affords an opportunity to better understand and respond to this risk. This accords with a 2020 study of populism and human rights that warned that apathy and unwillingness to adapt in the face of populist 'feedback' might be a greater danger to the democracy–constitutionalism–human rights agenda.[53] For Orentlicher, too, the populist challenge (to international law and institutions more generally) is not just something to condemn, since it raises 'perfectly legitimate questions' about the efficiency and legitimacy of international institutions.[54]

Fagan accepts, properly, that it would be 'absurdly reductivist' to attribute the rise of populism to the failures of liberal democracy to meet expectations around inequality and marginalisation.[55] If so, it would be an even longer bow to draw to blame human rights (as merely one plank of the rules-based liberal order) for fuelling populism. Where right-wing populist–nationalism is at play, it seems a curious logic for Left-leaning scholars to blame the human rights movement or discourse while criticising it for 'hiding' in legalism so as to avoid hard, inevitable political contests. This might symbolise nothing more than the reluctance of the political Left to admit shortcomings in terms of articulating a vision of society that is sufficiently compelling and reassuring to the 'ordinary person (voter).' If so, it is not really *about* human rights or the movement needing a hard self-examination or a re-immersion in politics at all. It seems like an easier pastime to criticise human rights than to do the so-called 'hard politics' that such critics say that human rights has avoided.

We have seen how one of the enduring criticisms of the human rights movement (and one of the explanations for the perceived decline in the traction of rights-based arguments) is that the modern human rights project is inseparable from the liberal or neo-liberal project (of market democracies). We saw too how a groundswell perception of having been ignored, sidelined, or patronised by supra-national and transnational systems of elite governance might be one explanation for the apparent popular appeal of populist narratives against human rights. Yet, if this is all so, by extension it is not necessarily the human rights movement that 'did this' but the playing out of a far broader set of

52 Taylor Swift, 'I Forgot that you Existed' from the album *Lover* (Republic Records, 2019).

53 Jolyon Ford, 'The Multilateral Human Rights System: Systemic Challenge or Healthy Contestation?' (2020) 35 *Maryland Journal of International Law* 90-103.

54 Diane Orentlicher, 'The Emerging Shape of Global Justice: Retrogression or Course Correction?' (2020) 35 *Maryland Journal of International Law* 61-72, 69.

55 Andrew Fagan, 'The Gentrification of Human Rights' (2019) 41 *Human Rights Quarterly* 283, 307.

forces, such that this is not necessarily a populist crisis of human rights but a far broader crisis of political inclusion and responsive governance. If this is so, too, the challenge for human rights is not the populist one addressed to rights themselves, but a much broader challenge related to the current zeitgeist: modes of governance (and public engagement about governance) in the face of popular disillusionment, distrust, disenchantment, dislocation in the context of a new sovereigntism, anti-globalism, and anti-institutionalism.

As human rights scholars, we might understandably feel singularly ill-equipped to write on such issues, let alone offer prescriptions relating to them. But scholars and activists can certainly shift from decrying or dismissing 'populists' so as instead to engage with lessons, from many disciplines and governance systems, on explaining the value of supposedly self-evident international governance regimes, repairing and deepening the legitimacy of norms and institutions, and being more responsive to those being globally governed. If the future of human rights is in question, what we would have is not necessarily the erosion or discrediting of the rules-based human rights international order due to 'populist backlash' or autocratic undermining or some other 'external' challenge. Instead, it would (at least in part) represent the failure – not of 'human rights' but of a far wider political and governance ideology – both to resonate and to offer tangible yield, a loss of credibility, a collapse under the weight of unmet promises, the 'light that failed.'[56] If the universalisation after 1945 (and especially in the 1970s and again post-1989) of human rights discourses and frameworks was a metaphor for or indicator of some wider globalisation processes,[57] perhaps counteracting forces might have a corresponding effect on reducing the profile and role of human rights in world affairs.

This aspect of the 'distraction' point is that the challenge of populism may not simply be to human rights themselves or even necessarily for their own sake. As innumerable commentators have observed, if the wider 'liberal world order' was indeed ever dominant, that dominance has been challenged geopolitically from the East while also having its legal and institutional architectures of global and regional integration questioned (including by populists) from within liberal democracies. The human rights project has been, or is seen as, a major plank of that 'liberal order,' Thus, the 'populist challenge to human rights' is only partly an attack on human rights and associated values of pluralism, inclusivity, and due process constraints; in part, the challenge is to the

56 Krastev and Holmes 2019: *The Light That Failed: A Reckoning* (Allen Lane, 2019): that the most powerful force behind the wave of populist xenophobia in Eastern Europe stems from alienation and resentment at the post-Soviet imperative to become Westernized.

57 See, e.g., André Siciliano, 'The Role of the Universalization of Human Rights and Migration in the Formation of a New Global Governance' (2012) 9(16) *SUR International Journal on Human Rights* 109.

wider order, and so to human rights incidentally, because of its prominence in that order.[58] Thus, Fagan observes that 'human rights' often features as a 'vaguely defined, or empty signifier' in populist political attacks on the wider order that invokes rights-based arguments.[59] There is a much bigger project at hand than arguments about the populist challenge against human rights: the need to defend and enhance liberalism and constitutional democracy by making these more responsive, equitable, and inclusive.[60]

It might be, then, that the 'anti-rights' narrative about populism is not accurate or at least is not sufficiently contextualised in the historical moment, such that it needlessly distracts our analysis. That is, the target might not be human rights *per se* (the idea, the movement, the institutions). What may be at play is a far broader trend, perhaps an anti-globalisation trend, of seeking greater control over things that are so exposed to broad forces, and so asserting 'the local' versus perceived external dynamics. If so, the supposed populist backlash in US rights constitutionalism or the Brexit-era UK 'rights tradition' debates are not necessarily about rejecting universal rights as such. They might reflect a deeper search for greater popular sovereignty, a desire not just to ground things in local governance modes (against an international system), but to find the original, to go back, to connect. Some dynamics might not be anti-rights as such, but more a case of 'we want to do things our way.' One thing common to a good proportion of both populist messaging in the last decade and prior critical human rights scholarship is a critique of elites and their exclusive, self-interested and falsely emancipatory modes of governance. This might require us to zoom out and see human rights, here, as under attack not necessarily for its own sake and faults, but as just one high-profile, over-promising aspect of a far wider critique of elite governance. If so, 'populism' itself is serving as a distraction or is merely the too-readily dismissed form in which some constituencies are trying to communicate a message that matters, or at least matters to them.

Finally, the 'populism' motif can distract us from continuities and convince us that there is something distinctive about an historical moment simply by adding an 'era of populism' label to it. For Marks, there is nothing particular new in 'populist' Brexit-era backlash against human rights in the UK criminal justice system: efforts at scapegoating rights and 'the Establishment' are

58 See Andrew Fagan, 'The Gentrification of Human Rights' (2019) 41 *Human Rights Quarterly* 283, 284.

59 Andrew Fagan, 'The Gentrification of Human Rights' (2019) 41 *Human Rights Quarterly* 283, 284-285.

60 Bojan Bugaric, 'Could Populism Be Good for Constitutional Democracy?' (2019) 15(1) *Annual Review of Law and Social Science* 41-58, 44.

all 'drearily familiar.'[61] Contrary to the alarmist narrative of rights scholars around the populist rhetoric of the Trump presidency, coming after an 'imaginary golden age,'[62] some have argued that US human rights state policy and practice has for decades been 'laced with ambivalence' along with 'sovereign realism and populism.'[63] Writing on the populist challenge, Sikkink argues that it is not empirically obvious that human rights, which have always been contested and resisted, are in a worse state than before.[64] The 'populist challenge' frame suggests that activists were popular at some point but are now being denigrated by populists, yet repressive (or merely opportunistic) governments have 'a long history of attacking and vilifying human rights groups.'[65] The backlash/exceptional moment thesis can, again, obscure such continuities.

'Populist backlash' as window (of opportunity)

The human rights movement in the face of the populist challenge may be seen as marked by either scepticism (rights were doomed anyway) or defensiveness (human rights will prevail but is the victim here, and not responsible for any issues that affect populism and its appeal).[66] Yet, a third way of approaching the backlash narrative is to perceive it as an opportunity to restore – albeit with the assumptions that word entails about the status quo previously – the legitimacy, credibility, and appeal of human rights in the eyes of governmental and popular stakeholders. Neuman's 2020 collection saw the value in examining some of the prominent populist objections to human rights (which Part II showed are not necessarily populist critiques, or 'pre-date' 2010s+ populist

61 Susan Marks, 'Four Human Rights Myths' LSE Law, Society and Economy Working Papers 10/2012, London School of Economics.

62 Gerald Neuman, 'Populist Threats to the International Human Rights System' in Neuman (ed.) 2020, 12.

63 Steven Pomper and Daniel Levine-Spound, 'US Human Rights Policy and the Trump Administration' in Neuman (ed.) 2020, Ch. 2, 22. They do concede that the open admiration for autocratic rule is something distinctive.

64 Kathryn Sikkink, 'A Cautionary Note about the Frame of Crisis and Peril in Human Rights Activism' in Cesar Rogriguez-Garavito and Krizna Gomez (eds.), (Editors' introduction) in *Rising to the Populist Challenge: a New Playbook for Human Rights* (De Justitia, Bogota, 2018), 171-184. More generally, see Sikkink's book *Evidence for Hope: Making Human Rights Work in the 21st Century* (Princeton University Press, 2017). Sikkink suggests that we may only think the state of things is worse because 'we care more and know more about human rights than ever before' (2018, 174), although it is hard to reconcile this outright assertion with her demand for greater empiricism.

65 Kathryn Sikkink, 'A Cautionary Note about the Frame of Crisis and Peril in Human Rights Activism' in Cesar Rogriguez-Garavito and Krizna Gomez (eds.), (Editors' introduction) in *Rising to the Populist Challenge: a New Playbook for Human Rights* (De Justitia, Bogota, 2018), 171-184, 173.

66 Cesar Rodriguez-Garavito and Krizna Gomez (eds.), (Editors' introduction) in *Rising to the Populist Challenge: a New Playbook for Human Rights* (De Justitia, Bogota, 2018).

trends), to see what lessons could be learned from them, to 'reduce the appeal of populists' or simply to improve the performance of the human rights.[67]

As Part II showed, for many scholars, the human rights motif is too compromised as a vocabulary to be able to address the populism apparently rising in many democratic polities.[68] As discussed below, such scholars see a need for alternative frames and discourses. Yet, there is undeniably an argument – from which the 'backlash' focus on the populist can, again, distract us – that once we can see and interrogate the backlash more clearly and less dismissively, opportunities arise for reformist strategies that might have the effects that Neuman mentions above. Some of this is quite familiar 'from crisis find opportunity' discourse in rights scholarship.[69] Yet of course, and notwithstanding the critiques in Part II, not all human rights scholars are pessimistic about the future of the project.[70] Sikkink is the flag-bearer for those who argue that see 'evidence for hope' including because human rights have 'persistent power.'[71] De Burca maintains that human rights ideals and language 'retain power and significance.'[72] Human rights can 'rise to the challenge'[73] and is not 'elitist, ineffectual, bureaucratic' but rather 'resilient and adaptive ... dynamic, diverse and evolving.'[74] She sees 'immense mobilising potential' in the rights project and detects 're-energization [sic]' of social movements more generally in the face of current challenges,[75] citing a study of current pressures on civil society that saw 'huge openings for progressive forces' and opportunities for 'real transformation and change.'[76] One does not need to

67 Gerald Neuman, 'Human Rights responses to the Populist Challenge' in Neuman (ed.) 2020, 258.

68 Amitai Etzioni, *Law and Society in a Populist Age* (Bristol University Press, 2018), 3-26.

69 For an 'opportunity' approach, see Luca Bonadiman and Ukri Soirila, 'Human Rights, Populism, and the Political Economy of the World' (2019) 37(4) *Nordic Journal of Human Rights* 301-328, 301.

70 For one characterisation of the debate between pessimists about the rights project's future and those optimistic about it, see Andrew Fagan, 'The Gentrification of Human Rights' (2019) 41 *Human Rights Quarterly* 283, 283-284.

71 Kathryn Sikkink, *Evidence for Hope: Making Human Rights Work in the 21st Century* (Princeton University Press, 2017). See too Risse, Ropp, and Sikkink, *The Persistent Power of Human Rights* (2013).

72 Grainne de Burca, *Reframing Human Rights in a Turbulent Era* (Oxford University Press, 2021), 231.

73 Grainne de Burca, *Reframing Human Rights in a Turbulent Era* (Oxford University Press, 2021), 208.

74 Grainne de Burca, *Reframing Human Rights in a Turbulent Era* (Oxford University Press, 2021), 191, 231.

75 Grainne de Burca, *Reframing Human Rights in a Turbulent Era* (Oxford University Press, 2021), 214.

76 Grainne de Burca, *Reframing Human Rights in a Turbulent Era* (Oxford University Press, 2021), 231, citing Ben Hayes and Poonam Joshi, 'Rethinking Civic Space in an Age of Intersectional Crises' (FICS, May 2020).

accept the 'optimistic' case (or the De Burca tendency to conflate social movements with human rights ones, but see below) to argue that we ought not allow the 'populist challenge/backlash' narrative to obscure opportunities for reflection and greater solidarity among rights advocates.[77] A leading scholar saw this early (2014) in the 'populist challenge' era, seeing:

> '... an unprecedented opportunity to reconsider some of our core assumptions ... for the first time, important tensions and asymmetries – South v. North, elite v. grassroots, national v. global – are being openly discussed with a view to overcoming such divisions and strengthening the collective capacity of the movement[78]

This entails, the argument would go, seeing a 'moment of transition and transformation' in the human rights field, creating opportunities for innovation, such that the populist era is also a 'creative and experimental' time.[79] The rise of populism could have an 'unexpected positive effect': to push the human rights movement to transform its architecture and strategy in ways that 'were imperative even before the new wave of populist governments, and that are now urgent.'[80]

The next section discusses the prescriptions that scholars advance for taking advantage of this opportunity and for countering the backlash. Whether or not one agrees with the scope or need for more ambitious 'creative thinking'[81] or productive 'disruptive reform,'[82] at very least there is an imperative to not allow 'backlash' thinking to obscure opportunities to understand how the human rights movement might have played into populist critiques. Alston was right, in this sense, to call for 'a concerted effort to understand the other side [populism's adherents], to address their formal as well as their real concerns, and to seek to identify constructive ways forward.'[83] Alston called for

77 Grainne de Burca, *Reframing Human Rights in a Turbulent Era* (Oxford University Press, 2021), 229.

78 Cesar Rogriguez-Garavito, 'The Future of Human Rights: from Gatekeeping to Symbiosis' (2014) 11(20) *SUR: International Journal on Human Rights* 499-510, 500.

79 Cesar Rodriguez-Garavito and Krizna Gomez (eds.), (Editors' introduction) in *Rising to the Populist Challenge: a New Playbook for Human Rights* (De Justitia, Bogota, 2018), 34.

80 Cesar Rodriguez-Garavito and Krizna Gomez (eds.), (Editors' introduction) in *Rising to the Populist Challenge: a New Playbook for Human Rights* (De Justitia, Bogota, 2018), 11.

81 Grainne de Burca, *Reframing Human Rights in a Turbulent Era* (Oxford University Press, 2021), 231.

82 Cesar Rodriguez-Garavito, 'Disrupting Human Rights: Existential Challenges and a New Paradigm' in Nehal Bhuta, Florian Hoffmann, Sarah Knuckey, Frédéric Mégret, and Margaret Satterthwaite (eds.), The Struggle for Human Rights Essays in Honour of Phillip Alston (Oxford University Press, 2021).

83 Phillip Alston, 'The populist challenge to human rights' (2017) 9(1) *Journal of Human Rights Practice*, 1–15, 11.

the human rights movement – which has not, historically, responded well to criticism – to respond to the populist challenge by developing both 'a spirit of introspection and openness.'[84] One intended message of this book is that this approach will require a degree of humility rather than merely righteous dismissal of the backlash. This accords with Braithwaite's call for greater scholarly and practitioner humility about the 'great expectations' of international law as a tool for advancing 'the good.'[85]

Writing for a 2020 special journal issue on populism and international law, Morales saw a need to find 'revelation out of rupture': new insights out of the exceptional pressures he observed on the international human rights and refugee law system.[86] Morales does not speak in terms of humility as such, but his argument resonates with that theme. He notes how we as scholarly experts think that we 'know how the world works' and so have found it very difficult (putting our heads into the sand) to accept that there may be things that we need to revise, such that we miss opportunities to enrich our understanding.[87] Populism may not be the real problem (see 'Populism as distraction'), but neither is it a set of outlier data to be ignored.[88] At many points in the 'populism and human rights' literature, one has the sense not that populism is ignored, but that it is condemned without a commensurate openness to exploring what lessons it might hold for increasing the legitimacy and effectiveness and coherence of a pluralist liberal constitutionalism based on universal human rights.

For example, some responses to [populist] arguments by senior office-holders that the UK should leave the Strasbourg system were to dismiss these as 'so ignorant, so illiberal, so misguided.'[89] One might well agree, but the wider point here is that it is difficult to counter populism if one merely dismisses it outright without pausing to consider whether there might be pragmatic but principled ways to address the perceived legitimacy gap that a populist is exploiting (and extending). This must be so unless one's view is that human rights institutions are so perfect (or so fragile) as to insulate them from robust

84 Phillip Alston, 'The populist challenge to human rights' (2017) 9(1) *Journal of Human Rights Practice*, 1–15, 4.
85 John Braithwaite, 'Conclusion' in Brett Bowden, Hilary Charlesworth, and Jeremy Farrall, *The Role of International Law in Rebuilding Societies After Conflict: Great Expectations* (Cambridge University Press, 2009).
86 Daniel Morales, 'Revelation out of Rupture: Building Human Rights from the Bottom up' (2020) 35 *Maryland Journal of International Law,* 127-133.
87 Daniel Morales, 'Revelation out of Rupture: Building Human Rights from the Bottom up' (2020) 35 *Maryland Journal of International Law,* 127-133, 128-9.
88 Daniel Morales, 'Revelation out of Rupture: Building Human Rights from the Bottom up' (2020) 35 *Maryland Journal of International Law,* 127-133, 129.
89 Conservative Party minister, quoted in 'UK must leave ECHR, says Theresa May' *The Guardian* 26 April 2016 (in the context of the Strasbourg court's decisions on the extradition and deportation, respectively, of radical Muslim clerics Abu Hamza and Abu Qatada).

debate about reform. The outright and righteous dismissal approach leaves no opportunity for adaptation, nor for undermining populist politicking about 'out-of-touch elites' by showing some degree of responsiveness to perceived concerns -- or at least engaging with the perceived issues so as to persuade the electorate, rather than dismissing outright those who proffer such views. Arguably, a case in point here is the mockery or dismissal and non-engagement from most US human rights and constitutional law scholars accompanying the July 2019 announcement, by the Trump administration, of a special 'Commission on Unalienable Rights'.[90] That commission can no doubt readily be described as a populist overture, if this helps analysis in any way. Yet the commission's report engages with some key themes of US rights policy and constitutionalism. It can even be read as highly reaffirming of human rights, overall. The tendency to deride the whole process is illustrative of an academy and bureaucracy that lacks humility and that has not – despite Trump's success with voters – learned any lessons about dismissing things as 'populist.' In his review of international rights bodies facing a populist era, Neuman rightly argues that such bodies should not complacently write off [populist] criticism of their work as mere 'bias and distortion' but rather be prepared to justify and explain their decisions in more fulsome ways.[91] One can see how without the humility to do so, such institutions might ironically fulfil the very criticisms that populists would make of them, of being remote elitist-driven patronising governance regimes.

The 'distraction' and 'opportunity' points are thus linked, of course, since dismissal removes the opportunity for reflection and refinement and reform. Dragic has analysed claims of the emergence of new norms of human rights in the face of the backlash phenomenon.[92] We can put aside that many of these have a very dubious jurisprudential basis even as still-emerging norms (notably 'the right of civil society to foreign funding'), although Part II covered arguments about how such tenuous claims can be seen as contributing directly to the discrediting or dilution of rights-talk. What Dragic has observed in her case studies is a pattern in recent years whereby the human rights 'community' tends simply not to engage, really, with the objections and arguments of states opposed to such normative developments. When a pro-rights author like this is writing that activists and advocates ought pause and 'actually hear' what states are saying about human rights, and not frame them necessarily as 'rebelling' against the rights order, it does support the argument that populist (or other) backlash cannot be effectively countered by dismissing contesting

90 See the Interim Report (July 2020): https://www.state.gov/wp-content/uploads/2020/07/Draft-Report-of-the-Commission-on-Unalienable-Rights.pdf.

91 Gerald Neuman, 'Human Rights responses to the Populist Challenge' in Neuman (ed.) 2020, 269.

92 Sanja Dragic, *Post-Backlash Human Rights Law* (Brill, Amsterdam, 2022).

views. Moreover, the tendency towards righteous outright dismissal might only feed the very forces that attack the human rights movement as being sanctimonious.

Reviewing

The stock response to the populist challenge is a 'vigorous re-affirmation of human rights' but also 'a strong popular reaction, using every means available.'[93] Yet, as the end of Part II noted, this 'just double down and do more rights stuff' thesis is precisely what requires questioning. As Waldron has argued (in the context of UK anti-rights populism), simply reiterating the applicability of standards such as criminal due process rights is unlikely to be enough to address those who reject the legitimacy of institutions such as the European Court of Human Rights.[94] Others argue that the response to the populist challenge is not to 'double down' on the existing human rights project, because it either has no impact against populist politics or may even be part of what feeds populism.[95] On this view, an approach of merely 'doubling down' (albeit with some adjustments such as 'better communication,' see below) does not follow from the diagnosis that the populist challenge is fundamentally different to anything that has come before. Moreover, such an approach avoids confronting 'uncomfortable' questions about how human rights may have contributed to the discontent (etc.) in which populists thrive, and may just result in 'doubling down on errors and mistakes.'[96] Yet, such arguments, as we shall see, still assume that powerful transformations could be realised if only made in human rights terms, albeit with more focus on 'neglected' areas (notably socio-economic concerns, or, since such authors see things in rights terms, socio-economic rights). To the extent that scholars have sought to see opportunities rather than just threats in the 'populist challenge' phenomenon, what are some prescriptions offered in terms of doing things differently, and not merely 'doubling down'? How might we evaluate these prescriptions, and do they reveal perpetuation of some of the problematic patterns and approaches and mindsets sketched in Part II?

93 Kenneth Roth, 'The dangerous rise of populism: global attacks on human rights values' (2017) 70th Anniversary Issue *Journal of International Affairs* 79-84, 83-84.

94 Jeremy Waldron, 'Rule-of-Law Rights and Populist Impatience' in Neuman (ed.) 2020, Ch. 3.

95 Luca Bonadiman and Ukri Soirila, 'Human Rights, Populism, and the Political Economy of the World' (2019) 37(4) *Nordic Journal of Human Rights* 301-328, 301.

96 Luca Bonadiman and Ukri Soirila, 'Human Rights, Populism, and the Political Economy of the World' (2019) 37(4) *Nordic Journal of Human Rights* 301-328, 307.

Prescriptions advanced for revitalisating human rights

Alston argued that in the face of the populist challenge, and while not giving up on the 'basic principles,' human rights proponents need to 'rethink many of their assumptions, re-evaluate their strategies, and broaden their outreach.'[97] Here, Part II's analysis adds important context since many of the ideas put forward below might be seen as addressing those critiques, such as the 'overreach and alienation' one. Yet, part of this book's point is that those are long-standing issues and not necessarily new to, much less the result of, populist backlash. Below is an effort to outline some of the prescriptions in the populist challenge literature, in addition to the various calls (above) for introspection and self-reflection:

- We saw in Part II that overreach (for example, overly expansive interpretations by supra-national rights judicial bodies) might gift to populist critics an easy target by explicitly disregarding important statist interests.[98] This explains exhortations to counter populism by more restrained approaches to judicial interpretation. At the international rights institutions level, Neuman argues that mechanisms such as human rights treaty bodies clearly cannot 'solve' the populist challenge by changing their modes of operating, but can change behaviour of their own 'that may have contributed to populism, and avoid making things worse.'[99] In particular, such bodies ought to be more careful and inclusive about efforts to justify and explain their decisions that constrain national ambitions and policies.[100]
- Helfer has advanced four 'survival strategies' for international human rights institutions.[101] These are 'play the long game'; be more deferential and 'circumspect' in interpreting rights in ways that constrain state action (a 'choose your battles' message for regional human rights courts); engage in more deliberate publicity, outreach and public education; and seek 'windows of opportunity' for wider mobilisation (whatever this means for a court).[102]

97 Phillip Alston, 'The populist challenge to human rights' (2017) 9(1) *Journal of Human Rights Practice*, 1–15, 2.

98 Gerald Neuman, 'Human Rights responses to the Populist Challenge' in Neuman (ed.) 2020, 266.

99 Gerald Neuman, 'Human Rights responses to the Populist Challenge' in Neuman (ed.) 2020, 250.

100 Gerald Neuman, 'Human Rights responses to the Populist Challenge' in Neuman (ed.) 2020, 269.

101 Laurence Helfer, 'Populism and International Human Rights Law Institutions: a Survival Guide' in Neuman (ed.) 2020, Ch. 10.

102 Laurence Helfer, 'Populism and International Human Rights Law Institutions: a Survival Guide' in Neuman (ed.) 2020, 228, 233-242.

- In domestic-level political debate, Neuman argues that we should adopt the view, to convince backlash constituencies in the context of the anti-elitist/foreign imposition narrative of populists, that human rights are not externally imposed but are 'consented obligations.'[103] This might conceivably allow, he would argue, for a link between human rights and popular or national sovereignty concerns in populist–nationalist contexts.
- Johnson argues that the principal challenge is how to make human rights also 'for' majorities.[104] We need, he would argue, a clear rights narrative that includes the majority. This is needed if (majoritarian) populism is the principal threat to human rights, and if it is the counter-majoritarian nature of rights that has alienated the majority.
- Unsurprisingly in the light of Part II's analysis as well as the socio-economic drivers of populist politics, scholars mention a shift towards a greater relative focus (by all actors in the human rights space) on socio-economic justice, economic inequality, insecurity and precariousness.[105]
- Neuman's conclusion has been that the movement (his topic is human rights treaty bodies, but one might generalise) should confront populism only in substance, and not in name. That is, they ought not attempt explicitly to address populism itself, but rather focus on the violations that populism causes (the backslide in Part I here) and the causes that might have driven populism (the backlash).[106]
- Johnson focuses his prescriptions on how to show those frustrated by the checks and balances of constitutional systems (that, in a populist critique, frustrate national progress) how these are there to guard against tyranny by a mob or monarch, such a narrative arguably having potential resonance with some US voters, for example.[107] Likewise, for Waldron, the challenge is how to convince populist critics that human rights (he means criminal due process rights) protect them too, from an over-bearing state.[108]
- For Waldron, more focus is needed on theoretical groundings of rights so that defenders of human rights can set out more clearly why people should continue both to respect and to place faith in them, and to identify what

103 Gerald Neuman, 'Human Rights responses to the Populist Challenge' in Neuman (ed.) 2020, 258-259.

104 Duncan Johnson, 'In Defence of Democratic Populism' in Neuman (ed.) 2020, 208.

105 Stephen Hopgood, 'Challenges to the Global Human Rights System' (2014) 11(20) *SUR: International Journal on Human Rights* 67-75, 69; VK Nagaraj, 'Human rights and populism: some more questions in response to Philip Alston' (2017) 9(1) *Journal of Human Rights Practice* 22–24, 23.

106 Gerald Neuman, 'Human Rights responses to the Populist Challenge' in Neuman (ed.) 2020, Ch. 11, esp. 251, 270; also 'Preface' in Neuman (ed.) 2020, xv.

107 Duncan Johnson, 'In Defence of Democratic Populism' in Neuman (ed.) 2020, 209.

108 Jeremy Waldron, 'Rule-of-Law Rights and Populist Impatience' in Neuman (ed.) 2020, 53. He thinks it unlikely that one could engage such an audience: 54.

'concessions' the movement needs to make to its critics.[109] For example, it is not enough simply to renounce the argument that those involved in serious crime have forfeited their due process rights; something more is needed to show persuasively why criminal liability can be reconciled with inalienable protections.[110]

- In directly addressing the populist challenge, Waldron argues that there may be a perception that rights (or rights-based argument) are being 'exploited for anti-social purposes' such that there is a 'sense' that we need to cultivate a stronger connection between rights and responsibilities (and avoid a blunt balancing narrative between perpetrator and victim).[111] Waldron's prescriptions include turning to so-called third-generation rights, which emphasise collective goals, as a model for addressing the perceived populist attack on the 'skewed' balance between rights and responsibilities.[112]
- Echoing Part II's 'overreach' critique, Waldron calls for more restraint on the proliferation of rights and rights-talk, and in the interpretation of rights, to undercut populist attacks by avoiding overreach and dilution. He argues that some populist critiques of human rights have resonance (are 'telling at a political level') because scholars have avoided addressing them (or, arguably, have assumed that these issues are self-evident).[113] The example he offers is the proliferation of rights from some moral minimums such as the prohibition on torture to cover the 'whole panoply or domain of socio-political life.'[114] If the discourse of human rights is 'often overblown,'[115] such constraint/restraint approaches might conceivably reduce exposure to backlash and fatigue or alienation.
- For some, the movement must (by reducing its legalistic and lawyer-heavy tendencies) 'tap into or use emotion' as the 'language of values,' to counter the populist's leverage of emotive rhetoric.[116] Salgado explores counter-populist 'emotion-based strategies': highly simplistic, passionate, and emotional discourse directed to the 'gut feelings' of the people.[117] This

109 Jeremy Waldron, 'Rule-of-Law Rights and Populist Impatience' in Neuman (ed.) 2020, 50.
110 Jeremy Waldron, 'Rule-of-Law Rights and Populist Impatience' in Neuman (ed.) 2020, 52.
111 Jeremy Waldron, 'Rule-of-Law Rights and Populist Impatience' in Neuman (ed.) 2020, 50.
112 Jeremy Waldron, 'Rule-of-Law Rights and Populist Impatience' in Neuman (ed.) 2020, 54.
113 Jeremy Waldron, 'Rule-of-Law Rights and Populist Impatience' in Neuman (ed.) 2020, 51-52.
114 Jeremy Waldron, 'Rule-of-Law Rights and Populist Impatience' in Neuman (ed.) 2020, 50.
115 Hilary Charlesworth, 'Author! Author! A Response to David Kennedy' (2002) 15 *Harvard Human Rights Journal* 127-131, 127.
116 Duncan Johnson, 'In Defence of Democratic Populism' in Neuman (ed.) 2020, 208.
117 Rosa Sanchez Salgado, 'Emotion strategies of EU-based human rights and humanitarian Civil society Organizations (CSOs) in times of populism' (2021) 22(4) *European Politics and Society*, 550-566, 551.

resonates with calls to develop powerful narratives using communicative tools to 're-engage the public on values and emotions in order to contest populist narratives and the politics of fear and anger.'[118] The movement must 'put narratives, emotions, values, and communications front and centre, rather than as afterthoughts in deploying conventional and technical tools of advocacy,'[119] including 'engaging with the majority of the population's values and emotions.'[120] Become more like the populist in strategy and technique and rhetoric, in other words, although such scholars would never say so explicitly.

- Activists are urged to put less emphasis on 'naming and shaming' strategies.[121] Instead, a 'broader effort' is said to be required at 'elevating communications from a tool to a strategy' because 'resonant narratives and stories are key in persuading the public -- not only the progressive camp – about the importance of human rights values.'[122] This seeks to mimic the exclusionary narratives of anti-rights populist rhetoric by seeking to garner 'citizen support' (because only one's opponents seek 'populist' support?) through language and values that resonate beyond the usual audiences of human rights activism. Indeed, Gready sees 'effective political communication' as the main challenge for the human rights movement, which ought to focus on being more persuasive, framing more compelling arguments, and explaining how human rights fit into a narrative of an appealing future society.[123]
- Rodriguez-Garavito, in criticising the dominance of legal knowledge in human rights debates and organisations (see Part II), writes of the need for human rights in future to borrow freely from other disciplines that have traditionally received scant attention in the field, including: cognitive

118 Cesar Rodriguez-Garavito and Krizna Gomez (eds.), (Editors' introduction) in *Rising to the Populist Challenge: a New Playbook for Human Rights* (De Justitia, Bogota, 2018), 36.

119 Cesar Rodriguez-Garavito and Krizna Gomez (eds.), (Editors' introduction) in *Rising to the Populist Challenge: a New Playbook for Human Rights* (De Justitia, Bogota, 2018), 38-39.

120 Cesar Rodriguez-Garavito and Krizna Gomez (eds.), (Editors' introduction) in *Rising to the Populist Challenge: a New Playbook for Human Rights* (De Justitia, Bogota, 2018), 38, 44.

121 Cesar Rodriguez-Garavito and Krizna Gomez (eds.), (Editors' introduction) in *Rising to the Populist Challenge: a New Playbook for Human Rights* (De Justitia, Bogota, 2018), 34.

122 Cesar Rodriguez-Garavito and Krizna Gomez (eds.), (Editors' introduction) in *Rising to the Populist Challenge: a New Playbook for Human Rights* (De Justitia, Bogota, 2018), 38, 44.

123 Paul Gready, 'Reflections on a Human Rights Decade, Near and Far' (2019) 11 *Journal of Human Rights Practice* 422. For Phil Bloomer, there is a need to be 'creatively tactical' in working with media and social media': 'Are human rights an effective tool for social change?' (2014) 11(20) *SUR: International Journal on Human Rights* 115-121.

biology, social psychology, artificial intelligence, and the neuro-science and the organisational psychology of cooperation.[124]

- For Nagaraj, to counter populism, the human rights movement needs to 'rescue' itself from an 'increasingly institutionalised and politically abstracted advocacy,' often framed within the confines of a 'single issue' window that makes human rights campaigns 'more spectacle and less substance.'[125] The need to leave 'abstraction' and law behind and engage in politics, especially mass movement politics, is a theme both of critical scholars canvassed in Part II, and now of the prescriptions of counter-populist scholars. Johnson argues (writing mostly for a US counter-populism context) that rights proponents need to 'listen harder,' avoid focusing on 'legal tactics,' and organise/mobilise a human rights culture within much broader constituencies who clearly seek economic and political systems that better meet their needs with dignity.[126] For Johnson the focus must be away from legal tactics and the 'excessive centrality' of law and lawyers in favour of advancing human rights through more broad 'social movements'.[127] Johnson argues that the human rights movement can only counter populism if it 'embraces antagonism and conflict,' rather than seeking consensus and avoiding offence.[128] This directly echoes the call from critical scholars in the last two decades (from Kennedy to Moyn)[129] for the human rights movement to descend from the safety and seclusion of law and abstraction into the messy programmatic contest of politics. From De Burca to Snyder, the prescription is to shift strategies from those steered by external legalistic elites to 'mass mobilisation'[130] and 'mass movements.'[131] Snyder exemplifies this strand of 'change strategy' scholarship in imploring a rediscovery of advocacy via mass movement politics that include locally based cultural and religious groupings. On this view, the human rights project is too focussed on large international organisations that do not

124 https://www.openglobalrights.org/the-future-of-human-rights/

125 VK Nagaraj, 'Human rights and populism: some more questions in response to Philip Alston' (2017) 9(1) *Journal of Human Rights Practice* 22–24, 23.

126 Duncan Johnson, 'In Defence of Democratic Populism' in Neuman (ed.) 2020, 208.

127 Duncan Johnson, 'In Defence of Democratic Populism' in Neuman (ed.) 2020, 211-213.

128 Duncan Johnson, 'In Defence of Democratic Populism' in Neuman (ed.) 2020, 208.

129 See Part II, "The legalisation' critique.'

130 Grainne de Burca, *Reframing Human Rights in a Turbulent Era* (Oxford University Press, 2021).

131 Jack Snyder, 'Empowering Human Rights through Mass Movements' in Stephen Hopgood, Jack Snyder, and Leslie Vinjamuri (eds.) *Human Rights Futures* (Cambridge University Press, 2018), Ch. 4.

or cannot represent 'local' views, impose top-down approaches, and perpetuate a certain distance between the global human rights elite and local activists.[132]

- Along with this 'do politics' call, a principal prescription for countering populism is to decentralise and localise, while enhancing networks and alliances both at various levels (local, national, transnational, international) and between various groupings ('conventional' rights groups and other social and justice movements, from unions to environmental defenders). The human rights community, it is said, needs to start expanding its horizons to work with non-traditional partners including business[133] and to work more with other social movements and with faiths and traditions.[134] Thus the movement needs involve a broader range of interlocutors[135] and to spend 'less time on gatekeeping' (guarding conventional strategies and boundaries) and more on 'symbiosis' ('finding more horizontal and effective modes of collaboration across borders').[136] This 'connective and collective' action[137] might involve connecting with new constituencies, combining online and offline mobilisation, and developing 'horizontal forms of collaboration' between global North and global South organisations and South-South groups.[138] De Burca also states that human rights require a wider base of social support, not just 'vertical networks between local activist elites and global expert ones.'[139] This echoes Alston's call for more effective synergies between international and local human rights movements, not relying on either level in isolation, and conscious that with

132 Jack Snyder, 'Empowering Human Rights through Mass Movements' in Stephen Hopgood, Jack Snyder, and Leslie Vinjamuri (eds.) *Human Rights Futures* (Cambridge University Press, 2018), Ch. 4, 94-97.

133 Phillip Alston, 'The populist challenge to human rights' (2017) 9(1) *Journal of Human Rights Practice*, 1–15, 9-10.

134 Stephen Hopgood, 'Challenges to the Global Human Rights System' (2014) 11(20) *SUR: International Journal on Human Rights* 67-75, 69, 72.

135 Phillip Alston, 'The populist challenge to human rights' (2017) 9(1) *Journal of Human Rights Practice*, 1–15, 4. See too Phil Bloomer, 'Are human rights an effective tool for social change?' (2014) 11(20) *SUR: International Journal on Human Rights* 115-121.

136 Cesar Rogriguez-Garavito, 'The Future of Human Rights: from Gatekeeping to Symbiosis' (2014) 11(20) *SUR: International Journal on Human Rights* 499-510, 501.

137 Cesar Rodriguez-Garavito and Krizna Gomez (eds.), (Editors' introduction) in *Rising to the Populist Challenge: a New Playbook for Human Rights* (De Justitia, Bogota, 2018).

138 Rodríguez-Garavito, C., & Gomez, K. (2018). Responding to the populist challenge: A new playbook for the human rights field. In C., Rodríguez-Garavito & K. Gomez (Eds.) *Rising to the populist challenge: A new playbook for human rights actors*, 14, 34, 44.

139 Grainne de Burca, *Reframing Human Rights in a Turbulent Era* (Oxford University Press, 2021), 198-199.

populist–nationalist around 'exclusively international advocacy' will be ineffective and perhaps counterproductive.[140]

- Some counter-populism scholars see positive trends such as a 'proliferation of place-based movements... increasingly visible and trans-locally networked … [with] broader possibilities for locally based human rights initiatives.'[141] Responses to populism must be 'at the local level … place-based efforts to realize human rights in localized settings.'[142] There are calls for more localised fundraising to reduce exposure to allegations of foreign agency.[143] Neuman joins this call for greater 'localisation' in terms of how rights arguments are framed in future (and presumably framed by 'locals') in ways that resonate with 'locally held values.'[144] That is, 'local activism' can supplement universal principles with 'culturally specific advocacy' that has greater local resonance.[145] Success is said to depend not on global rights organisations but on 'authentic and locally relevant rights movements' throughout the world.[146]
- Finally, one set of prescriptions proffered is to avoid the human rights language, frame, or mode altogether, either because of enduring problems or because of its limited traction (or counterproductive provocation effect) within 'populist circles.' We return to this below.

Some prescriptions expressly addressed to the populist challenge do not aim to confront the populist narrative as such but to focus (in a 'double down' sense) on fairly conventional structural reforms and investments, for example in the criminal justice system, that might revive public support.[147] Heydarian's study of populism in South-East Asia concludes that ordinary people have not been turned against human rights in the sense that the 'populist challenge' thesis suggests: they are not anti-rights but merely frustrated with a

140 Phillip Alston, 'The populist challenge to human rights' (2017) 9(1) *Journal of Human Rights Practice*, 1–15, 8.

141 Jackie Smith, 'Local Responses to Right-Wing Populism: Building Human Rights Cities' (2017) 11(2) *Studies in Social Justice* 347-362.

142 Jackie Smith, 'Local Responses to Right-Wing Populism: Building Human Rights Cities' (2017) 11(2) *Studies in Social Justice* 347-362.

143 Cesar Rodriguez-Garavito and Krizna Gomez (eds.), (Editors' introduction) in *Rising to the Populist Challenge: a New Playbook for Human Rights* (De Justitia, Bogota, 2018), 44.

144 Gerald Neuman, 'Human Rights responses to the Populist Challenge' in Neuman (ed.) 2020, 256.

145 Gerald Neuman, 'Human Rights responses to the Populist Challenge' in Neuman (ed.) 2020, 270.

146 Beth Simmons, 'The Future of the Human Rights Movement' (2014) 28(2) *Ethics and International Affairs* 183-196.

147 Richard Javad Heydarian, 'Penal Populism in Emerging Markets: Human Rights and Democracy in the Age of Strongmen' in Neuman (ed.) 2020, Ch. 7.

dysfunctional criminal justice system.[148] The context for such comments is the appeal of a narrative of societal order and collective security in the context of a democracy where the popular concern is not 'freedom' but effective governance and equitable access to services and where there is a culture of deference to authority or perceiving the state and society as indivisible.[149]

Such analysis is an important reminder not to be distracted by the 'backlash' thesis or to assume necessarily that all populist rhetoric is intended to undermine human rights itself, or in fact has that effect even if so intended. It is also a reminder to proceed, when it comes to prescriptions, from a contextualised basis that (as here, for example) does not assume that the backlash has extensive public traction or requires new distinctive shifts. 'Populism' is a catchy term – this book relies on that fact, too – but there may be nothing new under the human rights sun. For scholars such as Brysk, human rights are dynamic and resilient and require (and show) adaptive political strategies but require nothing more dramatic than a pragmatic reform agenda ('new pathways') of 'reconstructing rights in a post-liberal world..[150] Indeed what all of the above amounts to, really, is perhaps a rather now-familiar call for more 'pragmatism,'[151] being 'more instrumentalist,'[152] for stepping back from supposed 'absolutism' so as to engage in 'a creative exploration of the art of the possible.'[153] One set of writers on the populist challenge to human rights already perceive some 'meaningful reinvigoration of the movement' through measures taken to counter (survive?) populist and other challenges, steps that they argue already do address 'the weaknesses and blind spots of the current human rights architecture that populist governments exploit.'[154]

Evaluating prescriptions for revitalisating human rights

How are the various counter-populism prescriptions above to be assessed? At least four sets of observations may be made. First, we must accept that new

148 Richard Javad Heydarian, 'Penal Populism in Emerging Markets: Human Rights and Democracy in the Age of Strongmen' in Neuman (ed.) 2020, Ch. 7, 156.

149 Richard Javad Heydarian, 'Penal Populism in Emerging Markets: Human Rights and Democracy in the Age of Strongmen' in Neuman (ed.) 2020, Ch. 7, 143, 151.

150 Alison Brysk, *The Future of Human Rights* (Polity, 2018).

151 David Kennedy, *The Dark Sides of Virtue* (Princeton University Press, 2004), 4. See too David Kennedy, 'The International Human Rights Regime: Still Part of the Problem?' in Rob Dickenson et al (eds.) *Examining Critical Perspectives on Human Rights* (Cambridge University Press 2012), 27.

152 Phillip Alston, 'The populist challenge to human rights' (2017) 9(1) *Journal of Human Rights Practice*, 1–15, 11.

153 Phillip Alston, 'The populist challenge to human rights' (2017) 9(1) *Journal of Human Rights Practice*, 1–15, 11-12.

154 Cesar Rodriguez-Garavito and Krizna Gomez (eds.), (Editors' introduction) in *Rising to the Populist Challenge: a New Playbook for Human Rights* (De Justitia, Bogota, 2018), 44.

approaches might have little or no impact. Neuman concedes that one cannot make claims of causation with respect to the role that the populist backlash might have played in the success of populism.[155] Moreover, O'Connell's study of populism and human rights in Erdogan's Turkey suggests that populism's contributions – either to the human rights advances or regressions that he chronicles – are 'uncertain' and partial.[156] The reverse is also true: changed approaches in response to the populist challenge (in Neuman's example, less expansive or more deferential interpretations by human rights bodies) will not necessarily affect the trajectory of populism.[157] Such evaluations would need a proper empirical basis, and a credible rationale for what baseline is used to assess whether changed strategy reduced the supposed impacts of any populist challenge. There is not a great deal of precision offered or attempted in terms of the rationale and change logic of how particular prescriptions will have any impact whatsoever on the dynamics of populism. More broadly, scholarship that advances responses to populist impacts will need to be more specific and contextualised in terms of the impact of populism on the effectiveness and legitimacy of attempts to advance or defend the rights or activities of particular sub-national or transnational groups and/or international organisations.[158]

Second, the various prescriptions offered in the counter-populism literature are in many respects unobjectionable and comprehensive. On one level, what we can take away from the counter-populism prescriptions is essentially nothing more profound than familiar real-world campaign strategies (when to push a human rights frame, when to 'lead with law,' when to mass mobilise, what mix of the above?), albeit perhaps informed by greater consciousness of the criticisms, shortcomings, and backlash-generating potential of human rights. It is difficult to escape a sense that all analysis leads to reducing the forward-looking question from 'what is the future of human rights' to simply one of strategies, in particular communications and public engagement strategies. Addressed to a global movement, they are perhaps necessarily broad and fair, and it would be quite difficult to come up with an alternative 'to-do' list. Some (notably 'seeking to persuade rather than just assert') resonate strongly with the critique of 'backlash as [dismissive] blindness' earlier in this part. However, these prescriptions are often at a level of generality or even obviousness that might conceivably be quite irritating for an activist–practitioner at the now constantly valorised 'local' level. De Burca's prescriptions for human

155 Gerald Neuman, 'Human Rights responses to the Populist Challenge' in Neuman (ed.) 2020, 258.

156 Jamie O'Connell, 'Representation, Paternalism and Populism' in Neuman (ed.) 2020, 126.

157 Gerald Neuman, 'Human Rights responses to the Populist Challenge' in Neuman (ed.) 2020, 269.

158 See in this regard Nienke Grossman, 'Populism, International Courts, and Women's Human Rights' (2020) 35 *Maryland Journal of International Law* 104-126, 104-5.

rights responses in the face of the populist (for her, the 'illiberal') challenge are illustrative, even if we might agree with them. Activists and others need to 'remain vigilant'; to 'keep mobilising in an iterative way'; to 'be nimble' and play a 'long game,' playing the fragmented system through ad hoc and multiple coalitions; to 'democratise' and to go beyond litigation and legalisation strategies.[159] The movement is advised to embrace 'innovative thinking and creative strategizing'[160] and so on. In this way the 'new way forward' counter-populism literature is, ironically, similar to the internal critique scholarship in its generality, in being 'curiously paralyzing' and not really indicating how identified populism-based or other problems (or prescriptions for renewal, etc.) may be taken on board by those interested in achieving just outcomes in particular cases.[161] These prescriptions are much easier to list than to action. Moreover, they can come across as rather disconnected, by calling for a situation that arguably may already exist or by contrasting a monolithic status quo that does not. Calls for 'a much more diverse, decentralised and network-like human rights field,' an 'ecosystem, rather than… unified movement or institutional architecture' suggest that this is not already what the field comprises in fact.[162]

Given the centrality of anti-elitism to the whole notion of populism, it is right to focus here on a third avenue of assessment, directly related to this 'generality' point: scholars offering prescriptions for countering populism appear unaware of how deeply patronising and condescending they can sometimes sound, especially when counselling 'localisation' and 'mass mobilisation' at least in more oppressive settings. This really is quite ironic in a debate that recognises perceived elitism as a problem for the human rights movement. It is refreshing and motivating of Sikkink to call for an end to the 'epidemic of pessimism' among the human rights community in the populist era today, but exhorting everyone to embrace 'a culture of activism'[163] might be met with shrugs by the much-discussed 'local' actors for whom activism is

159 Grainne de Burca, *Reframing Human Rights in a Turbulent Era* (Oxford University Press, 2021), 209-213, 222-223. De Burca also suggests activists and others 'use' the SDGs (presumably where rights-talk is unpalatable) because 'all states approve these.' This is a somewhat problematic idea, but critique of it lies beyond this book's scope. For now, it relates to discussion, below, of seeking alternative non-rights frames.

160 Phillip Alston, 'The populist challenge to human rights' (2017) 9(1) *Journal of Human Rights Practice*, 1–15, 2.

161 Charlesworth 2002, 130-131. De Burca's own work (2021) is based on deep case studies.

162 Cesar Rogriguez-Garavito, 'The Future of Human Rights: from Gatekeeping to Symbiosis' (2014) 11(20) *SUR: International Journal on Human Rights* 499-510, 500, 505.

163 Kathryn Sikkink, 'A Cautionary Note about the Frame of Crisis and Peril in Human Rights Activism' in Cesar Rogriguez-Garavito and Krizna Gomez (eds.), (Editors' introduction) in *Rising to the Populist Challenge: a New Playbook for Human Rights* (De Justitia, Bogota, 2018), 171-184, 171.

their reality or necessity, not just a potential new mindset. Consider these two prescriptions to counter populism. First:

> 'Human rights – as slogans, values, methods, laws, and institutional machinery – are most effectively deployed not in the abstract but in conjunction with and in support of specific campaigns, and their role and function should be to assist such concrete struggles.'[164]

And second:

> 'Human rights activists should rely less on… so-called 'naming and shaming' and more on what might be called 'effectiveness politics' – identifying techniques and campaigns that have been effective to discern how best to improve human rights.'[165]

If detached paternalistic 'elitism' is a critique shared by both populist and critical scholars, it is arguably and ironically too prevalent in counter-populist scholarship itself. 'Local' activists around the world are no doubt very well aware and do not need to be told, that they are or should be involved in 'concrete struggles' and no doubt do not spend appreciable time attempting abstract deployments of rights. Nor do they need to be told that assessing the effectiveness of campaign choices is important, and that what might work is to sometimes look at ... what has worked or not. One could draw up a long list of this pattern: activists should be innovative and creative and network widely but also just explore the 'art of the possible,'[166] should be 'nimble,' 'vigilant,' and mobilise 'in an iterative way,'[167] and may need to accept (would you believe) that sometimes 'compromise will be the only option.'[168] Compromise!? What can scholars tell activists about real-world contestation and compromise? Some of this systemic condescension is clearly inadvertent,

164 Ron Dudai, 'Human rights in the populist era: Mourn then (re) organize' (2017) 9(1) *Journal of Human Rights Practice* 16–21, 18.

165 Cesar Rodriguez-Garavito and Krizna Gomez (eds.), (Editors' introduction) in *Rising to the Populist Challenge: a New Playbook for Human Rights* (De Justitia, Bogota, 2018), 34.

166 Phillip Alston, 'The populist challenge to human rights' (2017) 9(1) *Journal of Human Rights Practice*, 1–15, 11-12.

167 Grainne de Burca, *Reframing Human Rights in a Turbulent Era* (Oxford University Press, 2021), 209-213, 222-223. De Burca also suggests activists and others 'use' the SDGs (presumably where rights-talk is unpalatable) because 'all states approve these.' This is a somewhat problematic idea, but critique of it lies beyond this book's scope. For now, it relates to discussion, below, of seeking alternative non-rights frames.

168 Stephen Hopgood, 'Challenges to the Global Human Rights System' (2014) 11(20) *SUR: International Journal on Human Rights* 67-75, 72.

such as contrasting 'local activists' with 'global *experts*'[169] because of course only foreigners are experts in human rights. Who needs populist politicians to manipulate feelings of alienation and disconnection when scholars do such a good job of it?

When scholars say that responses to populism must be 'place-based efforts to realise human rights in localised settings'[170] what can they possibly mean that such local activists would not just understand as entirely obvious or axiomatic? No doubt the 'localisation' call is meant to consider how to outflank (populist) narratives of foreign interference and imposition and has merit in this sense.[171] Yet, as with the critical scholars before them, such scholars often offer very few examples or empiricism to support their prescriptions. Whereas critical scholars argue that the international human rights movement and lexicon displaces and undermines valuable local institutions, voices, and strategies, Charlesworth has observed that such scholars have not really offered examples of events where this has occurred.[172] Likewise, they tend to make into prescriptions things that are already a reality for activists (being judicious about strategies, when to 'go vertical' to involve other actors, and when not), and are inescapably condescending about their assertions that these activities are what activists need to do if rights are to work. As Charlesworth has already observed over two decades ago, the human rights movement already largely operates in this pragmatic mode and activists in particular contexts must always grapple with the negative consequences of making certain claims or using certain modes and make at least rough estimates of the net costs and benefits of doing so all the time.[173] Scholarship becomes offensive when it is premised on any other basis, at least where examples are not put forward.

The prevalence and depth of the patronising tone in human rights scholarship is an important issue if we are to use this 'window of opportunity' to reinvigorate (etc.) the movement. As noted above, Johnson's prescription for countering populism necessitates human rights actors embracing 'antagonism and conflict' rather than seeking (presumably weak and undesirable?) consensus and 'avoiding offence.'[174] Human rights and social justice activism and

169 Grainne de Burca, *Reframing Human Rights in a Turbulent Era* (Oxford University Press, 2021), 198-199.

170 Jackie Smith, 'Local Responses to Right-Wing Populism: Building Human Rights Cities' (2017) 11(2) *Studies in Social Justice* 347-362.

171 Alston notes that the 'localisation' trope is somewhat unrealistic (to abandon the international human rights regime and move all efforts back to the national or local level): 'The populist challenge to human rights' (2017) 9(1) *Journal of Human Rights Practice*, 1–15, 6.

172 Hilary Charlesworth, 'Author! Author! A Response to David Kennedy' (2002) 15 *Harvard Human Rights Journal* 127-131, 127.

173 Charlesworth 2002, 130.

174 Duncan Johnson, 'In Defence of Democratic Populism' in Neuman (ed.) 2020, 208.

advocacy are heavily contested and competitive even within the movement, let alone versus a potentially repressive constellation of state and private actors. 'Local' activists are unlikely to be strangers to 'antagonism and conflict.' When Snyder calls for shifting from elite-driven strategies to driving 'mass movements,'[175] it would not be unfair for activists, at least in less free societies, to find such an exhortation both naïve and patronising. If mass action was possible and effective, it would no doubt have been attempted. Hopgood sees apathy as the greatest challenge to human rights, which requires 'people, the citizenry, the populace, to say that these rights are important and to demand that their governments observe them.'[176] The dilemma for the human rights scholar is that the 'apathy' point is intuitively appealing, especially if 'human rights' become about everything (and so nothing) and/or disconnected from popular concerns. Yet, it is also incredibly patronising for academics to suggest to people – faced for example with an oppressive, tech-enabled surveillance state, or just with precarious living in notionally affluent societies – that if they just stood up for their rights, the human rights movement would flourish. This is so much easier said from an ivory tower than 'done' at the so-called 'grassroots' where so many scholars implore the human rights movement to reconnect. What do such scholars think that 'local actors' do all day faced with oppression and injustice?

Dudai argues that there is a need to reconnect human rights (as 'practised' in Geneva at multilateral forums) with grassroots social movements so as to ground human rights in particular contextual campaigns.[177] Yet, this diagnosis or criticism is an easy and now familiar one. Again, what do such scholars think that activists do? Of course they contemplate what might be the most effective and legitimate mix of local and transnational, legalistic and non-legal forums and methods, etc. Most activists are already 'acutely aware' of the internal and external challenges that the movement faces globally or in their own contexts: questions about 'how, where, and when to compromise when pragmatism seems necessary' are very familiar to them.[178] It is not obvious what value the anti-populist prescriptions to 'localise' or 'network' or

175 Jack Snyder, 'Empowering Human Rights through Mass Movements' in Stephen Hopgood, Jack Snyder, and Leslie Vinjamuri (eds.) *Human Rights Futures* (Cambridge University Press, 2018), Ch. 4.

176 Stephen Hopgood, 'What is the greatest challenge to human rights?' *The Conversation* 23 October 2018; https://theconversation.com/what-is-the-greatest-challenge-to-the-future-of-human-rights-we-the-people-are-105428:

177 Ron Dudai, 'Human Rights in the Populist Era: Mourn then (Re)Organize' (2017) 9 *Journal of Human Rights Practice* 16.

178 Beth Simmons, 'The Future of the Human Rights Movement' (2014) 28(2) *Ethics and International Affairs* 183-196. See for example Emma Larking, 'Mobilising for Food Sovereignty: The Pitfalls of International Human Rights Strategies and an Exploration of Alternatives' (2017) 21 *International Journal of Human Rights*.

form 'ad hoc coalitions' add for such actors. Others argue that human rights 'must be able to win back the streets, politics, and media' and be able to work with different actors from environmentalists to labour unions which are more equipped to deal with some of the issues that have contributed to the current situation.'[179] Only highly non-empirical, high-altitude scholarship could proceed on the assumption that human rights defenders and other social justice activists do not collaborate (even if they also sometimes compete). Only condescending scholarship would lack any self-consciousness of the implications of exhorting such actors to 'win back the streets.'

Moyn's argument was that rights advocates need to leave these legalistic abstract avenues behind and descend into the messy realities programmatic contest for power.[180] Part II explored how there is some merit to arguments that overly legalistic and litigious strategies might hinder the human rights project or its popular resonance and relevance. Yet, Moyn's is a weak argument, influential as it has been. First, it is based on the somewhat ironic assumption that things framed as 'legal' cannot also be highly political (additionally, that there is a binary choice of strategies, either legal or political). Second, this call to 'get your hands dirty in politics' is an extraordinarily patronising arm-chair-critic thing for a comfortably employed academic to say: most human rights defenders at the 'local' level (the level that Moyn and others urge us all to operate at) are very much engaged in contests for power. They are very aware of politics, of power, of the limits of legal strategies. They are not divorced from the political. Does rights discourse, if they adopt it, force them to abstract themselves from Moyn's so-called 'reality' of power politics? It is difficult to imagine a Moynist making this 'descend into politics, will you!' argument with a straight face, in person, to an activist trying to operate at the 'local' level in particular inside a highly oppressive or reactionary state. Perhaps these arguments should be seen as restricted in intent only to stable free societies. For Moyn, for example, the human rights movement's success depends not on articulating 'metaphysical principles' but on its own 'mobilisational strength and grassroots penetration' at the local level, as 'contingent tools of pragmatic social organisation.'[181] This sort of argument is not only presented without any real effort at examples of what 'descending into programmatic contest' would look like, or examples of actual patterns of such practices of supposed philosophising at the expense of street-level social mobilisation. It is also both unreal (most human rights activists, global or

179 Luca Bonadiman and Ukri Soirila, 'Human Rights, Populism, and the Political Economy of the World' (2019) 37(4) *Nordic Journal of Human Rights* 301-328, 327.

180 Samuel Moyn, 'The Future of Human Rights' (2014) 11(20) *SUR: International Journal on Human Rights* 57-66, 57.

181 Samuel Moyn, 'The Future of Human Rights' (2014) 11(20) *SUR: International Journal on Human Rights* 57-66, 62.

local, do not while away their time articulating metaphysics) and condescending to the point of offensive to those who, at the 'local' level, are just trying to make a difference.

Moyn argues that the human rights movement will need to put to the periphery its 'obsession' with civil and political rights issues especially in authoritarian states and rather engage in a larger campaign of 'economic welfare and inequality.'[182] In some ways, this prescription seems apt for re-engaging popular interest in human rights in more liberal but unequal populist-affected states, where economic insecurity issues are more relevant to the average person and civil and political rights may not be under immediate threat. Yet, not only is it curious to deride an entirely appropriate focus on the most immediate state-based human rights threats as an 'obsession,' Moyn would be the first kind of scholar to critique the human rights movement as insufficiently engaged in political contestation if it focussed away from such threats. Even De Burca, who dismisses Moyn and other critical scholars, argues that human rights is not an alternative to politics and 'social mobilization', and the movement needs to engage in those ways.[183] What does she assume activists think about and do? It is true that legalisation holds limited potential (and may foster populist backlash). It is important to take a step back and ask or evaluate what has been gained through the current model (of advocacy) and what has been lost, perhaps 'irretrievably.'[184] Yet it is much easier to call for politically-engaged, mass mobilization strategies than to be the person or group who must do them in particular settings.

Recalculating

This brings us to a series of questions that arguably fall from the doubts expressed about the utility, relevance, and traction of framing one's cause or claims expressly in human rights terms, including because of the potential for triggering populist backlash. Is a 'human rights' frame still powerful, or can that question only ever be answered in particular contexts? What arguments are made, in the counter-populist literature in particular, that alternative languages and frames offer more promise, or does that question assume we always face a binary zero-sum choice between rights-based or other strategies? And what, if anything, can we make (in the shadow of the populist backlash thesis) of situations where freedom, justice, or equality (and other)

182 Samuel Moyn, 'The Future of Human Rights' (2014) 11(20) *SUR: International Journal on Human Rights* 57-66, 62.

183 Grainne de Burca, *Reframing Human Rights in a Turbulent Era* (Oxford University Press, 2021), 209-213, 222-223.

184 Ratna Kapur, 'On *Gender, Alterity and Human Rights: Freedom in a Fishbowl*' (2019) 122 *Feminist Review* 167-171, 170.

issues are not pursued expressly or exclusively in human rights terms? Does it matter whether social justice and protest movements rely on human rights vocabularies, or is the question a moot one because it is inevitable (and, to avoid backlash may be desirable) that individuals and groups will just invoke rights frames and modes when it is convenient and possible in their particular circumstances? Engaging with these lines of questioning takes us to the book's conclusion.

Are human rights still powerful?

Rhetoric, semantics, and framing do matter in the contest of ideas in a populism context.[185] Alston famously argued that framing or naming a claim as a 'human rights' one 'elevates it above the rank and file of competing societal goals' giving it some 'aura of timelessness, absoluteness, and universal validity'[186] – or at least this once was supposedly the case. Part II explored the contrary 'end times' thesis, and whether human rights are still an effective language for producing social change,[187] while the populist challenge approach suggests that rights-talk has been disempowered and delegitimised. In any event, there has never been any guarantee that human rights would forever remain the dominant frame for the pursuit of social justice.[188] There is nothing 'inevitable, unidirectional, or unanimous' about the success of human rights.[189] If there is a populist backlash against human rights as a discourse – and/or if rights are otherwise compromised – is the answer an alternative vocabulary for the pursuit of justice or freedom? Kapur writing on the 'possibility of freedom in the aftermath of the critique of human rights' has recently asked whether, 'if human rights cannot give us what we want – namely, freedom – then what can?'[190] Gearty argued in the mid-2000s that human rights had come to do 'all the moral work' where once we had a range of other ideas and frames like 'socialism', 'social justice' and 'fairness'.[191] In Part II, we canvassed this 'rights hegemony' argument: that rights-talk has come to displace other 'lost vocabularies' that might be equally universal or

185 Jeremy Waldron, 'Rule-of-Law Rights and Populist Impatience' in Neuman (ed.) 2020, 54.

186 Phillip Alston, 'Making Space for New Human Rights: The Case for the Right to Development' (1988) *Harvard Human Rights Yearbook* 1, 3.

187 Stephen Hopgood, 'Challenges to the Global Human Rights System' (2014) 11(20) *SUR: International Journal on Human Rights* 67-75.

188 Conor Gearty, *Can Human Rights Survive?* (Cambridge University Press, 2006), 1.

189 Beth Simmons, 'The Future of the Human Rights Movement' (2014) 28(2) *Ethics and International Affairs* 183-196.

190 Ratna Kapur, 'On *Gender, Alterity and Human Rights: Freedom in a Fishbowl*' (2019) 122 *Feminist Review* 167-171, 167.

191 Conor Gearty, *Can Human Rights Survive?* (Cambridge University Press, 2006), 9.

(in strategy terms) effective, such as 'duty' or 'responsibility' or 'collective commitment.'[192] Mutua called for something to take the place of (irretrievably compromised) human rights, a 'universal inspirational ideology or philosophy' and 'new moral language to fill the vacuum.'[193] Indeed, a whole sub-literature exists on alternative framings and vocabularies, a search for some other kinds of non-negotiable 'absolutes' like rights.[194] In this context, one conceivable counter-populism strategy might be for 'the movement' to focus rhetorically and substantively on some other powerful concept. Etzioni, for instance, has argued that a 'more comprehensive moral language' is required to counter populism.[195]

One such alternative often put forward to escape the 'baggage' of rights is 'human dignity.'[196] This approach might foreground dignity as the universal concept (and in relation to which human rights may then be more significant in their background and instrumental value in securing, enabling, or protecting dignity).[197] Rather than the 'my rights, versus yours' connotations that legally-protected human rights are said to engender, the concept of dignity might be thought to better focus on our perception and treatment of the other as human.[198] Dignity expressly underpins the *Charter of the United Nations* 1945 as well as the *Universal Declaration of Human Rights* 1948 and the twin 1966 *International Covenants*, and human rights scholars have long triumphed it as the one truly universal idea (if human rights did not 'make it' to that status).[199] For Habermas, for example, since human rights developed in response to specific violations of human dignity, rights are merely specifications of human dignity, which is their moral if not positivist source.[200] Yet, if one of the problems with human rights is that rights language has 'begun to

192 Kennedy, 'Dark Sides' (2004), 9-10.

193 Mukua Mutua, 'Is the Age of Human Rights Over?' in Sophia McClennen and Alexandra Schulthesis Moore (eds.) *The Routledge Companion to Literature and Human Rights* (Routledge, 2016), Ch. 42, 450-458.

194 Martti Koskenniemi, 'Human Rights Mainstreaming as a Strategy for Institutional Power' (2010) 1(1) *Humanity* 47, 47–8.

195 Etzioni 2018, 3-26.

196 Mark Lagon and Anthony Clark Arend, *Human Dignity and the Future of Global Institutions* (Georgetown University Press 2014). For one defence of a dignity-based account of human rights, see Katherine Eddy, 'On Revaluing the Currency of Human Rights' (2007) 6(3) *Politics, Philosophy and Economics* 307-328.

197 Jeremy Waldron, 'Is Dignity the Foundation of Human Rights' in Rowan Cruft, Matthew Laio and Massimo Renzo (eds.) *Philosophical Foundations of Human Rights* (Oxford University Press, 2015).

198 See generally the essays in Christopher McCrudden (ed.), *Understanding Human Dignity* (Oxford, Oxford University Press, 2013).

199 Oscar Schachter, 'Human Dignity as a Normative Concept' (1983) 77 *American Journal of International Law* 849.

200 Jürgen Habermas, 'The Concept of Human Dignity and the Realistic Utopia of Human Rights' (2010) 41(4) *Metaphilosophy* 464-480.

lose [its] power to move us,'[201] this may also now by the case with concepts like 'dignity.' This is because while it seems to offer some new convening and consensus-building power, it also has its drawbacks (for example, 'dignity' is understood in just too many different ways;[202] or perhaps its origins make it dependent on belonging to a particular political community).[203] Dignity may also just as easily be dismissed as 'nothing but a phrase'[204] or over-used and so merely 'kitsch.'[205] In any event, the 'let us switch to dignity' argument has not gained traction, and (as argued below) the 'alternative framing' approach proceeds on a false binary that there can only be one language or vector for social contestation, emancipation, and so on.

One encounters a range of other proposals. Waldron, concerned about populist backlash, ponders whether we should all focus on the 'rule of law' concept instead of human rights.[206] It is not necessary here to explore this other than to note how problematic (status quo, and susceptible to capture by autocratic regimes) the 'rule of law' frame potentially is. Some writers suggest that given the issue that populist constituencies are said to have with 'human rights,' the human rights movement might focus on 'solidarity' as a term, concept, or idea. Thus, the 'path forward' could be 'provided by unearthing the forgotten concept of solidarity and thus drawing from a now marginalised but more radical tradition of human rights thinking,' the movement could 're-appropriate the notion of solidarity to vindicate its original promise.'[207] This argument is that 'returning' collective solidarity 'to its place of honour' may 'help re-programme the human rights movement and gain back some ground that it has lost to nationalist populism.'[208] For Fagan too, disillusioned with rights, the future in responding to the populist challenge will involve

201 Christopher McCrudden, 'On Portraying Human Dignity' Research Paper #12, Queen's University Belfast School of Law, 2016, 31.

202 For one attempt to address some drawbacks with the concept of 'dignity' in relation to human rights, see Peter Schaber, 'Human Rights and Human Dignity: A Reply to Doris Schroeder (2014) 17(1) *Ethical Theory and Moral Practice* 155-161.

203 Jürgen Habermas, 'The Concept of Human Dignity and the Realistic Utopia of Human Rights' (2010) 41(4) *Metaphilosophy* 464-480.

204 Charles Beitz, 'Human Dignity in the Theory of Human Rights: Nothing But a Phrase?' (2013) 41(3) *Philosophy & Public Affairs* 259.

205 Avishai Margalit, 'Human dignity, between kitsch and deification' in C Cordner (ed), *Philosophy, Ethics, and a Common Humanity: Essays in Honour of Raimond Gaita* (London, Routledge, 2011).

206 Jeremy Waldron, 'Rule-of-Law Rights and Populist Impatience' in Neuman (ed.) 2020, 54.

207 Luca Bonadiman and Ukri Soirila, 'Human Rights, Populism, and the Political Economy of the World' (2019) 37(4) *Nordic Journal of Human Rights* 301-328, 308, 313, 328.

208 Luca Bonadiman and Ukri Soirila, 'Human Rights, Populism, and the Political Economy of the World' (2019) 37(4) *Nordic Journal of Human Rights* 301-328, 308, 313, 328.

developing an 'ethic of solidarity'[209] instead. For some, the trend is of 'localisation' and displacement of human rights in the context of a perceived increasing demand for vernacularisation whereby the promotion of rights – at least outside Western democracies – is 'translated into normative alternatives based on local culture.'[210] This is akin to the 'pragmatic partnership' view of the future of human rights whereby activists tire of trying to promote universalism and 'localise' their work, accepting that some universalist aspirations must be given up.[211] Ignatieff's 2017 diagnosis (and prediction) meanwhile was of people turning away from human rights to localised 'ordinary virtues.'[212] For Ignatieff, there is a link to populism: human rights might be the language of states and liberal elites, but 'ordinary' everyday values (for example, tolerance, forgiveness, trust) are the moral language that resonates with most people and that privilege the local over the universal, and fellow group members' claims over those of strangers. Ignatieff saw such values as easily exploited in the politics of fear and exclusion (denied to others but claimed for one's own) but concluded that these are the only 'moral community' possible, such that universalistic human rights had little future prospect of traction. Like the wider 'localisation' prescription, it is not clear that 'local virtues' have displaced retreating rights-talk (which might always have had some contingent traction) or that rights advocacy is untenable in all respects in this sort of either/or portrayal.

Nagaraj's response to the populist challenge is to speak of human rights as deriving from a 'deeper place' than the state and law, from 'a sense of relational ethics, love, compassion, and solidarity,' or to focus on 'human' and not 'rights' and indeed to move beyond rights to re-centre around 'a political concept of love.'[213] This sort of generalised call is the high-water mark, as it were, of any number of such alternative framings. These are either advanced normatively or, like Ignatieff, are based on claimed observation of trends. Hopgood speculated some years ago that China might see value in adopting an alternative international language about 'values' or 'a just social order' and saw it as inconceivable that China would 'capitulate' and adopt the

209 Andrew Fagan, 'The Gentrification of Human Rights' (2019) 41 *Human Rights Quarterly* 283, 308.

210 Stephen Hopgood, Jack Snyder and Leslie Vinjamuri (eds.), 'Editors' Introduction' in *Human Rights Futures* (Cambridge University Press, 2018), 20.

211 Stephen Hopgood, Jack Snyder and Leslie Vinjamuri (eds.), 'Conclusion' in *Human Rights Futures* (Cambridge University Press, 2018).

212 Michael Ignatieff, *The Ordinary Virtues: Moral Order in a Divided World* (Harvard University Press, 2017).

213 VK Nagaraj, 'Human rights and populism: some more questions in response to Philip Alston' (2017) 9(1) *Journal of Human Rights Practice* 22–24, 23-24.

human rights frame.[214] This is what Hopgood and others call the 'sideshow model' of the future of human rights: they enter a severe decline because rising non-liberal powers reject liberal rights-talk, which also finds limited traction amid increasing inequality in Western societies.[215] It is related to the potential future of the so-called 'global welfarism,' a shift to collectivism and a decline in the use of individual-focussed rights-talk.[216] This is not the place to engage with the misconceptions in Hopgood's prediction (including about how non-threatening 'human rights' can be to autocratic states when approached and co-opted selectively in certain ways). However, there is certainly a rich research agenda on how influential actors might, over time, reshape discourse to focus more on duties or responsibilities, or communitarian considerations,[217] ethics as non-law free-standing principles for socio-political dialogue and contestation, or other frames. It is enough to note this debate, but for the most part, scholars have proven reluctant, in the face of populism, to put aside the rights project altogether.

A persistent belief in the rights frame

As noted, both the 'backlash' motif and critical scholarship suggest that the rights framing and discourse is part of the problem for many stakeholders. Yet, some of the prescriptions for countering the populist challenge can appear to assume that advancing claims in rights terms will remain effective and legitimate in a populist era (and that the movement only needs to 'localise' or 'politicise' and so on, as above). Fagan used the UK human rights community's silence around the Grenfell fire disaster in London (which affected people near the bottom of London's socio-economic strata) as evidence that the human rights community is elitist, out-of-touch, and its frameworks unable to see or respond to structural inequalities that affect large parts of the population.[218] For this reason, he argues that human rights in its contemporary forms contributed to the conditions that make populist anti-rights (anti-rights defender) talk effective. Yet, this reasoning, even while it describes human rights as diminished and ineffective, also assumes that framing Grenfell in human rights terms would have given its victims or its wider issues greater

214 Stephen Hopgood, 'Challenges to the Global Human Rights System' (2014) 11(20) *SUR: International Journal on Human Rights* 67-75, 71.
215 Stephen Hopgood, Jack Snyder and Leslie Vinjamuri (eds.), 'Conclusion' in *Human Rights Futures* (Cambridge University Press, 2018), 320-324.
216 Stephen Hopgood, Jack Snyder and Leslie Vinjamuri (eds.), 'Conclusion' in *Human Rights Futures* (Cambridge University Press, 2018).
217 Kathryn McNeilly, 'What should human rights in the future look like?' *The Conversation* 3 October 2017.
218 Andrew Fagan, 'The Gentrification of Human Rights' (2019) 41 *Human Rights Quarterly* 283.

relief, priority, transformation. There is an irony in decrying the 'blind faith' in human rights as a panacea,[219] yet arguing that what really might resolve social ills is … to ensure they are dealt with explicitly in human rights terms and by those identifying as human rights defenders.

There is a reluctance to let go of the rights frame even as one castigates it as entirely compromised, co-opted by capitalism, disconnected from normal people: if the human rights movement had responded using their rights-talk and rights frameworks, so Fagan implies that this would have had some impact. We saw earlier how a small number of scholars *have* reflected on how the shortcomings of the human rights movement are a part of the success of populism, as it were. Their argument is about elitism and legalisation in the rights movement, but mainly about how the human rights project's [perceived] focus on civil and political rights and [at least perceived] neglect of socio-economic issues contributed to (or had little to say about) the very conditions that feed populism. Alston, for example, argues that in the face of populism we do not need to change our frame to 'poverty' or 'dignity' or 'development,' but to construct 'an appropriate human rights framework' and 'treat economic and social rights as full-fledged human rights.'[220] Yet, such scholarly critiques nevertheless carry the same Fagan assumption with them. This is that if the human rights movement found ways to engage more explicitly with the 'bread-and-butter' issues to which socio-economic rights relate by framing issues such as Grenfell in rights terms, this would address the substantive concerns while also restoring credibility and legitimacy to the idea and language of human rights.

This simply presumes or assumes too much. First, notwithstanding all the ink spilled on the problems with human rights, it is an approach that assumes that the human rights frame automatically, inevitably, or still brings power and urgency to an issue, such that framing these issues in rights terms and focusing there will turn things around. This reminds one of the 'mistaken assumption that a bit more human rights can never make things worse.'[221] Second, it assumes that human rights modes, and practices and advocates are suitable lead agents or vectors for the wider social and political work of the agenda around economic insecurity, socio-economic inclusivity, and inequality. Rather than asking whether other strategies and frames better address these issues, there is the sense that if these are not pursued in the language of human rights, they either will not work, or do not count, or will result in the irrelevance of human rights. Yet, it is not obvious exactly how this complex

219 Andrew Fagan, 'The Gentrification of Human Rights' (2019) 41 *Human Rights Quarterly* 283, 305.

220 Phillip Alston, 'The populist challenge to human rights' (2017) 9(1) *Journal of Human Rights Practice*, 1–15, 9.

221 Kennedy, 'Dark Sides' (2004), 29, 34.

societal situation is amenable to rights framing. This may not be because human rights are deficient, but because there are other more powerful or effective or appropriate ways of characterising the situation. There remains something contradictory about critical scholars' arguments that say 'human rights contributed to populism by having nothing to say about structural inequality' but 'human rights is not the way forward here, other political forms and modes of action are.' Human rights might not be an effective vocabulary for change in relation to some structural societal issues. Instead of populists scapegoating human rights, it is scholars scapegoating rights for not having an impact on issues that the same scholars say are not really susceptible to being addressed in rights terms (or perhaps, in human rights as articulated in laws).[222] The answer might be some boring medium position. Sometimes rights-based approaches (whether in part law-focussed or not) are effective and legitimate and coherent for justice, social justice, equality, or fairness, sometimes other forms of action are, and often it is a mix of such strategies. Scholarship can tend to apply binary positions about whether rights-based approaches work or are legitimate or not.

Finally, and without straying into debates about hierarchies of generations of rights, such approaches perhaps do not give enough weight to the truth that without a suitable environment of civic space and freedom (in civil and political rights terms), concerted action on socio-economic issues is not easy. In this sense, there seems to be something inappropriate, and inaccurate, about the implicit or sometimes explicit view that those living in affluent liberal democracies have the luxury of focusing on civil and political rights, but have neglected socio-economic rights issues that are the principal concern of those in the developing world. Only a moment's pause-for-thought will reveal the problem with this mindset.

Another manifestation of this is arguments that if human rights are to stay relevant, the human rights movement 'must also become an environmental and climate change movement.'[223] On the one hand, this is simply an argument for strategic relevance, but on the other, it reveals both the anxiety that societal causes be framed in rights terms and the belief that so framing any cause will considerably advance it. We do not need to canvass the attempts to frame climate change in human rights terms to note that it is not obvious that human rights adds much or that it may do but this will entirely depend on the

222 Fagan, the example being analysed here, himself argues in this piece that human rights have displaced other vectors for advocacy and change on social justice. Yet, his Grenfell argument smacks of reluctance, ironically, to accept that maybe human rights was not the appropriate frame for the complex socio-economic conditions that underlie this tragedy.

223 Sherif Elsayed-Ali, 'The Future of Human Rights' 'Next Strategy' Series (Amnesty International, 2019) https://nextstrategy.amnesty.org/2019/08/09/the-future-of-human-rights/.

context, audience, and so on.[224] Bloomer argues that human rights defenders and those who work on 'broader social justice' issues are increasingly combining their narratives to drive action, for example, on inequality.[225] This does not necessarily imply that rights-led campaigns are less effective, or that adding rights-based approaches to other movements will enhance these invariably. Such things depend on context and need to be studied as such.

Great expectations?

Part of the problem with debating the health or future of human rights comes from definitional assumptions and/or the lack of any agreement or objective notion of when things were better, or worse, than they are now.[226] Mutua argued that the human rights era has ended, but its 'norms and values' were not necessarily 'impotent' because it is 'irreversible' how deeply embedded the notion had become in the 'psyches of states and cultures around the world.'[227] The 'new compact between the state and the citizen' is a 'civilizational shift' and here to stay.[228] Yet, this is simply a claim (that human rights action drove this or that activity) – just like the claim, that Mutua also makes, that human rights let us all down. Both the 'successes' and the 'deficits' can come across simply as claims with no other basis than their declaration by the critical author themselves. They are also full of contradictions: human rights dominated and displaced other ways of thinking but actually did not really penetrate many parts of the world.[229] Critical scholars (at least within the legal tradition) make claims that in any serious social science would not pass for peer review. Notably, sweeping claims of cause and effect: 'human rights helped shift whole mindsets' but also 'human rights sold out the world.' The same scholars who deride human rights or declare its demise do so on the back of no other real basis than their own declarations that, until their thesis, human rights dominated world politics in distorting and illegitimate ways. It is not just attacking straw men, but manufacturing them oneself before turning to attack them.

224 See in this regard Sarah Knuckey and Margaret Satterthwaite, 'Should Human Rights Practice Be Rights-Based?' in Nehal Bhuta, Florian Hoffmann, Sarah Knuckey, Frédéric Mégret, and Margaret Satterthwaite (eds.), *The Struggle for Human Rights Essays in Honour of Phillip Alston* (Oxford University Press, 2021).

225 Phil Bloomer, 'Are human rights an effective tool for social change?' (2014) 11(20) *SUR: International Journal on Human Rights* 115-121.

226 See in a similar vein Philip Alston, *Does the Past Matter? On the Origins of Human Rights* (2013) *Harvard Law Review* 2071.

227 Mutua 2016, 155.

228 Mutua 2016, 155.

229 See Mutua 2016, 454 (human rights a 'civilisational shift' yet not really embedded very deeply in most of the world).

Mutua wrote (on the advent of this 'populist era') that the human rights movement's deficits ('the failure to change the abusive proclivities of humans and states') have 'dimmed' the human rights era.[230] Yet these are extraordinary expectations for a legal-political idiom that critical scholars like Mutua simultaneously exalt and dismiss. An undergraduate student would be penalised for writing such a naïve statement in an essay that 'human rights did not stop or transform the worst of human nature' and so lost its shine such that we need something else. Critical scholars deride human rights for 'assuming' an exalted, messianic position, yet hold it to standards that no Messiah could meet. Critics argue that human rights seem 'toothless and ill-equipped to deal with the root causes of socio-economic inequalities in contemporary societies.'[231] Yet, this is to judge human rights by standards that any alternative moral language or system would struggle to meet too. When critics argue that 'perhaps the movement bit off more than it could chew,'[232] they might be ascribing to human rights some great expectations that no-one has shown 'the movement' promised.

The critics' position does require further unpacking. It is that the failure to fulfil socio-economic rights (while being associated with the promise of market democracy) might have undermined the legitimacy and credibility of the human rights system.[233] This makes sense in a 'disappointment critique' sense (Part II). But it presents a rather unreal notion that societal failures are failures *of human rights*, its system and movement. True, this may not matter to the credibility of rights in a populism context if the perception is that it is 'human rights' – rather than governments, business, or others – that did not deliver. Yet, from the 'populist challenge' literature to date we do not really have much evidence that populists have in fact expressly deployed anti-rights arguments in this way.

Questions of substance versus form

A final observation in terms of evaluating anti-populist or 'post-populist' prescriptions is to develop further the earlier observation about how critical scholars still cling to the rights frame that they describe as so problematic. Some like Moyn who foreshadow the end of the human rights movement (as

230 Mutua 2016, 155.

231 Luca Bonadiman and Ukri Soirila, 'Human Rights, Populism, and the Political Economy of the World' (2019) 37(4) *Nordic Journal of Human Rights* 301-328, 315-318.

232 David Kennedy, 'The International Human Rights Regime: Still Part of the Problem?' in Rob Dickenson et al (eds.) *Examining Critical Perspectives on Human Rights* (Cambridge University Press 2012), 22.

233 'Report of the Special Rapporteur on extreme poverty and human rights' (UN Human Rights Council, 26 April 2016), A/HRC/32/31, 9 (para [18] and [19]).

insufficiently radical or politically embedded or savvy) with 'something else' to take their place nevertheless appear, as discussed earlier, reluctant to let the idea go. Such scholars sometimes seem to prefer this new global politics be one of human rights, in human rights terms, but with different strategies.[234] Critical scholars can be seen as remaining within the 'fishbowl' of the liberal rights order that they critique[235] and have tended to offer 'reformulations' and, in effect, 're-install the project of human rights through proposals of pragmatic renewal and reinvestment.'[236] Hopgood – who penned the 'end times' of human rights thesis – argues ultimately that if we want long-term change '... the discourse of human rights can still help us.'[237] Bonadiman and Soirila's work represents the contradictory argument that rights are compromised and limited, but if we could find a way to 'do' various issues (especially economic inequality) in human rights terms, great change is still possible.[238] Kapur argues that we urgently need to advance alternative (non-liberal, rather than illiberal) understandings of freedom than those associated with the 'human rights' lexicon.[239] She rightly diagnoses the 'anxiety and fear' among critical voices about 'letting go' of the human rights project.[240] Yet, she would not abandon it.

This reluctance is curious, arguably, because it points to a tendency to focus ultimately on *form* rather than *substance*. From 'Occupy Wall Street' to '#MeToo' to 'Rhodes Must Fall' and 'Black Lives Matter,' many of the most significant mass social phenomena in recent years were arguably not organised or coordinated by conventional movements (let alone explicitly human rights ones). Issues were often expressed in terms of economic or social justice, rather than rights.[241] For some, this prompts soul-searching over whether human rights are no longer seen as an effective language for producing social change or that that human rights organisations have lost their represent the wronged

234 Samuel Moyn, 'The Future of Human Rights' (2014) 11(20) *SUR: International Journal on Human Rights* 57-66, 63.

235 Ratna Kapur, *Gender, Alterity and Human Rights: Freedom in a Fishbowl* (Edgar Elgar, 2018). I am grateful to Fiona de Londres for drawing my attention to Kapur's work.

236 Ratna Kapur, 'On *Gender, Alterity and Human Rights: Freedom in a Fishbowl*' (2019) 122 *Feminist Review* 167-171, 168.

237 Stephen Hopgood, 'Challenges to the Global Human Rights System' (2014) 11(20) *SUR: International Journal on Human Rights* 67-75.

238 Luca Bonadiman and Ukri Soirila, 'Human Rights, Populism, and the Political Economy of the World' (2019) 37(4) *Nordic Journal of Human Rights* 301-328, 308.

239 Ratna Kapur, *Gender, Alterity and Human Rights: Freedom in a Fishbowl* (Edgar Elgar, 2018).

240 Ratna Kapur, 'On *Gender, Alterity and Human Rights: Freedom in a Fishbowl*' (2019) 122 *Feminist Review* 167-171, 168.

241 Sara Burke, 'What an Era of Global Protests Says about the Effectiveness of Human Rights as a Language to Achieve Social Change' (2014) 11(20) *SUR: International Journal on Human Rights* 27-33.

and disenfranchised.[242] One sees De Burca at pains to try to argue that the 'Black Lives Matter' movement was not 'just' a civil rights movement but a human rights movement.[243] She seems determined, even desperate, to be able to claim that human rights is relevant, moving around with an eye attuned to picking up any mention of human rights in modern social and protest movements. De Burca sees human rights as 'dynamic, diverse, and evolving'.[244] Yet De Burca may simply be speaking of human rights movements defined so broadly[245] that any evidence of assertive, vital social activism, and protest can be seen as evidence that 'human rights' is alive and well. Again this seems to indicate a pre-occupation with identifying 'human rights' rather than with the state and status of human rights in substance.

Yet, what matters is the pursuit of social justice, not the terms in which this is done. Sometimes rights-talk and rights-based (including litigation-based) strategies will gain traction, and sometimes they will provoke backlash. Sometimes social movements will adopt rights frames or be led by those explicitly self-identifying as human rights defenders, and sometimes they will not. Or things might be messy and non-uniform (sometimes rights-talk is used, sometimes not). This does not require us to descend into the complex debate about whether rights are merely instruments for underlying values such as 'freedom' or 'justice.' Nevertheless, it is advancing and protecting those values that ultimately matters, not their form or frame. When women's groups in the Pacific mobilise around land tenure issues, or environmental defenders in the Amazon resist land-clearing activities in defence of indigenous groups, we can understand such actors to be 'doing' human rights. They are clearly doing so even if they are not invoking rights explicitly, they are not 'categorised' or self-identify as rights groups, and notwithstanding that they might not themselves think to frame their struggle in rights terms. Some scholars have argued that one challenge for human rights advocates in many US cities is 'to convince political activists and leaders to view human rights as a useful organising framework' because this uptake is rare given the

242 Lucia Nader et al (eds.) 'Human Rights in Motion: a Map to a Movement's Future' in (2014) 11(20) *SUR: International Journal on Human Rights* (editors' introduction).

243 Grainne de Burca, *Reframing Human Rights in a Turbulent Era* (Oxford University Press, 2021), 199, fn. 7, and 226.

244 Grainne de Burca, *Reframing Human Rights in a Turbulent Era* (Oxford University Press, 2021), 191, 231. For some other positive outlooks, see too Kathryn Sikkink, 'Human Rights: Advancing the Frontier of Emancipation' *Great Transition Initiative* (April 2018), http://www.greattransition.org/publication/human-rights-frontier, and Beth Simmons, 'The Future of the Human Rights Movement' (2014) 28(2) *Ethics and International Affairs* 183-196.

245 De Burca defines the human rights movement to include social and mass or protest movements of all kinds: Grainne de Burca, *Reframing Human Rights in a Turbulent Era* (Oxford University Press, 2021), 227-228.

experience that 'American exceptionalism' sees the language of human rights as referring only to places outside the United States, not within it.[246] Yet, on one view, this anxiety about whether groups use human rights framing or not is an enormous distraction from more worthwhile questions about what frames and strategies might best advance their cause, including in a populism context. There are questions to be asked about the power of the rights frame. One can ask whether, in a US context for instance, calling women's rights 'human rights' has helped advance these. However, it seems unlikely we might arrive at useful, reliable conclusions without concerted studies of particular contexts and generalising from there. Charlesworth noted two decades ago that claims that human rights are a dominant vocabulary for seeking emancipation may be the case in countries where debates about freedoms and entitlements are mainly conducted in terms of constitutional guarantees of rights. In many other contexts, rights-talk is unfashionable and has little impact in legal or political debates about freedoms or social justice.[247] This remains true.

De Burca is right that most of the critical scholarship relates really to parts of the international human rights system, not the wider movement at all levels, yet treats the latter as a monolithic extension of the former.[248] In particular, the calls for 'make it local' come across now as just a fashionable prescription, often without much empirical basis or attempt at such. The human rights 'movement' is obviously far more diverse and complex than the familiar transnational NGOs such as Amnesty International and Human Rights Watch that critical scholarship seems to focus on.[249] De Burca argues (using case study empiricism) that the system is neither 'top-down' nor bottom-up but a complex ongoing series of 'iterative interactions' and internal friction and contestation, or even competition.[250] This is undoubtedly correct, even if she is really taking a plural messy internally and externally contested reality ('plural, dispersed, fragmented' and comprised of a multiplicity of 'mutually constitutive' multi-level networks)[251] and making of it an ideal approach or deliberate strategy.

246 Finnegan, Saltsman, and White, 'Negotiating politics and culture: the utility of human rights for activist organizing in the United States' (2010) 2(3) *Journal of Human Rights Practice* 307-333.

247 Charlesworth 2002, 127.

248 Grainne de Burca, *Reframing Human Rights in a Turbulent Era* (Oxford University Press, 2021), 191, channelling Charlesworth 2002, 129.

249 Beth Simmons, 'The Future of the Human Rights Movement' (2014) 28(2) *Ethics and International Affairs* 183-196.

250 Grainne de Burca, *Reframing Human Rights in a Turbulent Era* (Oxford University Press, 2021), e.g., 192, 227-229.

251 Grainne de Burca, *Reframing Human Rights in a Turbulent Era* (Oxford University Press, 2021), 192-194, 209, 227-230.

Rather than asking whether social mobilisation enhances human rights, De Burca seeks to ask whether human rights framings and strategies enhance social mobilisation.[252] First, there is some risk that we simply erect another fashion ('social mobilisation') that is not necessarily, or universally, a pre-requisite for change that advances human rights. Second, it might be very difficult to say whether something was 'enhanced' and if so whether rights strategies (etc.) were part of this, as De Burca herself points out. Both critical and proponent scholars tend to assert that 'human rights did this or that,' whereas a more defensible approach might be that 'human rights were likely or potentially a part of this change.' Often we might not be able to distinguish the relative roles that rights framing, discourse, values, institutions, or mechanisms and tools or strategies might have played in success or failure.[253] In much of the literature, one does not see any attempt to unpack things in such ways. Human rights may or may not offer a moral, political, or legal frame giving activists (local, or networks) 'leverage for reform'.[254] This – the success or otherwise of invoking rights, and in which ways – will always be a highly contextualised question. 'Populism' and other such categorisations seem unlikely to add much analytical value or insight.

Human rights do not necessarily need to play an explicit role in advocacy, even if the objectives are capable of being described or advanced in rights terms. Perhaps this is what Kennedy meant by calling for 'calculation' (costs and benefits of pushing a human rights frame) rather than 'veneration.'[255] On some issues, either because of populist backlash or some other reasons (including those outlined in Part II), it seems hard to deny that activism may need another mobilising and legitimating language than the often law-based rights framework. Yet, these are strategy issues, they are not either/or questions that commit us either to pursue or abandon human rights altogether. Advocates might use complementary frames not necessarily alternative ones. Populist backlash might be only one reason why particular activists, diplomats, or others opt for another frame, or mix things up in a non-binary way. What we may be witnessing is greater circumspection about deploying human rights discourse or strategies. The populist backlash may or may not have something to do with that, generally or in particular settings. However, it will

252 Grainne de Burca, *Reframing Human Rights in a Turbulent Era* (Oxford University Press, 2021), 199.

253 Grainne de Burca, *Reframing Human Rights in a Turbulent Era* (Oxford University Press, 2021), 195.

254 Grainne de Burca, *Reframing Human Rights in a Turbulent Era* (Oxford University Press, 2021), 195-196.

255 David Kennedy, *The Dark Sides of Virtue* (Princeton University Press, 2004). See too David Kennedy, 'The International Human Rights Regime: Still Part of the Problem?' in Rob Dickenson et al (eds.) *Examining Critical Perspectives on Human Rights* (Cambridge University Press 2012).

be difficult for those advocating a move to a post-human rights paradigm to argue against the idea that in advancing humanistic social, political, and economic causes in some new or alternate (non-rights) language, activists are not advancing 'human rights' in the sense that these have come to be understood. This is a distinct argument to Hopgood's prediction that human rights frames and arguments will in future either be used so loosely as to provide no solace to global advocates worried about the decline in resort to rights-talk, or be used so selectively that their universality is undermined.[256] Here, the point is that much of the anxiety in the literature seems to be based around the curious idea that if human rights (substance) are pursued not in the language of human rights (form), all is lost. Human rights rhetoric, discourse, and modes need not be at the explicit forefront of social activism or pacific diplomacy or corporate accountability (or any other cause), just as explicit *anti*-rights rhetoric was not at the forefront of some populist backsliding on rights, such as in Poland.

One project on the future of human rights has argued that it is not realistic to assume that human rights will remain the common universal moral language and that the future will require the human rights project to be 'more hybrid' and will depend on the capacity of human rights advocates to build bridges with 'other frames of justice.'[257] Yet, it is not necessarily a crisis in the future of human rights (the substantive values) if social movements do not use rights discourse or strategies, or self-identify as human rights groups. In any event, some of the anxiety about whether rights frames are used or not (i.e., are in decline or not) is based on questionable assumptions about how dominant rights discourse was before now. For example, in general, the United States has not, in foreign policy terms, necessarily put human rights up front, preferring (at least under Republican administrations) to talk about 'freedom' and 'democracy' and 'rule of law,' while as observed earlier 'human rights' is little used in domestic discourse there and in various other countries. Even if we could demonstrate a decline in use of the 'human rights' frame (form), this would not necessarily signal a decline in human rights or societal agitation to achieve those (substance). The relevant question might not be 'how are human rights faring [in an age of populism]?' but rather 'how are civic and other struggles (whether or not framed in human rights terms) faring?'

The protection of human rights faces challenges other than illiberalism and populist–nationalism in electoral democracies: autocracy and geo-political shifts, the accountability of non-state (corporate and financial) actors, new technologies in the context of state and corporate surveillance of individuals

256 Stephen Hopgood, 'Challenges to the Global Human Rights System' (2014) 11(20) *SUR: International Journal on Human Rights* 67-75, 73.

257 https://www.openglobalrights.org/reimagining-human-rights-as-a-frame-of-justice/

and groups, the climate emergency, and so on.[258] Yet, and while it is no consolation, these are not just challenges to human rights as some self-contained normative system and associated infrastructure. They are wider challenges to a whole order of which human rights is but one part. It is not obvious that the dysfunctions or trajectory of this wider order can usefully or properly be evaluated or approached through analysing the state and status of human rights. It is quite absurd, ultimately, for critical academic scholarship to proceed as if 'human rights' (ideas? frameworks? actors?) is to blame for not preventing or fixing the whole political economy of globalisation, inequality, or the state of democracy in the developed and developing world. It is also absurd to proceed as if 'human rights' (and tweaks to the strategies and framings thereof) – or any supposed unspecified alternative meta-narrative – might, if we just get it right, hold the answer to all these challenges. If rights discourses, framing, institutions, and techniques are useful in the future to states, to corporations, to social groups, these actors will no doubt use them here and there. They might appropriate or coopt the discourse in ways that require critical assessment. But focus on the form in which social or global justice contestation is pursued seems useful only if it can in some way offer us a hold on whether and where there is 'progress' or otherwise, howsoever, and by whomsoever defined. This is an apt point on which to turn to our conclusion.

258 For one recent characterization of these threats or challenges, see generally Grainne de Burca, *Reframing Human Rights in a Turbulent Era* (Oxford University Press, 2021) 200ff. See too the three challenges raised by Stephen Hopgood, 'Challenges to the Global Human Rights System' (2014) 11(20) *SUR: International Journal on Human Rights* 67-75.

CONCLUSION

In a sentence, this book cautions against kneejerk dismissal or condemnation of the messenger (populist leaders and parties) where this obscures their potentially important message (things that are popular about populist themes). From a human rights perspective, populist leaders can often justifiably be condemned. Yet, this book has explored what we risk missing if the focus is disproportionately on the populist figure, on labelling and dismissing them. It suggests the need for a greater degree of self-reflection by human rights scholars and advocates (and indeed political representatives and policymakers more broadly) on why populist messaging might have some broad popular appeal, or why it might offer a valuable opportunity to reflect on shortcomings in human rights activism, practice or governance.

This shorter-form book has engaged with the literature around an identified 'populist challenge to human rights,' especially within electoral democracies in the last decade (from Brexit to Trumpism, from Poland to the Philippines) and towards 2030. The 'populist challenge' narrative is not just about backsliding by various governments on human rights commitments and associated legal, constitutional and institutional systems, along with increased encouragement of divisive and discriminatory rhetoric in society more generally. These backslide trends challenge the protective and emancipatory effectiveness of human rights, but the 'populist challenge' thesis goes further. It also sees a more profound threat to the very credibility and legitimacy of human rights as a universalist legal–political project. That is, the thesis of an explicit, deliberately engineered and politically motivated populist backlash against the idea, modalities, language, and defenders of human rights. On this thesis, since the mid-2010's so-called populist leaders – especially on

DOI: 10.4324/9781003311140-5

the political 'Right' – have sought political advantage by expressly dismissing, deriding or delegitimising human rights. Human rights is increasingly portrayed, on this thesis, as a set of undue, sometimes externally imposed or foreign constraints on popular sovereignty and national flourishing, administered by an out-of-touch, patronising, lawyer-heavy elite. This class ignores the legitimate economic, security, and cultural integrity concerns of 'ordinary people' and uses rights-talk to give undue protection and preference to undeserving (often immigrant) minorities. According to the 'populist challenge' narrative, the combination of this backslide and backlash is new and distinctive, still growing, a worldwide phenomenon, and represents a fundamental, existential threat to the future of the modern human rights project.

Yet, this book has questioned that narrative in two principal ways. First, we need to put the 'populist challenge' thesis into perspective, given the whole range of forces and factors *other than populist words and actions* that might help explain the problems that are perceived to exist around the contemporary legitimacy, relevance, and salience of human rights language and systems and of the so-called global human rights 'movement.' For many scholars, the human rights project or experiment was in decline anyway well before the 2010s. Part of putting the 'populist challenge' in perspective also required exploring how the practice of human rights might have itself contributed to its supposedly decreased state and status, rather than its poor health just being a function of external attacks or threats. This relates to the second way in which this book has questioned the 'populist challenge' thesis. It was necessary to ask whether, in what ways, and to what extent it is arguable that the practice of and movement for human rights might have contributed to the conditions that support anti-pluralist, anti-elite, anti-institutional populism and so helped drive or shape the backlash against human rights. It is arguable that the 'populist challenge/backlash' thesis does not adequately account for this. At very least, in its simpler form, it called out for an exploration of why human rights might have become vulnerable to populist scapegoating or delegitimisation. What it is about how human rights have come to be seen or practiced that might have made it more difficult for rights proponents to respond credibly and effectively to populist criticism or dismissal?

One contributor on the populist challenge issue titled his piece with a call to 'mourn' the impact on the movement.[1] Now, the objective impact of the backslide on rights is undoubtedly a grave issue. Yet, one risk with the parallel backlash narrative is that the orientation is towards 'look what populists have done to us' as victims of their discrediting strategy, at the potential expense of asking 'how did human rights generate populist pushback or become so

1 Ron Dudai, 'Human Rights in the Populist Era: Mourn then (Re)Organize' (2017) 9 *Journal of Human Rights Practice* 16.

exposed to populist delegitimisation techniques?' The book's aim was to serve as a provocation, really, to the human rights movement and academy: how did we get to a place where the universal rights of all people were apparently so easily dismissed as just niche minority-favouring obstructions to the general will of the 'true people'? The risk of focusing outward on populism or populists might be missed opportunities to reflect on where and how the human rights project perhaps lost some vital connection, or attraction, or traction, such that framing a claim in human rights terms now does not necessarily give it any particular power and urgency. Indeed, it may bring on a backlash (whether populist or not).

At the outset, in defining 'populism' in Part I, we noted the caution that would be needed in deploying this label and foreshadowed its very real limits as a diagnostic or analytical tool (let alone as a target in human rights strategy terms). Indeed, we came in Part III to discuss whether focus on a populist backlash against human rights might adversely affect the clarity of our vision in three main ways. Populism as 'blindness' relates to the argument, above, that the 'backlash' concept risks obscuring how human rights as practiced or preached might have fostered not just apathy or indifference but also resistance and reactance, things that potentially help fuel populist strategies. Populism as 'distraction' meanwhile represents the related risk of a misplaced diagnosis of the challenges that human rights practice and practitioners face, and to the future of human rights as a vocabulary or discourse of power and contestation and emancipation more generally. For one thing, autocracy that does not necessarily qualify as 'populist' is nevertheless deeply problematic even while a 'populism' lens means that we focus on illiberalism within democracies. For another thing, while populist regimes are not limited to developed liberal democracies, they are also not the principal human rights issue or threat to many people's lives in large parts of the contemporary world. The 'populist challenge' literature can come across as slightly Euro-centric, with just a faint sense of shock still that this sort of crude, low-brow politics is for 'other places' and could not happen *here*. 'Distraction' also refers to the need to unpack whether there is anything unique about the backlash against *human rights* as such. That is, human rights scholars in future may need to situate any backlash analysis within a far broader context of the implications of a possible generational *zeitgeist* phenomenon involving widespread feelings of disconnection and distrust and misgivings about economic and cultural globalisation, mass migration, values-projection, and elite governance more generally. The backlash may be against a much broader status quo than against 'human rights.' It may be against a world order that flew the rights flag but perhaps never recovered its overall legitimacy and credibility from the co-existence of Gross Domestic Product (GDP) growth with economic inequality and economic and debt crises, in the context of both environmental degradation and perceived imposition of external cultural and identity-related agendas. In the background, always, is the challenge to liberalism of the hypocritical disaster of the illegal 2003 invasion of Iraq, justified as it often was in terms of bringing democracy and human rights. Refining some human rights advocacy strategies might hold promise of making the rights agenda less alienating to some majoritarian communities, but it is a far wider project to respond to the legitimate and often entirely reasonable questions about the order to which human rights are seen to belong.

Finally, populism as a 'window' (of opportunity) relates to the calls by some scholars, in advancing prescriptions for facing the populist challenge, to 'use' this moment in history to reflect on where the human rights movement might approach things differently (including to counter the populist attack and backlash). On the one hand, there is certainly a perception that there is excessive undue negativity about the future of human rights and its challenges. After all, the opening of the 2022 Qatar International Federation of Football Associations (FIFA) World Cup, the world's most-watched sporting event, saw FIFA's head feel obliged to address human rights concerns expressly in the language of human rights,[2] not some other superseding frame that has replaced it. Yet, it is also true that there remains a good degree of denial or reluctance to engage with the nature and scale of some of those challenges.[3] For example, the editors of a recent 'special issue' journal seemed to suggest that all the human rights movement/system needs are 'certain adjustments,' a few tweaks here and there, especially to its institutions, and it would run smoothly:

> [While] some of the criticism towards the international human rights system is misplaced, it must be admitted that its institutional machinery has grown piecemeal and might need certain adjustments to function optimally.[4]

This book has taken as given, for argument's sake, that human rights faces *some* significant challenges and crises and has not sought to evaluate the empirical basis for this, other than to pose fairly obvious questions around what historic baselines, expectations and success criteria are used for positions either of pessimism or optimism about the future trajectory of human rights. In relation to this, there is perhaps a forward research agenda around what might be the appropriate 're-' term here, and what that word-choice would assume:

2 'Fifa president Gianni Infantino accuses West of "hypocrisy" *BBC Sport*, 19 November 2022, https://www.bbc.com/sport/football/63687412.

3 Ironically in terms of using it to show the persistent relevance of rights discourse, the Qatar example above illustrates just how rights-talk can legitimise situations that we should find very problematic.

4 Gentian Zyberi et al, (eds.) 'Special Issue: The Future of Human Rights' (2022) 40(1) *Nordic Journal of Human Rights*, 1-12, 2.

're-imagining,' 're-vitalising,' 're-evaluating,' 're-thinking,' 're-framing,' etc. Indeed (and, as ever, conscious when around semantic issues that English is only one language in the world), does *any* 're' word itself imply something that we ought to question, a return, a restoration, something intrinsically backward-looking or at least perhaps overly nostalgic and utopian? Part III also involved briefly canvassing the arguments that – in light of the problems perceived or associated with human rights – societies and polities may need other, non-rights frames or discourses or vocabularies for advancing freedom, justice, dignity, equality, flourishing, pluralism, and various other fundamental values and goals, within what our planet and its changing climate might accommodate.

Such arguments highlight a key theme of this book: the role that arguably unfounded 'great expectations' about the human rights project and movement have come to play in narratives about its future and relevance and worth. The critical scholars canvassed in Part II at times position human rights in ways that can only result in relative disappointment: in the view of scholars from Mutua to Moyn, human rights is discredited or even deceased because it has not, as a phenomenon, resulted in fulsome equality, freedom, safety, inclusion, etc. Yet, the same critical scholars exhibit, ultimately, a deep reluctance to let go of the human rights frame even as they ask too much of it as merely one factor and framework in human affairs and governance. Implicit in many of their arguments is the idea that if we just re-orient and re-commit (more 're-' words...), 'human rights' is capable of almost anything. The conclusion of this book is that even in some 're-' form, this might be asking too much of a discourse, a set of mechanisms, a disparate, uncoordinated, often-competing collection of movements and actors. Indeed, the populist backlash shows that it might, in some contexts, be not just futile but counter-productive (in strategy terms at least, if not out of principle) to foreground an expressly rights-based argument or framing. This is nothing new to many activists and rights strategists, but the rise (again) of populism in so many polities in the last decade certainly highlights it. The human rights movement and academy is rightly concerned about political trends such as populism. However, these actors have agency and with this comes a degree of responsibility, since the problems with 'human rights' are partly a function of how the human rights movement curates the rights project and cannot simply be put down to their historical origins or associations. At least, there is a responsibility to engage in self-reflection on how rights-based strategies might trigger backlash or not bring a critical mass of people along on the journey of explaining just why universal minimal protections and entitlements matter to all.

Perhaps, in conclusion, the key term here is 'expressly' or 'explicitly.' This is in two senses. First, a curious feature of the 'populist challenge' narrative is that we can chronicle a host of ways in which populist administrations have undermined substantive rights protections and affected the culture of and conditions for human rights fulfilment ('backslide' in Part I). Yet, authors do not actually offer us *that* many examples of overt or express and deliberate stigmatisation and delegitimisation of human rights by populist leaders that are so distinctive as to really ground an indisputable 'backlash' thesis and moment. In addition to the limited global scale of the handful of geographies that recur in analysis, some of the examples advanced are somewhat 'business-as-usual' governmental complaints against supra-national institutions or the apparently ever-productive politics of decrying 'rights for criminals.' More work remains to catalogue the populist backlash in its probable varying degrees of explicitness: this book has not attempted to, but has explored some responses to the backlash *as advanced* in the literature after about 2015.

The second sense in which 'express' or 'explicit' is a key term is as follows and relates to the comments above about a search for discourses other than 'human rights.' Both generally and within the 'populist challenge' trope, analysis of the future of human rights arguably displays a desire (and, at times, almost desperation) to find evidence that societal activism and contestation is still being conducted by reference to, and in the language and systems of, human rights. Notably, we saw in Part III just how curiously keen De Burca was to be able (in her 2021 study) to present recent mass social movement phenomena such as 'Black Lives Matter' as *human rights* movements. Unless human rights really is a quasi-religious creed, does it really matter if social activism expressly invokes human rights or sees itself as part of that 'movement?' Does it matter if social activism, political contestation, diplomacy (etc.) in pursuit of freedom and other goals or values is conducted in human rights terms, or by actors that define themselves as human rights defenders, or whether such claims and struggles and dialogue are capable of being categorised, in a narrow sense, as 'human rights' work? It is just not obvious how it matters (especially in a US domestic context) whether the Black Lives Matter phenomenon 'is' a human rights movement or uses human rights language or frameworks or not. At the same time, individuals and organisations around the world working to advance the interests to which the international human rights normative superstructure relates are still doing 'human rights' work irrespective of whether they choose to frame and label things this way (or are framed or labelled by others). In this sense, calls for human rights groups to work more closely with 'wider civil society' such as workers' unions or environmental activists can be seen as having an unduly narrow idea of what counts as 'working on human rights.' There must obviously be a distinction between *doing human rights* in substance and *doing human rights through human rights language, law, mechanisms, etc.* To the extent that their varying power-for-agency allows, activists, diplomats, and others in particular strategic and tactical contexts will no doubt choose whether, when, how, and to what degree to invoke human rights or rights law explicitly. The risk of populist backlash or distortion might well be one factor in that choice: it depends.

If there is a backlash, perhaps it is a corrective, and part of the contestation that is inescapable in law, politics and human rights: overreach or under-sell, then backlash, then countering pushback or compromise or engagement, and so it goes.[5]

Is this how all attempted sweeping analyses of human rights futures end, with a call to be pragmatic and context-sensitive?[6] Is that it? Are we left with the argument that human rights peaked as a political phenomenon some time ago, but still has 'some strategic uses in some institutional contexts?'[7] If so, this might not be something particularly novel: sometimes a legalistic, litigious or rights-up-front approach is useful, sometimes it is not, and very often one does not have this highly artificial, academic binary either/or choice of frames or modes of advocacy anyway. People and organisations will choose their strategies. A decade before the 'populist challenge' narrative emerged, Gearty argued that human rights 'can survive' but its supporters:

> … must think harder, run with rather than against democracy, not be afraid of making powerful enemies, and be choosier about what they stand for, while willing to build alliances with the forces of justice and fairness wherever they find them.[8]

This injunction has some force in an era of populism, in particular the tension of human rights with democracy. Yet, 'thinking hard' and selecting issues, partners and strategies are issues that human rights movements large and small, from Albania to Zimbabwe, must perforce face all the time. Although somewhat inevitable, there is something unsatisfying or troubling about calls by scholars – presumably addressed to members of 'the movement' out there at the 'local level' – to counter populism or any other challenge by being more

5 In a somewhat similar vein, Voeten would counsel patience: 'populism comes in waves and populists face difficulties organizing large multilateral coalitions in favour of reform': Erik Voeten, 'Populism and Backlashes against International Courts' (2020) 18(2) *Perspectives on Politics* 407-422.

6 'Be more pragmatic' is David Kennedy's message for the human rights movement: 'The International Human Rights Regime: Part of the Problem?' (2002) 14 *Harvard Human Rights Journal* 101-126; *The Dark Sides of Virtue* (Princeton University Press, 2004); 'The International Human Rights Regime: Still Part of the Problem?' in Rob Dickenson et al (eds.) *Examining Critical Perspectives on Human Rights* (Cambridge University Press 2012), 22-23. In the latter Kennedy describes swinging between idolatry towards the creed of human rights (the remedy for which is pragmatism) and pragmatism (compromising participation in governance, for which the remedy is to return to ethics, and dangers of idolatry).

7 Marti Koskienemmi, 'Human Rights: so 90s', address, Oxford Martin School, March 2014.

8 Conor Gearty, *Can Human Rights Survive?* (Cambridge University Press, 2006), 15-16.

'pragmatic' or now 'nimble,'[9] taking 'innovative steps'[10] and standing 'ready to mobilize'[11] and so on. In this sense, the scholarly writing (see Part III) about the need to 'localise' or 'mass mobilise' to counter populism is quite problematic, at least in less free polities. It suggests – almost certainly inaccurately – that this is not exactly what activists and others already do, deciding when to use law, invoke rights, engage transnationally, or not. Too much of both the critical and prescriptive literature is advanced without any particular effort at contextualised empirical study of how and with whom activists *do* try to work. Kennedy famously criticised the human rights movement for lacking strategic nous and insufficiently engaging in a costs-versus-benefits analysis in terms of which rights issues to pursue, how, when, and where.[12] There is some force to this. After all, we saw in Part II that overreach and alienation, among other things, can certainly result where rights issues are pursued (or issues are pursued as rights) at all costs or in ways that do not account for others' sentiments and sensitivities, and even how this might explain part of the backlash. Yet, Kennedy offered no real 'cost-benefit' examples at the time he made that critique. It strains belief that activists or coalitions thereof would not weigh up various factors and seek (to the extent that they can agree) to mobilise more broadly, or connect 'vertically' or 'laterally' with other groupings, if they thought it would advance their cause or interests in particular contexts.[13] Moreover, the idea of a highly strategic 'costs–benefits' analysis (costs to the overall rights project of this strategy or tactic or the other) tends, ultimately, sometimes to assume some fictional monolithic single coordinated and coordinate-able global movement. One is, in effect, asking individual rights-holders or organisations to constrain their program so as not to damage or generate backlash against the wider rights project, something that implies a far more united, single vision/voice 'movement' than will ever likely exist in practice.

The other reason such prescriptions are problematic relates to a final point about scholarly voice and role. This is that prescriptions to 'mobilise' or 'localise' more are, of course, deeply condescending or patronising. It may well be that rights-work became, generally or in some places, too focused on legal frames or litigation strategies, vertical networking vectors, or judicial

9 'Pragmatic': Kennedy 2002; 'nimble': De Burca 2021.

10 Stephen Hopgood, Jack Snyder and Leslie Vinjamuri (eds.), 'Editors' Introduction' in *Human Rights Futures* (Cambridge University Press, 2018), 2.

11 Nienke Grossman, 'Populism, International Courts, and Women's Human Rights' (2020) 35 *Maryland Journal of International Law* 104-126, 126.

12 Kennedy, 'Dark Sides' (2004), 5.

13 See Hilary Charlesworth, 'Author! Author! A Response to David Kennedy' (2002) 15 *Harvard Human Rights Journal* 127-131 (responding to Kennedy's call for more 'pragmatic' and strategic approaches).

enforcement. Yet it is just too easy – from one's professorial chair – to suggest that activists generally or in country X or Y should rely less on legal-judicial strategies or on ties to global governance elites and should 'get their hands dirty' or 'be prepared to descend into programmatic contest' and ugly politics. In many places, 'local' activists might just be trying to advance their cause and constituency (and/or manage their donors and others) as best and as safely as they can. Alston is right that defending human rights has never been a consensus project or inevitably winning cause but involves 'constant struggle.'[14] The 'local activists' and mass publics that some scholars both lecture to and put on a pedestal no doubt experience this truth in a different way to us scholars.

The book's introduction reflected briefly on the place of critical scholarship on human rights. Even if the human rights idea, and its proponents, are in significant difficulties, there seems to be no need to curb critical perspectives (as futile as such a prescription would be). Some argue that the language of human rights being still relevant in the world, the focus of discourse should shift 'from criticism to lesson-learning' and exploring new ways to make human rights relevant to all.[15] Extreme political ideologies do make for a more difficult space in which to promote critical self-reflection on the part of human rights proponents. Yet, refraining from criticising human rights in scholarly terms hardly seems likely to strengthen them (and we have not seen particular evidence of populists drawing directly on such critiques); the movement's problems, such as they are, are arguably not really a consequence of critical scholarship.[16] Yet, as scholar-practitioners of all sorts who work in and around the human rights motif, we could aim for more contextualised, empirically grounded work. There is a *lot* of literature lately about 'the future' of the 'ongoing experiment'[17] that is human rights. There always is, though. Most recently, a renowned academic journal – in convening yet another 'special issue' on the future of human rights – observed that human rights seem permanently to be at a crossroads.[18] This book's conclusion is a call for human rights scholarship that attempts to understand what frames, strate-

14 Phillip Alston, 'The populist challenge to human rights' (2017) 9(1) *Journal of Human Rights Practice*, 1–15, 3-4.

15 Kirtika Kattel, 'Are Human Rights Enough? Exploring Ways to Reimagining Human Rights Law' (2022) 40(1) *Nordic Journal of Human Rights*, 13-27.

16 Martti Koskenniemi, 'Rocking the Human Rights Boat: Reflections by a Fellow Passenger' in Nehal Bhuta, Florian Hoffmann, Sarah Knuckey, Frédéric Mégret, and Margaret Satterthwaite (eds.), *The Struggle for Human Rights: Essays in Honour of Phillip Alston* (Oxford University Press, 2021). See too James Loeffler and Mila Versteeg, 'The Future of Human Rights Scholarship' (2018) 81 *Law and Contemporary Problems* i.

17 https://www.openglobalrights.org/reimagining-human-rights-as-a-frame-of-justice/.

18 Gentian Zyberi et al, (eds.) 'Special Issue: The Future of Human Rights' (2022) 40(1) *Nordic Journal of Human Rights*, 1-12, 1.

gies, or models worked well or not in particular settings (and what counts as 'working well' and to whom, and with what associated consequences for other strategies, etc.). Such studies may try to draw wider conclusions, for other places or issues, or for the future. Ideally, in that future, there will be less need for 'grand narrative' studies like those that this book relates to (or this book itself). As scholars in this field (especially of law and regulation), we are too prone to sweeping, unfounded statements about the trajectory of human rights (whether ending, declining, enduring, reviving…) that would not withstand scrutiny in many other disciplinary fields. Like the impact of populism and the nature of any 'backlash,' the emancipatory potential of human rights – which places, what issues, which vectors, what actors – *is* ultimately an empirical question.[19] It is not an easy one but is central to the future relevance of human rights scholarship.

19 Gentian Zyberi et al, (eds.) 'Special Issue: The Future of Human Rights' (2022) 40(1) *Nordic Journal of Human Rights*, 1-12, 1.

INDEX